Looking For Home

Memoirs of a Sephardic Jew From Morocco

By Robert Ben-Nun Benayoun

Looking for Home: Memoirs of a Sephardic Jew From Morocco

All rights reserved
Copyright © 2019 by Robert Ben-Nun Benayoun
Photos by Robert Ben-Nun Benayoun and family

Printed in the United States of America

No part of this book may be reproduced or transmitted in any form without written permission of the author, except for brief passages in connection with a review.

ISBN 9781951776121

Disclaimer: The stories herein are of the author's lived experiences as he remembers, with some details from research. This is not to be taken as historical documentation.

This book is dedicated to my family:
my wife, Deborah, the love of my life, our two sons,
David and Daniel,
and to my grandchildren, Adam and Lia,
so that one day they might want to know
the life story of Papi

TABLE OF CONTENTS

Introduction – 9
My Family – 13
19 Rue de Tanger – 37
Synagogue Ettedgui – 47
Rabbi Eliahou – 61
Albert Sonsol Elementary School – 65
Fishing With Father – 71
22 Rue Berthelot – 81
Hiloula Rabbi Yehya Lekhdar – 97
Jewish Holidays – 105
Monsieur Elie Bittoun – 119
Samy, Jacqueline, and Armand – 123
Haim Douck and the Decision to Leave Home – 133
Alonei Itshak, Israel – 153
To Haifa and Jerusalem – 195
Israel Military Service (Tsahal), 1972–1975 – 201
Yom Kippur War, 1973 – 227
Road to the Suez Canal – 253
Visit to France, 1974 – 263
Bir Tmadeh – 269
Simon – 283
Civilian Life and Neot Hakikar – 287
Prosper (1952–2007) – 307
Visit to Morocco, 1977 – 311
Sinai – 315
Military Reserve Duty (Miluim) – 321
Turkey – 327
Deborah – 333
A Texas Wedding, 1979 – 351
Evelyne, Michel & Nanou – 357
Visit to France, 1980 – 361
My Father (1923–1980) – 363
Austin, Texas – 369

Montreal, Canada – 375
The Kerrville and Giddings Ranch, Texas – 379
Constantina – 391
Jews in Canoes – 395
Estepona – 401

Introduction
My Story

As I am entering my sixty-sixth year of age, I would like to recap my journey and my memories from early childhood to my adult life. For many years I have been wanting to write down my mémoires—my recollections and the souvenirs of my life. I was one child out of nine, born in the early 1950s in Morocco. At the age of fifteen, I left my parents' home and lived for ten years in Israel, far from my family. Then I got married and settled in Texas and started a family of my own.

In the last few years, I have been trying to investigate, collect, and document as much information as I could find through personal interviews of living elder relatives, old photo albums. I wanted to know the origins and history of my parents, my grandparents, and my great-grandparents. Until the coming of the French government to Morocco around 1906, no written civil records or family records existed to document the origins and history of our family.

It is thought that Jews have been in Morocco in the sixth century B.C., since just after the destruction of the first temple in Jerusalem. Under Arab rule in the seventh century, there was generally a tolerance of Jews, who were considered *dhimmi*, or non-Muslim "protected persons." They could practice their religion, but they had to pay a special tax, dress in a special way, and were not allowed to have certain occupations. Sometimes there was violence against them. Jews first came into Morocco in ancient times, but the Sephardic Jews of Spain came in great numbers during the later years of the Spanish Inquisition, around 1492, to escape persecution and death. In 1492, any remaining Jews were expelled from Spain.

From *Wikipedia*, "The French presence in Morocco began during the end of the nineteenth century. In 1904, the French government was trying to establish a protectorate over Morocco and had managed to sign two bilateral secret agreements with Britain and Spain. France and Spain secretly partitioned the territory of the sultanate, with Spain receiving concessions in the far north and south of the country."

In 1906, France and Germany reached an agreement where France gave up some control on its eastern border with Germany, in Alsace Lorraine, in exchange for a full mandate to control Morocco. In 1912, the French government took over control of the Moroccan Kingdom, establishing a protectorate. The Jewish population started to change, evolving and adapting themselves to the new, wide-ranging opportunities for education as new schools from the Alliance Israelite Universelle were opening in most cities. This organization, founded by Jews in Paris, had a goal of educating and assisting Jewish people, especially in countries where they were discriminated against.

In the middle of the twentieth century, Jews left Morocco in waves — after the founding of Israel, at the end of the French protectorate, and during the Six-Day and Yom Kippur Wars. Many Jews in Morocco felt that their Arab country was becoming unsafe for them.

My family had been established for many generations in Morocco among the Arab population, adapting and assimilating to the same way of life, except for keeping our Jewish faith and sticking to our own Jewish religious lifestyle and customs within our own separate Jewish community. I belong to the generation that felt for many reasons the need to leave our native country of Morocco and seek a better future somewhere else. I find it is almost a duty to record and document the events leading us to be the "transitional generation."

I strongly believe leaving behind a written, personal record describing my own sequence of events could first benefit me as a kind of mental therapy, recapping my own

Introduction

journey, and second, be a small written legacy for future generations of the Benayoun Ben-Nun family.

Looking for Home

Memoirs of a Sephardic Jew
From Morocco

> We grew up in the age of transition
> and have become the generation of nostalgia.
> – Kisty Mea

> People need history in order to know themselves,
> to build a sense of identity,
> and to have pride, continuity, community,
> and hope for the future.
> -- Douglas Preston

My Family

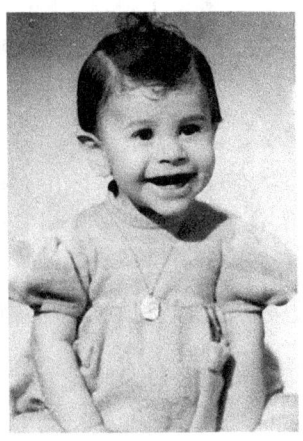

Robert, a few months old, 1954

I was born in Casablanca, Morocco, in October 1953, the fifth child of nine of David and Suzanne (Saada Aisha) [née Suissa] Benayoun. As was customary under local French law, our parents had to give us French names to be legally registered, but each one of us always knew our individual Hebrew name.

My parents had four children before me: Samy (Shlomo), born in 1945; Jacqueline (Esther), 1948–2010; Armand (Amram), born in 1949; and Prosper (Messod), 1952–2007. Then came me, **Robert** (Reuben), born 1953.

Four more were born after me: Evelyne (Yaffa), born in 1955; Simon (Shimon), born in 1956; Michel (Meyer-Shalom), born in 1959; and then Annie, or "Nanou" (Hninah), born in 1960.

That makes me the middle child, which is fitting since I was born in October under the astrological sign of Libra, the balancing scale.

Nine Benayoun brothers and sisters with our mother in the center, reunited in Casablanca, 1991. Standing in birth order from right to left: Sam, Jacqueline, Armand, Prosper, Robert, Evelyne, Simon, Michel, Nanou.

Parents and Grandparents

My parents met and were married in Casablanca around 1942 or 1943. My father, David Benayoun, was born in Settat, a small town inland about forty-five kilometers from the Moroccan Atlantic coast. Settat was where his own parents, Amram Benayoun and his young bride, Mryem (Miriam) [née Lousky, or Lousqui], came to settle and start a new life, escaping turmoil and unrest in Salé around the turn of the century.

Both of my father's grandparents were originally from the small coastal town of Salé, across the river from Rabat, the capital city of the kingdom of Morocco, on the Atlantic coast. Salé is a city in northwestern Morocco on

My Family

the right bank of the Bou Regreg River, opposite the national capital, Rabat. Founded in antiquity as a Phoenician colony, Salé became a haven for pirates as an independent republic before being incorporated into Morocco under the Alaouite royal dynasty.

Trying to research the origins of my family going back more than the turn of the century was not an easy task, since written documents or government archives are practically non-existent before the French arrival to Morocco around 1912. My original family name, Benayoun, with different spelling variations like Ben Hayon, Ben Hayoun, Benhayon, Benaion, Benaioun, and Ben Yahyon can be traced and found in old Spanish-archive documents starting around the twelfth century. The name is found in various files and documents in regard to commercial, real estate, and tax transactions in different cities throughout Spain, from Pamplona and Tupelo in the north of Spain to Toledo, Cartagena, and Murcia, as quoted in the book published by Abraham Isaac Laredo in 1978, *The Origins of Names, Jews of Morocco*.

My great-grandfather (father of Baba Amram) was Jacques (Yishak) Benayoun, married to Istir [née Afflalo]. Jacques Benayoun was born in Salé, Morocco, where he was a kind of currency trader or moneylender by profession. He died in Salé of old age and is buried in the small local Jewish cemetery there. Jacques and Istir had five children: Abraham, Amram (my grandfather), Shalom, Shabba, and Yossef.

A few years ago, I came across an interesting book, published in France in 1978, that gives a small description of the Mellah of Salé, the Jewish quarter, at the turn of the century, even mentioning by name my great-grandfather Jacques (Yishak) Benayoun and the Lousqui family. Lousqui, or Lousky, was the maiden name of Mama Mryem, my grandmother.

Quote from the book *Les Juifs du Maroc, Identité et Dialogue*, published in 1980, pages 188, 200:

"At the beginning of the French Protectorate in 1912, the Mellah of Salé included some two hundred houses, more than twenty shops, two ovens, and two mills. The layout of the Mellah was similar to that of the city. A large gate, which closed every day at sunset, gave access to a long street, relatively narrow, parallel to the southern wall. Along this street were shops, homes, and synagogues. On the north side of the street, there were nine small, dead-end, narrow streets, which bore the names of prominent householders. Toward the end of the century, the streets bore the names of <u>Jacques Benayoun,</u> Joseph Dahan, Samuel Cohen, Shaul Ben Zvi, Yehuda Amzallag, Rabbi Raphael Encaoua, Benarroch Yehuda, <u>Yehuda Lousqui,</u> and Al-Caid Sbihi."

My grandparents, Amram Benayoun and Mryem Lousky, escaped the Mellah of Salé circa 1903 because of unrest and local warfare, to seek refuge and settle in the interior town of Settat, where my father, David, was born in March of 1920. I never had the chance to meet my grandfather Amram Benayoun. He passed away in the late 1940s, way before I was born in 1953. Many years later, I was able to gather some information about him through interviews with cousins and older family members, mainly Jack Bitton, a cousin who grew up in Settat, and recently my aunt Tata Fiby Ifergan, Amram Benayoun's daughter. She is my father's sister, the youngest and currently the last living sibling of my father. She lives in the northern part of Israel in the town of Migdal Haemek.

Amram Benayoun, my grandfather, second from right

In 2010, I was able to videotape an interview with Tata Fiby in Paris, where she came to attend my nephew's bar mitzvah. She was born in 1928 in Settat. She related to me her childhood memories growing up in her parents' house in Settat, the house of my grandparents Amram and Mryem. Baba Amram was apparently an artisan *ferblantier*, or tinsmith, shop owner. Before electricity came to rural Morocco, most of the households used lamps made from tin. This metal was commonly used for making windows, lamps, platters, utensils, and such.

My grandfather owned his own house in Settat. He was a hardworking, deeply religious man dedicated to his family of seven kids, to his faith, and to his work. He had a beard and wore a head covering, black *djellaba*, and *babouches*, the leather Moroccan slippers. It was customary then for Jews to wear black djellaba, a long, hooded robe, to always stand out and be distinguished from the rest of the population, one of the requirements under the *dhimmi* laws of the local authorities for non-Arab people. This was the traditional, typical menswear before the French takeover of Morocco in 1912 and before the widespread adoption by the younger generation of conventional European modern attire.

Much later, around the early 1960s as a young child in Casablanca, I have some memories of Baba Amram's wife—my grandmother Mama Mryem—coming to stay with us at 22 Rue Berthelot when my mother was away visiting her own mother, Meme Hninah, in Israel. My father, Mama Mryem's only surviving son, asked her to move in with us during that period to assist and help with the household. She was a very stern, rigid, and serious woman. She had the bad habit of occasionally pinching us kids in either the arm or leg to get our attention or to discipline us. She was also known to bestow nicknames on her grandkids, and not necessarily complementary ones.

Sam's nickname was "Bourogeot," more than likely coming from the name of General Thomas Bugeaud, a famous French general who won a great military battle against the Moroccan army in 1844, and I imagine he left behind an impact on the local population for his bravery and courage. Jacqueline's nickname, and later on

My Family

Mama Mryem Benayoun [née Lousky], my paternal grandmother

Evelyne's, was "Ouwah Jikah," referring to seagulls, and the squawking sound they make flying around town.

Armand was "Bouchaieb el Khel," due to his slightly darker skin compared to the rest of us and the resemblance to a black-skinned vendor of charcoal in our old neighborhood when Armand was born.

Prosper was "El Pernakh," which could be interpreted as lazy, slow moving, not very efficient in running errands.

I was called "El Htipi," which means short in height, or dwarf. As a young child, I was slightly shorter than average for boys my age.

Simon was "Bou Sbaa," meaning "the owner of the finger," as a result of an unfortunate accident when he was three or four years old. Falling on a broken glass bottle, Simon had a tendon on his finger cut, and after a small surgery he could not bend one of the fingers on his left hand very well while making a fist—not corrected to this day.

Michel was "Einine el Hout," or "eyes of a fish," due probably to a sensitivity of his eyes. He was always blinking his eyes as a nervous tick.

Mama Mryem's family came from a small coastal town, Azemmour. She dressed in the old-fashioned way as was customary for old Moroccan Jewish women, always in black or dark colors, probably because she was already a widow when I first met her. She wore the traditional scarf tied and covering her long, graying hair.

Shortly after being widowed from my grandfather in her late forties in Settat, she moved in to live with Tata Sol, my father's sister. Tata Sol, also known as Sulieka, was living at the time with her husband, Shimon Bitton, in the same town of Settat. Later, they moved to the big city of Casablanca, in the old Jewish quarter on the other side of Place de France, in the prolongation of la Rue du Commandant Provost at Rue de la Croix Rouge. The name, La Place de France, was later changed to la Place des Nations-Unies — the United Nations Square.

Very often on Saturdays after Shabbat morning services at the Synagogue Ettedgui, located in our old neighborhood near the port in Casablanca, while walking along Rue de Tanger and Rue de Safi and crossing the old Jewish quarter, we would stop by to pay a visit to Tata Sol. Her apartment was located on Rue de la Croix Rouge, not far from le quartier de la Ibanse, named after one of the first and most famous ice cream parlors located there. We would spend time visiting with my aunt and grandmother, so my father could wish his mother a good *Shabbat Shalom* with a traditional kiss on her forehead. We would have a cup of tea or a quick snack before getting back home for the traditional Saturday *dafina* meal of slow-cooked stew.

A few years later, in the early 1960s, whenever staying with us at Rue Berthelot, my grandmother would have her own sitting area on the floor, against the wall in our long entry hall. She sat cross-legged on her white, furry lambskin, peeling vegetables and directing our house cleaner. She would occasionally reach for her silver snuffbox, apparently a gift from my father to her, engraved with her name in Hebrew, "Miriam Benayoun," and the date of June 5, 1952. I ended up inheriting somehow the silver snuff box, and I always keep it on my desk.

My Family

Sometimes at night, she would gather us kids around her sitting area in the long corridor and tell us tales and stories from her past. Mama Mryem spoke only the Moroccan Arabic dialect and communicated to us in that language. At that time, my understanding of it was somewhat limited since our father strongly emphasized and insisted on only speaking and communicating with us in French. He would rarely speak to us in the Arabic dialect of Darija, the everyday colloquial language. My father, like most of the Jewish families established in the big cities, embraced with open arms the French culture. He believed very strongly that French culture and education was the only way forward, offering a better future for his children in education, progress, and future development.

The trend back then within most upcoming Jewish families was to distance themselves and somewhat reject or look down on the Arab culture and language—the culture and language that had been our parents' and grandparents' unique culture before the French takeover of Morocco. They embraced every aspect of the new French ways. France was a synonym for emancipation, civilization, education, a better future, and total freedom, particularly for the new generation. Our old Moroccan culture and language were probably associated with the limits and restrictions previously imposed on the Jewish population as a minority living in a Muslim country.

I do remember vividly some of the words Mama Mryem used while one night recounting her escape from possibly Rabat or Salé. Particularly, one phrase kept coming back—Blad el Sibah—when she was referring to escaping the turmoil, warfare, and the rampage taking place around her small town on the coastline. She and my grandfather were trying to escape and seek shelter inland, toward the small town of Settat.

For a long time, I confused the word *shibah*, a commonly used, fragrant herb for making tea. It is the Moroccan Arabic word for wormwood, also known as the *Artemisia absinthium* plant. Only many years later did I understand what Mama Mryem had been saying, when I read about the history of Morocco around that time regarding the division of the country between "Blad el Makhzen," where the sultan or king had full control, and "Blad el Sibah," where different tribes and religious sects were at times rebelling against the authority of the Moroccan ruler, the sultan. I learned that when fighting each other, these warring factions would sometimes in the process raid towns and Jewish quarters in the mellah.

In Mama Mryem's youth, she had to escape the conflicts, turmoil, and massacres with her young husband, our grandfather Baba Amram, and escape the Mellah of Salé. They made their way out of the mellah with Mama Mryem riding a mule or donkey, with her face all blackened and dirty to hide her features and not attract attention in the ongoing confusion. Baba Amram followed behind on foot as they went to seek refuge and start a new life in the agricultural town of Settat, located forty-five kilometers from the Atlantic coast.

Amram Benayoun, my grandfather, on the right with his brother Abraham on the left

David Benayoun, My Father

My father, David Benayoun, was born in Settat in 1920 and grew up there until the age of thirteen — the age of his bar mitzvah. He was the youngest boy of seven siblings. His four sisters were Simy, Perla, Suleika (Sol), and Fiby. There were three brothers: Shlomo, Simon, and David (my dad).

Shlomo, the oldest of the boys, had his own store in Rabat, wholesaling or trading spices. He died in his late twenties from a lung disease, leaving his wife and two young daughters, Suzanne and Georgette. My brother Sam was named after him.

Simon, the other brother, was assassinated in 1955 in Rabat, where he lived with his wife, Rosa, and six children. He suffered and later succumbed to a fatal gunshot wound by a Moroccan militant fighting for independence from France, also mentioned in the French book *Les Juifs du Maroc Identites et Dialogue*, page 281.

My uncle Simon was a store owner in Rabat, selling tobacco products. Like in mainland France, all cigarettes and tobacco products were regimented and controlled by the French authorities. The underground Moroccan party fighting for independence from France wanting to disrupt and hurt the local economy, and they called for a strike to all merchants and store owners. The French authorities forced my uncle to stay open and guaranteed his safety by posting an armed police officer near the store. Both my uncle Simon and the police officer were gunned down. My brother

My father, David Benayoun, late 1930s

Simon, born in 1957, a couple of years after this terrible event, was named after him.

My father attended French elementary school in Settat as well as Hebrew religious studies under a traditional rabbi in a local synagogue. He graduated from elementary school and obtained his Certificat d'Etudes, which was quite an achievement at that time in the early 1930s in a small town like Settat. I remember as a child seeing a big, heavy book around the house from the famous French author Alexander Dumas. The name of the book was *Georges: Un Drame a l'Ile Maurice en 1824*, which had been given to my dad as a special award at his graduation from elementary school at the age of twelve or thirteen, or not long after that according to later interviews with my aunts, his sisters. I learned that my father was sent off to the big city of Casablanca to live and work with his uncle Abraham, called Braham, who was one of Amram's brothers. It was quite typical at the time for a young Jewish boy recently graduated from the local French Alliance Israelite Universelle to get some kind of apprenticeship to learn a new profession.

Braham Benayoun, my father's uncle, was the owner of a retail store of dry goods in Casablanca and needed a young assistant to help around the store, together with his own son about the same age as my dad and named exactly as my dad, another David Benayoun. The son was later to be known to our family as "David el Kraah," the bald one, in reference to his prematurely balding head.

Tonton David, our cousin, was a joyous, gregarious, lively man who seemed to always enjoy life and was quite a prankster. Tonton David led an interesting life. He was married to Alegria and they never had any children. Early in his life, he was not as religious as my dad was, and he had a passion for hobbies such as photography, filming, playing musical instruments like the mandolin and accordion, traveling, raising singing birds, and fishing.

I owe him for some of the only existing old photographs of my parents, particularly my father. After my dad passed away in December of 1980, and knowing that Tonton David was an avid photographer, I took the initiative of contacting him in Casablanca around 1990. I wrote him a letter from Texas asking him to share any old photographs he might still have, and luckily, he was able to forward me about a dozen remaining photos he had saved while in the process of cleaning out his old files and documents. I was so happy to get these old black and white photographs as it gave me a glimpse of my father in those early years as such a handsome young man.

Whenever I think of Tonton David Benayoun, it brings a big smile to my face. He had a long professional career working for the main local newspaper, *Le Petit Marocain*. My dad and his cousin with the exact same name always enjoyed getting together. Many years later, we would run into Tonton David on Sunday mornings while fishing at the end of the long, massive rock jetty, called the Jetée Delure, within the port of Casablanca. Both Davids as teenagers had to spend a couple of years together sharing a room when my father was sent from Settat to work for his uncle Braham. During this time, they both evolved as teenagers, discovering life in the mid-1930s in the booming, vibrant, and ever-expanding bustling city of Casablanca.

Many years later, in early 1972 while in boot camp in northern Israel, while I was training in the Israeli army as a recent recruit, Tonton David came from Casablanca on a short trip to Israel to visit family. He got the great idea to go to the Israeli military headquarters in town and request special permission to see his supposed son—me. Tonton David, having exactly the same name as my dad and probably wanting to fulfill the special promise to his cousin to visit his son while in Israel, presented himself as my own father, showing his passport which resulted in me getting a welcomed 48-hour special break to visit him in the middle of a strenuous training period.

After working for his uncle and having a few other small jobs, and while still in his teens, my father was able to get hired by la Minoterie Algérienne, a mill involved in wholesaling and processing grains and cereals. At the time, the business was owned by two partners, Mr. Boumendil and Mr. Sabah, both Jewish originally from Algeria. This is where my father got his start, at the age of sixteen or seventeen, as a young clerk for a long, productive career, until his last day in December 1980 when he succumbed to a fatal heart incident. He worked there for all those years going through different promo-

My father standing on the right, first cousin David Benayoun wearing a white shirt and kneeling in the center

My Family

My father on the left, at the beach with his first cousin with the same name, David Benayoun, on the right

tions to become later in his life a master grain buyer and specialist in the storage and distribution of imported grain, such as wheat, through all of Morocco.

Traditionally, wheat flour, cooking oil, sugar, and tea were the basic major staples throughout Morocco and essential in the daily diet, always subsidized by the government to help regulate the price and to feed the growing population. In order to meet the demand, most of the wheat, or sixty or seventy percent, was imported into the country, brought by large French cargo ships coming into the port of Casablanca, the largest port in all of North Africa, recently completed by the French.

Dealers, buyers, distributors, and mill owners from across the country met these ships upon docking at the port to bid and buy the grain to store, resell, distribute, and process for flour. The labor to unload these large cargo ships of thousands of grain sacks from the bellies of the boats to the trucks on the docks was done manually, mostly on the backs of several hundred strong Arab laborers freshly arrived from the countryside. This was one of the reasons why my father, and later my brothers and I growing up, knew very closely some of these workers, who would become so attached to my father and our family they were almost like family members. Among them in the early years was a Jewish worker by the name of Moshe that I only have some vague memories of as I was very young then.

I recall Moshe accompanied my father once a week to the local street market of Bab Marrakech to haul on his back all the fresh vegetables and fruits purchased by my father and bring them all the way back home. My father made the rounds, making his selections among the many colorful stands loaded with piles of vegetables and fruits. He would then have the almost required, conventional, friendly price haggling with each merchant. Poultry was always bought alive before being ritually slaughtered on the spot by the Jewish *shohet*, a person officially licensed to slaughter and knowledgeable about Jewish food laws. Moshe made *Aliyah*, (the immigration of Jews from the diaspora to the land of Israel,) in the mid-1950s.

I grew up knowing Ali, Omar (El Frizzy), Bouazza, and Hmed. Most of them many years later came to pay their respects during the shiva for my dad after he passed away in 1980. Ali was the closest to my dad and the one we remembered so fondly. Ali was a Berber, or *Chleuh*, from the region of Marrakech in the Atlas Mountains. Berbers are the original people of northern Africa. Ali was a sweet, proud, sincere, honest, and gentle man working for and loyal to my father.

My father, in his office at the Minoterie Algerienne located on Route de Mediouna on the east side of town, supervised several hundred laborers at the big warehouses for grain storage. From early on, my father liked

Ali and trusted him. It seems that they developed a strong complicity because of Ali's honesty and straightforward attitude, not intimidated in the least by the difference in social class, religion, or professional hierarchy, always showing respect and admiration for my dad. While I was growing up, Ali was often around our home to help with all kinds of chores, especially during big preparations and cleanups for holidays, bar mitzvahs, or any big celebrations.

There is a famous story about my older sister Jacqueline, when she was in elementary school and one day my father could not pick her up after school. Ali was dispatched with his Mobylette moped to bring her home safely, to the slight embarrassment of Jacqueline who the next day had to explain to her schoolmates who Ali was. Ali would also at times pick up my brothers and me from the traditional Hebrew classes with Rabbi Eliahou and walk us through the old quarters.

Many years later, in the mid-1980s while on a short visit to Casablanca with my brother Simon, we went walking around the old neighborhood of Rue de Tanger, as we often do whenever we are in Casablanca, to revisit the Ettedgui Synagogue and the old quarters by the port, and we were able to track down Ali. We found his street address and paid him a visit in his home located in the old medina, an area of shops and cafés. We were so happy to reunite with him and exchange many stories regarding his old friendship with our father. Ali shared with us many details of my dad's days as a young husband starting a family. Ali was, of course, present at work that day of December 16 when my father suffered his fatal heart attack and had to be rushed to the Clinic d'Anfa.

We had a great visit with Ali in his home, where we were introduced to his second, younger wife and little kids by her. We had tea and snacks, looked at old pictures, and talked mostly about old memories of my father and the special bond and friendship between him and Ali. He gave me the name of a village back in the Atlas Mountains, as he was planning to sell his house in Casablanca and retire at last to his Berber village where he came from. Ali insisted one last time to accompany us and walk with us a little way back toward the modern quarters, while on the way pointing out for us the old home of Meme Hninah before her immigration to Israel in the early 1950s, as well as the home of Simy Levy, the first fiancée to my father.

Suzanne, My Mother

My mother was born in Casablanca in March of 1923, the eldest of six children—Suzanne, Perla, Rachel, Simy, Raphael, and Armand. Their parents, Messod Suissa and Hninah (née Asseraf), were married at a very young age in Casablanca. Messod was born in Marrakech around 1903 in a neighborhood called Rmillah, his parents moving there from Demnate, a rural village in the Atlas Mountains surrounding Marrakech. Messod was a shoemaker practicing his trade out of a small shop located in Bab Marrakech, the old Jewish quarter of Casablanca.

Meme Hninah was promised by her parents at the very young age of twelve, and within a few years after being officially married to Messod Suissa and able to conceive, she had several stillbirths. Hninah was losing hope of bringing a healthy child to the world, and as traditionally done in those days she was praying and seeking help by visiting holy shrines throughout the city, including the famous Muslim holy site tomb known as Sidi Belyout, not far from Casablanca's old train station. It was accepted back then that sometimes Jews and

My Family

Muslims would commonly visit each other's holy shrines, such as a tomb of a holy man, to say a special prayer or to wish for a remedy. When my mother was born, she was named Saada Aisha, loosely translated as "to help survive."

My grandfather Messod Suissa died at the relatively young age of thirty-nine years after he suffered a knife wound from a street robber going for his leather side bag. Due to a subsequent infection and complications from the wound, he succumbed a few months later, passing away and leaving his wife, my grandmother Hninah to care for their six children, the last two boys only a few years old.

Messod and Hninah Suissa, my grandparents on my mother's side

Meme Hninah

In the late 1930s in Casablanca, with six kids being left without a bread-winning father to help raise the family, that put the whole family in dire, very hard times. My mother's two younger brothers, Armand and

Raphael, had to go live with other relatives who could provide for them, and they grew up away from their mother. In order to survive and feed the family, my grandmother Hninah became a seamstress with a small portable sewing machine, in the market square and going to private homes to sew clothes, curtains, and other things. My mother, the eldest daughter, was a teenager, and as soon as she could she found employment, becoming a salesgirl in the local Bata shoe store.

My mother, Suzanne (Saida Aisha) Benayoun [née Suissa]

My mother met my father through common friends, probably around the late 1930s. The two seemed to hit it off very well from the start and fell in love right away, even though at the time my father was officially dating and under pressure from his family to be engaged to another young woman by the name of Simy Levy. The two families, on the woman's side and on my father's, were already anticipating and finalizing the future union. My father's family from the beginning didn't take well to my father's choice of my mother. One obvious reason was that Simy Levy's family and social background was much more appealing and seemed more appropriate than my mother's modest background and family status.

Many years later, an unusual coincidence came when my sister Evelyne recently arrived in Montreal, Canada, with her baby son, Nathan. Evelyne was looking for a babysitter in her building to stay with Nathan. She met one of her neighbors, an older lady also originally from Casablanca, and after a few polite exchanges regarding family names and background, it turned out to their total surprise that this lady was the same Simy Levy, the first girlfriend to my dad.

My parents around the time of their marriage in the early 1940s

David and Suzanne, my parents, seem to have gotten married in Casablanca around the early 1940s. No wedding pictures exist. The closest thing to a wedding portrait is around those years they appeared in a picture together with another couple getting married.

Our parents' first child was stillborn due to a complicated birth at home with the help of a midwife, as back then was customary. After that sad event, my parents made sure we were all born in a private, modern medical clinic. My brother Sam was born in November 1945 in a private clinic, the first of eight more children to come.

Samy, being the firstborn, has some memories as a child spending time visiting our grandparents' home in Settat. Meme Mryem, telling us about his visits to Settat with my parents as a young couple coming from Casablanca, recalled one day Samy was riding his tricycle not too far from my grandparents' house and was almost swept away by the rising muddy water of a nearby *wadi*, a stream bed that fills up after a rain.

19 Rue de Tanger

My first recollection as a child was in our home at 19 Rue de Tanger. Prior to that my parents as a young couple were living in a neighborhood called Jemaa el Chleuh, or the Mosque of the Berbers. That first home is where most of the older siblings—Sami, Jacqueline, Armand, Prosper, and I—were born. I don't have any recollection of that house, being too young, but my older brothers seem to recall it. While on a family visit to Casablanca in 2007, Armand took me there to show me the street and the house.

Many years later, after moving to Israel at the age of fifteen and meeting my grandmother Meme Hninah in the small town of Tirat Hacarmel on the outskirts of Haifa in North Israel, she related to me her memories of pushing the baby carriage with me in it during the big move from Jemaa el Chleuh, Rue Sidi Fateh, to Rue de Tanger. Since I was born in 1953, this must have taken place probably sometime during 1954, shortly before she and her two sons, Raphael and Armand, immigrated to Israel, leaving behind my mother and her two sisters, Simy and Rachel, and one other sister I never knew existed until much later, named Perla.

Perla, my mother's younger sister, apparently fell in love in the early 1950s and eloped to get married to the young man who had been secretly courting her. Perla decided to convert to her new husband's faith, Islam, and abandoned her Jewish faith, severing all ties to her family. During those days back in the early 1950s, this was considered a big taboo and an embarrassment to the two families and both communities — one of the reasons we were probably never told or made aware as young children of her existence. Many years later, after the sudden passing of my father in December 1980 and during the subsequent mourning period, I finally was able to meet my Aunt Perla, aka Zohra Sebati, and help her younger son, Zoair, come to Austin to study at the University of Texas, where he graduating from. We reconnected with my Aunt Perla and her husband then, meeting their children who grew up in Casablanca never knowing that their own mother was born in the Jewish faith. My Aunt Perla later insisted on wanting to travel to Israel in the company of our mother, to visit one last time her own mother, Meme Hninah, who was then in her late eighties.

Samy, Jacqueline (1947–2010), Armand, Prosper (1953–2007), Robert, Evelyne, circa late 1950s

19 Rue de Tanger

Our upstairs apartment at Rue de Tanger was located near the Casablanca maritime port. Our main entry door was at the end of a long, narrow courtyard, near a massive wooden front door to a dispensary for treating young nursing mothers and their babies. A set of two flights of stairs led to our four-room apartment.

Our second-level apartment had four large rooms, a small kitchen, and a bathroom, with an open area in the center covered by a glass skylight dome, called a *verriére*. From the main central room, a small staircase gave us access to a big terrace — *el stahh* in Arabic — on the rooftop, overlooking the commercial port in the distance and the surrounding neighborhood buildings and homes with lower rooftops. *La terrasse* on the roof played a big role in the daily activity in the house as an open-air extension used constantly for different activities, among them cooking and laundry washing and drying.

My mother was assisted by at least one maid who, with a growing family like ours, was always busy doing necessary chores around the house. Cooking was always going on in the kitchen and also on the rooftop terrasse where we had a small charcoal fire in a typical small Moroccan clay brazier, called *el mezmar*, which was where flavorful *tagines* would simmer for hours.

La terrasse had in one corner a wooden cellar shed used for storing root vegetables, bags of flour, and wicker baskets full of different kinds of beans, rice, potatoes, etcetera. The space was also used as a laundry room where our Arab maid would do on a regular basis the laundry for our expanding household. The clothes, bed sheets, blankets, and other things were, of course, laundered by hand as in a typical Moroccan household in the 1950s, using the traditional washboard, *el louha de sabon*, rubbing the garments with large brown cubes of Arabic soap, *sabon el arbi*. The laundry was hung out to dry on metal wires crisscrossing the terrace. Very often after school, the terrace would become an ideal playground for us kids, exploring the view, running around the rooftop, and just enjoying the fresh air, with the deep blue Atlantic Ocean not too far in the distance.

*On the rooftop of 19 Rue de Tanger,
my sister Jacqueline and I, circa 1956*

I have some vague memories of the wedding of my father's niece Suzanne Elbaz that was celebrated on that rooftop, shortly before she moved away to live in France with her new husband. I believe my brother Sam's bar mitzvah also took place there.

I have a clear memory the day King Mohammed V died, in February 1961. I was not quite eight years old, and it was during the day. Our maid and some neighbors all gathered up on the rooftop to watch very anxiously as the news spread in the city and all were concerned of possible civil unrest. From our rooftop we stood above, watching as the whole city reacted in shock to his sudden death, apparently following a routine surgery. The transition to his son Hassan II went smoothly, despite everybody's concerns.

On the rooftop of 19 Rue de Tanger: my brothers Armand on the left and Samy behind me, with our dog, Diana, in the background and the cranes on the waterfront of the Casablanca maritime port

King Mohammed V became quite popular among the Jewish segment of the Moroccan population, particularly during World War II as he took a strong stand to protect the status of the Moroccan Jewish community, making it clear to the French collaborating government of Vichy. He made sure the treatment of the Moroccan Jewish population was equal in all manners to the rest of his Moroccan subjects. A German delegation with the assistance of the local French representative was already initiating a general Jewish population census in Casablanca. Luckily, not too long after that the Allied forces led by the US Navy landed in Casablanca on November 1942 on their way to start the battle to liberate North Africa and fight the German forces and their French Vichy allies. Mohammed V was the grandfather of the current king, the much liked and respected Mohammed VI.

The facade of 19 Rue de Tanger facing Rue de Safi. Our apartment was the upper three windows plus the rooftop

19 Rue de Tanger

*The stairs entrance to
19 Rue de Tanger
on the left side*

*Visiting
Rue de Tanger
with my family
in 1991*

In the dining room, there was a large window overlooking the street below. I remember the big walled compound across the street, with gardens and living quarters of the French resident general protected by a big white wall. Each corner of the wall was reinforced with a big, ancient cannon buried mouth first in the ground. We also had a view of the public water fountain that was a gathering spot for the neighborhood, serving many of the locals who did not have running water and had to rely on the fountain. This was quite a busy spot where people would gather daily to get their containers filled and hauled back to their home or business.

Among the frequent visitors to the public fountain to haul fresh water was the typical *guerrab*, or water carrier, a common sight in the streets of Casablanca, ringing his shiny brass bell as he walked, dispensing for small change some fresh water from a large, black goatskin carried by his side. Upon request, he would pour some cold water into shiny brass cups. The inside of the goat skin was typically lined with a special *goudron de bois de thuya*, cedarwood tar, that added a special aftertaste to the cool and fresh water.

In our home, fresh bread was baked daily. Dough was taken by the maid to the local neighborhood wood-burning public oven, *el ferrane*. Most households would have their daily fresh bread sent there to bake. This public oven was a place where most of the maids from the neighborhood households would gather almost daily, bringing in the batch of bread to be baked in the oven on large, flat, metal pans. The maids would gossip and exchange the latest happenings in the neighborhood and in the different families. Each family had a special marking on their bread dough or a particular pattern to recognize their own pan.

Friday was a big and busy day at the ferrane, as all the Jewish household families in the neighborhood would send challah bread to bake in the morning. Every Friday while retrieving the delicious baked Shabbat bread in the afternoon, the maid would deliver to the ferrane at the same time a large pot containing the traditional Dafina dish. The Dafina famous Shabbat dish is a typical slow cook stew composed of meat brisket , chickpeas ,rice or wheat grain, potatoes, oignons , whole eggs in the shell. The Dafina will slow cook overnight while parked inside the wood burning public oven and will be retrieved the next day .Every Saturday as my father and brothers after returning home at the conclusion of the morning prayers and services, we will gather around the festive Shabbat table to enjoy the weekly special family meal and the traditional aromatic Dafina Stew, almost as a symbol marking the Jewish Sabbath.

Further down on our street was a big wall with a large gate in the middle. When the gate was sometimes left opened, you could glimpse the imposing Spanish Catholic Mission, with its large chapel dominated by the bell towers. The chapel was surrounded by nice landscaped grounds. We could hear the bells tolling every Sunday for special Christian religious celebrations.

Right across from the Spanish Catholic Mission was a narrow street by the same name of Rue de la Mission, where our childhood synagogue was located. So within one block, almost on the same street, we were in the vicinity of a Spanish Christian Catholic church, with the weekly sound of its bells, and several mosques a couple streets away, with their imposing minarets dominating their surroundings and from where emanated loud, daily calls to prayer by the *muezzin*. Perched on the top of the minaret, the muezzin, and much later, loudspeakers, spread the traditional invitation to prayer throughout the neighborhood, starting in the early morning hours before sunrise. My early childhood at Rue de Tanger consisted of attending elementary school at Ecole Albert Sonsol and Rabbi Eliahou's Hebrew studies every day after school and on Sundays.

Synagogue Ettedgui

My father, who came from a religious background, received a good religious education while growing up in Settat. While he attended school at the local Alliance Francaise, he also attended a local *yeshiva* and studied under a rabbi. With his father, he attended the local synagogue for daily prayer services. Later, the synagogue played a big role in our upbringing and in interactions with all the Jewish families in the neighborhood on a daily basis, and especially every Shabbat and on Jewish holidays.

The history of the Synagogue Ettedgui goes back to around 1860 when the family Ettedgui, originally from Tetouan, a small town in the Spanish region of northern Morocco, moved to the recently established and expanding new city of Casablanca. As more Jews started to be drawn from surrounding small towns and villages to move to the Jewish quarter, the Ettedgui family, who were traders and wholesalers with connections to the local Arab government, obtained in 1873 a special authorization from the King of Morocco, Moulay Hassan I, to build a small room for community worship and prayers for Jewish members of their community. A site close to the main port was selected. Some years later, after the French took over Morocco around 1912, a new building as it stands today was erected on the same original spot and continued to be owned and managed by the descendants of the Ettedgui family for the use of the local Jewish community.

The Synagogue Ettedgui was located off the narrow street, behind a big, white wall. Two massive, green wooden doors gave access to a courtyard surrounding the synagogue building. Several marble steps led up to the beautiful, arched, wooden double doors to the actual synagogue entrance.

At one side of the yard, right against the wall, was a water well, which is now encased with a metal lid and padlock and has a green wooden bench over it. The old water well, probably dug originally when the synagogue was built, would serve the purpose for the ritual of *Tashlich* done once a year before Rosh Hashanah. During this special service, congregants gathered around the open well to symbolically cast away their sins before starting a new slate for the upcoming new year.

On one side of the synagogue building was a small apartment that served as living quarters for the synagogue caretaker, or *shamash*, and his family. Right across the front yard, another wall with a small gate in it separated the main courtyard from access to the garden. Le *jardin* and the standing ruins in it were apparently the remains of a small apartment compound where several Jewish families lived up until November 1942, when the military Allied forces and the US Army under General Patton appeared on the Moroccan Atlantic coast to start the battle to push the German army and the Vichy French collaborators out of North Africa.

The battle for Casablanca, named "Operation Torch" lasted about three days. The Vichy French collaborating forces, comprised of warships and fighter airplanes, refused to surrender and fought the American forces. Several airplane dogfights and artillery bombardments took place all around the coast and the port of Casablanca. The apartment compound adjoining the synagogue was destroyed and a family of four was killed.

The shells were probably intended for another compound in the vicinity less than a block away, where it was rumored that the German military delegation was headquartered. In the same vicinity was the residence and main compound of the Vichy French military governor. The synagogue building was left intact and did not sustain any damage.

Years later these ruins, that we as kids commonly referred to as "le jardin de la synagogue," became our playground—an amazing, fascinating playground and elaborate maze among the ruins. We would look for any excuse to explore the many hidden corners and play while escaping the watchful supervision of our parents gathered to pray inside the synagogue. Any excuse or break during the long religious services found us kids quickly escaping and roaming in the garden.

The sons of the different families attending prayer services were les Benayoun, Zekri, Abittan, Elmaleh, and Assayag kids. We would venture exploring the half-demolished rooms with roofs caved in and wide open to the sky. Several of the original painted walls and the stairs leading to old, dangerously standing rooftops remained, with weeds, wildflowers, and vegetation growing wildly everywhere. We would ambush and chase wild cats roaming through the ruins, watch wild birds, and divide ourselves into smaller groups to play war games in the many hideouts in the small compound.

One small portion of the garden, close to the entrance door and surrounded by a couple of large peach trees, was cleared in order to accommodate a small, open space where every year the traditional *sukkah*, a temporary hut or shelter, was erected during the fall, a few weeks after Rosh Hashanah, for the festival of Sukkot. The sukkah reminds us of when God provided for the

Israelites in the wilderness after they were freed from slavery in Egypt.

I recall the different families of the synagogue that we were close to, like Menahem Zikry, the tailor, who sat in front of my father, closer to the *tevah*, the raised platform where the rabbi read the Torah. Mr. Wazanah was leading services in the synagogue and was the community's *mohel* who did the traditional, ritual circumcisions. Isaac Carciente sat near my father, and there was the family Assayag; Abraham Elmaleh, the textile merchant; Eiyouch, a trader; and David Niddam, a saddle maker.

Iyahou, a carpenter, sat on the right side of my dad, always sharing around his little silver snuff box full of the brown, fine-powdered tobacco, slightly perfumed. There was a complete ritual involving sharing snuff. First, when offered, make a quick acknowledgement by touching the tips of your fingers to the hand offering the open snuff box, then bring your fingers to your lips. Then you may reach inside the small box, using two fingers to grab a small pinch. Bring the snuff directly to your nostrils, or another way was putting the powdery brown snuff on the back of your hand, right behind the thumb, then bringing it to your nostril to snuff it up.

Every Saturday morning after services we were allowed by our father to pay a visit to El Hssin, the owner of a tiny pastry and fresh milk products shop in our neighborhood. We would get a treat like a *petit pain au chocolat* or *un palmier* that was put on tab for my father to settle later, since on Shabbat we were not to handle money.

Isaac Carciente, being part of the Ettedgui family probably through his mother, was the actual day-to-day manager of the synagogue and played a big role in making sure the daily operation of the synagogue and its services flowed smoothly. Every Saturday afternoon, a group of friends, namely Zekri, Abittan the fabric merchant, Elmaleh, Benayoun, and a few others gathered at the synagogue for a group study of religious text and commentaries and particularly Zohar, which is the North African Jewish Cabala, or Jewish Mysticism. Our dads made us come with them during these afternoons and we looked forward to our escape into the exciting playground that was the adjacent ruins.

Many times, while playing within the walled compound of the synagogue or on our way there from home, some local Arab kids would tackle us or bother us. On one of the Saturday afternoons while the adults were inside, gathered around their weekly study session, we were running around playing in the front yard and the garden while outside the synagogue wall in the small street just in front of the entrance, a band of Arab kids were playing ball. They decided to start throwing small sticks and rocks over the wall to annoy us. We kids inside decided to reciprocate by opening the big wooden gate and throwing the projectiles back at them.

After a few minutes of this game of cowboys entrenched behind the wall and Indians on the outside, we noticed my oldest brother, Samy, walking down the street, making his way to the synagogue. He must have been about fourteen or fifteen years old. Watching him as he made his way from the top of the narrow street down toward us, we felt relief and were reinvigorated, as if the cavalry was coming to the rescue. We told him of the little harassment we were being subjected to by the neighborhood kids.

Samy, having lived in France the last couple years, was not very intimidated by the band of Arab kids. He noticed the leader of the band and the instigator of the rock throwing and went right away to confront him and try to tackle him. We stood close to the wooden gate entrance of the synagogue, afraid to venture out. We watched as Samy wrestled down the leader of the band, but while he had him on the ground one of the other kids grabbed a big piece of lumber and came up behind. Before we could warn Samy, he hit him on the head with it and we watched in horror as Samy collapsed, knocked out on the ground.

The Arab kids immediately scattered. We panicked, rushing to alert our parents inside the synagogue, thinking the Arab kids had just killed my brother. The adults came immediately, carried Samy inside the courtyard and got some fresh water on his face. After a few slaps, he regained consciousness and recovered with just a minor bruise showing on his head.

My father became very active after Mr. Wazanah moved away, probably to Israel or France. My dad started leading services and reading the portion from the Torah roll during the weekday services on Mondays and Thursdays and reading the expanded portion at Shabbat morning services. At home he was always studying and rehearsing the long Torah portion for Shabbat, reading and chanting to be sure he knew all the right notes.

He would ask any of us kids to check on his performance. He would read and chant from a book that had a reproduction of the text like on the Torah scrolls while we looked at another book with regular text and punctuation and, most important, the cantillation for the chanting notes. We could monitor or correct him if necessary.

My father led prayer services at Synagogue Ettedgui well into the end of the 1960s. The Jewish population was gradually moving away from the old neighborhood and it became difficult to get a *minyan*, the necessary minimum ten Jewish participants required to conduct daily services and be able to read from the Torah.

Synagogue Ettedgui

My family, as well, around the early 1960s decided to move to the center of town, into the heart of the modern French quarters, to Rue Berthelot.

At the entrance of Synagogue Ettedgui, after my brother Simon's and my bar mitzvahs, 1968. My father on the left wearing a hat, my brother Michel behind me, left side, and brother Prosper upper right.

After my brother Simon's and my bar mitzvahs, 1968, with my mother. Sister Evelyne is behind me.

Recent pictures of Synagogue Ettedgui converted to a Jewish museum

Synagogue Ettedgui

Bimah platform for the Torah scrolls

Revisiting Synagogue Ettedgui in 2007

Monsieur Isaac Carciente

After our move from Rue de Tanger, I believe services were held only on Shabbat. My father would still make the long walk from Rue Berthelot on Friday evenings and on Saturdays for Shabbat, since he could not drive. My brothers and I would follow him, walking by his side all decked out in our dressy Shabbat clothes. The walking distance separating our new home in the center of town to Synagogue Ettedgui in the old quarters was probably a couple kilometers, taking us through the wide, modern Boulevard de la Gare, la Rue de l'Horloge, the Tazi passage lined with shops, and the Place de France where Isaac Carciente would usually pick up French magazines and the French newspaper from the newspaper kiosk.

We crossed the big, open, modern Place de France, busy with car traffic, before entering the old Arab quarters through la Rue du Commandant Provost. The narrow streets here were lined with clothing merchants and shops with shoes hanging from strings and dangling in the wind. We passed by the Cinema Imperial, and across from it was the store where we usually got our school supplies the first week of each new school year. We walked by the studio of the photographer, where the now-famous black and white family portrait of the Benayoun brothers and sisters was taken in the late 1950s. In the picture, we are all six of us lined up in our best outfits, in chronological order by birth from Samy to Evelyne. We passed by the big warehouse full of wooden barrels of wine. Then we walked by the main entrance to the big mosque adjoining the Arab girls' school across from the nearby port and finally turned onto Rue de la Mission to enter Synagogue Ettedgui.

Isaac Carciente developed a close relationship with my father, becoming very good friends. He often visited our home and was always welcomed to share Shabbat and Jewish holiday meals with us. Isaac liked to bring us sweets and interesting articles to read and loved having long talks and playing quiz games with us. He was an old bachelor, never married. The rumor was that as a young man, he fell in love and was engaged to a nice Jewish girl, but she for some reason ended up marrying and having a family with his brother, causing a huge love deception for him and big fallout with his own brother.

Isaac was also very close to another family, the Elmaleh, who were also very active within the synagogue. Isaac was the godfather of one of the Elmaleh boys, Dov, who was about my age, and he played a big role in teaching, tutoring, and taking care of Dov and spoiling him with sweets, toys, and comic books.

Mr. Isaac Carciente with baby Dov Elmaleh

Isaac was probably living off some limited income from his family real estate holdings. He lived in a modest, clean, one-bedroom apartment in a nice neighborhood. The apartment did not have a full kitchen, and I remember how he managed to use the large bathroom as a made-up kitchen. He would put a large wood cover on the bathtub and use that as a countertop to cook on. The main room had a big wooden armoire full of folders containing his large and diverse collection of stamps.

When I visited to play with Dov Elmaleh, Isaac many times showed us his stamps and shared with us his love of them, trying to initiate us to start collecting them ourselves. I started my own collection with Isaac contributing many stamps to get me started. Isaac's two passions in life were the total dedication, management, and upkeep of his family synagogue, which for him was a *raison de vivre*, and secondly, his large collection of stamps.

Collecting stamps and being a philatelist was Isaac's true passion, which I imagine produced little income through the years. He was a self-taught philatelist and was very knowledgeable about the whole world of stamps. He corresponded with many philatelists from all over the world. He would show us some of the most beautiful, colorful stamps from exotic countries, some I never knew existed. With his network of worldwide collectors, he constantly was exchanging monthly new issues of Moroccan stamps, with their official postal markings, or *tampon*, from the local main post office.

Isaac was notorious as well in recycling slightly used stamps, or stamps that came in on regular mail without the usual stamp marking, mainly from France or Morocco. He showed me how after cleaning and putting a new light coat of adhesive on them they could be reused — not exactly a legal practice.

Isaac did not drive and did not own a car. He liked to walk or use cabs to run his errands in town. One of his regular, almost daily stops was visiting the main post office for his stamp business. Sometime in the mid-70s, one Friday afternoon as he was leaving the main post office on his usual route and getting ready to cross the big Boulevard de la Gare, he was fatally hit by a motorcycle. In the resulting fall he must have hit his head against the hard pavement, dying on the spot. I was living at the time in Israel and was very sad when I finally learned about it.

Rabbi Eliahou

My father, being from the old school, believed strongly in a good, modern French education for his children. This education was easily available and offered by the schools of the Alliance Israelite Universelle. At the same time, my father wanted to keep the old tradition of Hebrew studies, mainly prayers study, under the supervision of the old, bearded, traditionally dressed rabbis, in this case Rabbi Eliahou Ibgui.

Rabbi Eliahou Ibgui and his brother Rabbi Braham came from a small village in the Atlas Mountains. Both typically dressed in the traditional garb of Moroccan Jews before the French influence and the new European trend, consisting of the black djellaba, a black tarbouche on the head, and the typical Moroccan footwear called babouches, the leather slippers in white or yellow.

Hebrew prayer study, Rabbi Eliahou

Both Ibgui brothers were managing a small synagogue in the old Jewish quarter and, for extra income, a prayer study program for children of all ages that acted as a mix of kindergarten and after-school Hebrew study. Sitting all of us in a room, under his watchful eye, Rabbi Eliahou had us reciting prayers and chanting proper tunes of the weekly *parasha* Torah readings and other daily prayers.

Rabbi Eliahou, our old-timer bearded teacher, always had with him a small black leather strip in his hand used occasionally as a whip to discipline us. The whip was used on us to correct our lack of focus or our mistakes in chanting, in the same manner as the typical Quranic *madrasa* or the *heder* schools in the old Jewish *shtetls* of Eastern Europe. I have to admit that for a long time I was scared and intimidated while being around the rabbi, even much later as a teenager.

I recall one Sunday morning making my way from home to attend the usual Sunday morning Hebrew study with my brother Simon. I must have been ten to twelve years old with Simon four years younger. My father entrusted me with a few coins to later pay for our haircuts. I got distracted by a common street scam, the three-card trick. This consisted of a person kneeling on a street corner shuffling three cards in front of a small crowd gathered around, then showing clearly to everyone which card was the ace. After shuffling the three cards some more, he would lay them face down on the ground. One of his accomplices acting as a bystander would put his foot on a card, successfully betting a few coins that it was the ace, guessing right each time and cashing in for the small crowd to see his easy winnings.

He made it seem so easy, thereby enticing everyone else to make a quick win and double their bet. I, of course, went for it and decided to try my luck and double the haircut money entrusted to me by my father. I chose the wrong card every time, or rather quick magic fingers made sure some way or another that I always ended up with the wrong card. I lost all my money, and once back home and confessing my gambling adventure, it did cost me one of the most memorable belt whippings by my father.

Albert Sonsol Elementary School

Albert Sonsol School, a preschool and elementary school, was located on Rue Fayolle *dans le quartier de la ferme blanche*, meaning in the quarter of the White Farm, which is the name of the area. The school belonged to the Alliance Israelite Universelle de France and was renamed in 1928 by the French authorities to honor the memory of Sonsol, a young Jewish man from Tetouan, Morocco, who fought in WWI for France and was killed in 1915. The school was divided in two, separating on one side the boys, the other for girls, and in the middle was *la maternelle*, or preschool.

    Most of the teachers were French nationals. Mr. Olivero, the principal, was a well-dressed, elegant, good-looking French gentleman with a strait nicely trimmed mustache. He was probably in his mid-forties then and in charge of the whole school. Occasionally students were sent to his office to be disciplined. Mr. Olivero, as common in most French schools in those days, would administer physical punishment by beating us on our lower legs, mainly on the backs of our calves, using a one-meter-long wooden ruler. He would make us stand against the wall and then he would administer a number of strikes, depending on the gravity of our mischief or the reason for being sent to his office.

    I recall one day when I was dispatched to his office and had to wait there for him to return. I took the liberty of taking a peek into a couple of shoeboxes on top of a file cabinet. Inside I discovered several silkworms crawling around in the box, probably a student school project. Shortly after that, growing silkworms was to become my first pet project.

I got some of these worms of my own and kept them in a shoebox, and with a couple friends went on an expedition to search for mulberry trees, the recommended food for these worms. Some of the villas in a certain neighborhood were known to have these trees. Once we located one, we had to be quick and discreet to climb to the lower branches and harvest leaves before escaping quietly to avoid attracting the local villa watchman.

Once I got home, I nicely placed the freshly harvested leaves in a plastic bag for storage in the refrigerator. I kept feeding my voracious worms until the little magic took place. The worms wove in one corner of the box the yellowish silk cocoons where, at the proper timing, the worm would slowly crawl into one and disappear, to reappear a while later as a beautiful little moth that in turn will lay eggs, where eventually more worms will come out from.

Madame Amant, our French teacher, liked me very much and bestowed on me the privilege of helping get the classroom ready in the morning before class, sometimes coming in earlier than the rest of the students. My big assignment was refilling *les encriers,* the white ceramic inkwells sunken in the center of the wooden desks. Using a one-liter glass bottle with a special pouring spout, I went through the classroom with the bottle of violet-colored ink and filled up all the inkwells in the small desks that each would seat two students.

From those early days at Ecole Sonsol, I am still in contact with some of my best friends. Lazar Oiknine and Albert Danino both live in Paris. Lazar's parents owned a small shoe factory no more than one block away from the school, and their apartment was above the factory. When we were in high school, me in Israel and he still in Casablanca, Lazar came to pay me a visit one summer and brought me some gifts sent by my parents. Lazar went on to medical school in France and is practicing as a physician in Paris. Recently after many years, I was able to track him down and we reconnected. Lazar was kind enough to share with me some great old photographs of the two of us back then, including some class pictures from our days in elementary school and high school.

After school, at around five o'clock, while all my friends and classmates went home to snack, play, and do homework, I would walk with my older brother about two blocks, carrying my *cartable*, the typical leather school bag, to attend the Hebrew school under the watchful eye of Rabbi Eliahou. We would remain there until my father came after work to attend the *Arvit* evening services, and only after services would we finally get to go home, riding with him in the family car.

Recently my brother Samy, born in 1945, mentioned his memories of my father's first bicycle, then a few years later upgrading to a motorcycle, used mostly to be able to commute to work at the warehouse and offices on Route de Mediouna on the other side of town. Only much later was he able to afford his first car, the Simca. That Simca Aronde left in me some very strong memories from my childhood. My father drove us every morning to school, most Sundays to fishing or to the beach, and once a year to the big *hiloula* celebration for remembering the great rabbis of the past. Recently I was able to find online some vintage flyers and original marketing brochures from the 1950s that have some great photographs of that particular model car. They are now framed and hanging in my study at home.

Preschool Albert Sonsol, 1959. Robert standing upper right

Elementary School Sonsol, 1962. Robert second row from top, first on the left

Outside our school every day as we were let out, numerous street vendors waited for us, selling snacks from their small wicker baskets. There were fried grasshoppers, sunflower seeds called *papaghayo*, pumpkin seeds, black seeds of watermelon, small cups of sour fermented milk called *rayb*, the white nougats *laban koule ouban* on a metal stick, and large apples on a stick that

Albert Sonsol Elementary School

Elementary school, Sonsol, 1963. Robert second row, standing, first on the right

were coated with bright red sugar syrup. Sometimes when we walked home our way took us through the narrow street of Bab Marrakech, the municipal old market and the busy fruit and vegetable stands with the hectic crowds of merchants and street vendors and their small wheeled carriages hauling goods and merchandise. The street was busy with a good many bicycles, the small mopeds called Mobylettes zooming by, and porters hauling goods on their backs and yelling *"balak, balak!"* which means "make way, make way!" Carts were pulled by donkeys, horses, or mules, and there was the heavy smell of manure in the streets. We were accustomed to making our way through this big, hectic, noisy street activity, holding hands together while holding tightly to our school bags.

Fishing with Father

Besides his dedication to his family and his faith and religious practices, my father had one other big passion—fishing. In my first memories of him, every Sunday morning he would try to escape from his busy routine of work, synagogue, and family and for a few hours he would disconnect from his intense schedule to go fishing in the port of Casablanca.

The preparation for Sunday morning fishing expeditions started on the previous day. One of his Arab workers, usually Bouazza, would go on his bicycle on a mission for several hours to catch live bait on the coast for my father. He carried a small burlap seine and looked among the rocks and in the small pools of sea water left by the receding tide, using his net to seine for shrimp, crabs, and worms. Bouazza would put his catch in a small wicker basket and bring it to our home. That small basket, with a wet towel covering it, would spend the night in our refrigerator until Sunday morning. It was kept in one of the vegetable drawers emptied for the occasion.

When Bouazza on his bicycle stopped by our home on Saturdays, my father always welcomed him, but if the catch of live bait was good, my father got really excited in anticipation of a good fishing day the following morning. Usually Bouazza enjoyed getting fed a generous plate of our Saturday dafina served to him in the kitchen, to thank him for his efforts in harvesting the live bait.

Saturday night after the Havdalah end-of-Shabbat ritual, my father would start his preparation for the next day's outing. He had special clothes and a hat dedicated for fishing. The pants were *daim gris*, which is what my father called blue jeans, and the shoes were typical French espadrilles with soles made of coiled rope. His fishing gear was quite basic, besides several fishing poles; he had a large wicker basket completely wrapped and lined with a heavy, brown burlap canvas stitched tightly by hand on the wicker frame. Inside he had an assortment of plastic and rusted metal boxes holding hooks, weights, and handmade corks and bobbers. His fishing pole was a long piece of natural cane bought from a merchant shop not far from the port. The dried, flexible cane was drilled through to receive an old wooden thread spool mounted on a metal screw. The spool was wrapped with several meters of fishing line to serve as a fishing reel. Metal loops were taped on the fishing pole every foot or so for the transparent fishing line to go through.

On Sunday mornings my father got up early as usual, around four-thirty, going first to attend Shacharit, the morning service at the synagogue, and then returning home for a quick breakfast of French baguettes, spreading his bread with butter and marmalade, accompanied by the traditional café au lait. After that, he would grab his fishing gear and head out to the port to enjoy his weekly leisure fishing escapade. Usually he would ask one of us boys to accompany him.

Once at one of the port entrances, past the guarded gate staffed by an armed police officer, we had access to the Jetee Delure. My father drove a couple kilometers on this very long breakwater, getting toward the end of it before carefully deciding on a particular spot to try his luck. Driving along, he would stop and greet other regular anglers and inquire on the conditions for the day, like the water clarity and the times of the sea tides. Some of the men were neighbors, like Messoud who drove a French Citroen 4CV having four horsepower. Another neighbor worked in a printer shop and was notorious for his exaggerated fish tales, always embellishing his experiences. Some anglers were professional locals making a living catching fish to sell, but most were just enjoying the outing and hoping to bring home some fish that was always highly appreciated as an ideal meal.

Many anglers were fishing for big mullets. The black mullet, *el burry*, was a small-mouth fish that could be seen sometimes in large schools skimming the water surface. They were commonly found at the fish markets. Fishing for the black mullet required using a whole different setup and a bait called *pelota*, which is Spanish for "ball." This was made of sardines, fine sand, and fish oil mashed together to create a very fishy dough, effective as bait for that particular fish but messy and stinky. Once handled in your fingers, it was hard to get rid of the scent. My father relied mostly on live bait like shrimp or worms.

The jetty was at least one-hundred feet wide and about a couple kilometers long. A set of stairs enabled us to climb to the side facing the open sea. That side was lined with enormous square boulders, to break the constant, pounding waves of the Atlantic Ocean. On some days the sound of the battering waves against the rocks was very powerful and intimidating, almost shaking the ground we were standing on.

When my father was younger, on the days when the sea was calmer he would venture to fish on the rough side of the jetty, facing the open ocean. He would use his specially equipped surf rod while standing on the boulders, casting far away from the rocks. In those days, he was apparently able to catch much larger fish like drum, sheepshead, and sea bass. When I started accompanying him on the fishing outings, I noticed that my father would favor the calmer side of the jetty. My mother, apparently out of concern for my father's well-being out on the jetty by himself, insisted that one of us kids tag along with him. That is one of the reasons my older brothers and later myself got to accompany him sometimes on his Sunday fishing outings.

The first thing my father would do was to bait the water surrounding his chosen fishing spot. He accomplished that by collecting a few small crabs and some already dead shrimp from the bait basket and putting them inside a rag to smash them against a rock and create a mush. The mush was cast into the water as chum to attract fish. He called this *grommege*, and once this was done, he would bait his hook with a lively shrimp and drop it into the water.

As my father focused on his line, I sat next to him, sometimes leaning on one of the large black mooring bits evenly spaced along the edge of the jetty. We sat facing the calm waters, enjoying the open blue water and watching the occasional maritime cargo ship traffic coming in and out of the large port, as well as the occasional ski boat or weekender sailboat going by. After a while, once he felt relaxed, he would sometimes chat or have a short conversation with me, unusual for us because he was always extremely busy with his schedule between the synagogue and long hours at work.

    One Sunday, when I was just starting high school, probably twelve to thirteen years old, I was sitting next to my father on the jetty watching him totally focused on his pole and the dancing little float on the water surface. That morning, the conversation led to my studies, and my dad wanted to know how I was doing in school with my classes and my grades. In French high school, the regular school year was divided into three trimesters, and at the end of each three-month period, if your grades were above average even slightly, you were awarded *un tableau d'honneur*, or an honor roll. The three options were honor roll granted, suspended, or refused.

    A student needs at least two out of three honor rolls granted that school year in order to pass to the next grade. In my case, that day answering my father's inquiries, I told him that my first three-month grade was slightly below average. I had a suspended honor roll. If I was able to make it to honor roll after the second trimester, the previously suspended roll would convert to honor roll granted, giving me the minimum two honor rolls required to pass class that school year.

    My father, wanting to encourage me to make a special effort for the next three months, made me an offer on the spot. Having seen that I really liked coming with him on a regular basis and I was eager to fish on my own, he promised that if at the end of the next trimester I got good grades, he would get me my own fishing rod. I thought it was a generous offer, because until then none of my older brothers ever had the option of having a fishing pole of his own. Occasionally my father would let us hold his fishing pole while he had a snack or took a quick break for a few minutes, but fishing on our own was very limited. I don't know if this promise made me double my study efforts, but in the end, I came through on my side of the deal. My grades improved, and I was very anxious to see if he would make good on his side of the bargain.

Indeed, when the day came, as promised my father took me to the local Arab store not far from the port. After carefully checking many canes lining the back wall of the store, he finally chose a long, flexible, smooth, and well-balanced cane perfect for me. With that, he added a few other minimal hardware purchases. He had one of his Arab workers put together the whole fishing pole with wooden reel and metal loops, the same as his other poles. One more condition was added as part of the deal. On Sunday mornings, I had to attend with him the morning prayer services starting at five-thirty, before having the privilege of going fishing with him.

Once I started fishing with my own pole, my father coached me on the different tricks of the trade—how to tie and attach the hook to the line, how to make the different types of knots to connect two fishing lines together, how to bait the hook, how to gently cast the line, how not to jerk too hard on the pole once the floating cork started to sink under the water surface, how to gently fight a hooked fish, and how to never rush. He always insisted on giving it one or two extra seconds before jerking the pole to set the hook, thus increasing the chance for a hooked fish. In the beginning when I started hooking fish on my own, my father would rush to my side and take the pole away in order to safely land the catch, but after a while I decided to resist his takeovers and try to do it myself and land my own fish.

Most of the fish we caught were small drum, sea bass, and sea bream—all sorts of pan-fry fish. Sometimes we would get lucky and catch some bigger fish to bring home and display for all the family to see before it was cooked for everyone to enjoy. I will always remember one Sunday when we came back home with a great catch of some very nice-sized sea bass and proudly displayed them in the kitchen for all my brothers and sisters to admire. Once the excitement was over, the fish were left in the kitchen sink waiting to be properly cleaned.

Next to the sink was a large window, usually wide open. One of the street cats that were always roaming on the rooftop of the moped shop below our apartment must have noticed the irresistible fresh fish smell. In a moment of inattention, while nobody was present in the kitchen, the feral cat snuck in through the window, grabbed in its jaws one of the fish from the sink, and made a run for it. By the time our maid walked in and took notice, the wild cat was already some distance away. My father was so upset, swearing to come up with a final solution on how to get rid of the street cats once and for all, especially after one of these street cats harvested his most precious fishing catch.

On the way to the port, next to the main entrance gate, we would pass a big building that was a school for merchant marine sea officers. Fishing with my dad those long hours on Sundays, sitting on that jetty keeping an eye on my floating bobber and watching the occasional large ships sailing away into the open blue sea, I gradually became enamored with the idea of maybe one day becoming myself a sailor or a sea merchant officer, sailing the big seas and discovering the world. That dream stayed with me for a long time, and later in Israel when the time came to enlist for my three years mandatory military service, I chose to apply for the course for Israeli Navy officers. After passing successfully a series of oral tests and making it to the final batch of fifty candidates, we were sent for a one-week intensive training and testing called *guibouche*. At the end of that week only thirty candidates were selected to proceed, and to my big disappointment I was not one of them.

Many times during the summer, after sitting in the sun for hours, my father, before packing and leaving to get back home, would decide to take a swim in the fresh, cooling waters of the port. He changed into his swimsuit in an area more like a long boat ramp under the pipeline. He was a very good swimmer.

Many years later, my brother Samy would tell a story about one such occasion when my father decided to take a quick swim after long hours fishing under the hot sun. Before jumping in the water, he had trusted Samy with the car keys of our famous Simca Aronde, but Samy accidently dropped the keys in the water. With no keys, the situation turned very upsetting for my father. Fortunately, he noticed two French scuba divers on a Sunday leisure outing swimming and spearfishing along the shoreline. He got their attention and enlisted their assistance to save the day, and they gladly volunteered to go on a treasure hunt and dove to try to retrieve the keys at the bottom of the sea. Luckily for Samy and my dad, the divers were successful at recovering the lost keys and my dad and brother were able to drive home after the big scare.

Samy was the one with the great merit to later take the initiative to produce a short historical video of our family in the early '60s. At the time, he had recently acquired a used Super 8 film camera bought from a cousin and was able to produce a short video film during visits in 1963 and 1964. This was the only color video of our family during those years, including some detailed visits to our apartment on Rue Berthelot, the bar mitzvahs of Armand and Prosper, the Synagogue Ettedgui, and fishing with my father at the port. A great video that I was able to convert and improve recently for better preservation and for family records.

Back to fishing. Sometimes when nothing was biting and the sun was beating on my head, I grew impatient, wanting to get back home. My father was adamant at staying at least until noon, even with nothing biting our bait in the water. One day I made the decision not to wait for my dad, and I walked on my own all the way home, a distance of about four or five miles away.

While walking on the jetty, halfway to the entrance I noticed a small crowd and heard music being played. As I walked closer, I realized there was some kind of military ceremony taking place, with some men in military uniform on shore next to a navy warship and two submarines lined up at the moorings. It was a Russian navy boat making a short visit to Casablanca, and I was witnessing the departing of the small fleet to the open sea. Probably most of the Russian representatives in Morocco had come to bid farewell to their compatriots. I was able to get very close and was so impressed by the sight of the military vessels. A national anthem was played and everybody on shore and on board stood at attention while the mooring ropes were cast away and the two submarines and the warship started making their way toward the open sea at the end of the jetty. The experience of witnessing a real submarine with my own eyes for the first time and the fact that it belonged to the Russian navy—the big Cold War enemy behind the Iron Curtain—made a big impression on me.

I must add that the fact that my father went fishing every Sunday while my mother was at home with all my brothers and sisters created some friction between my parents, especially when my father would sometimes extend his fishing hours and come back home past the usual midday return.

Sundays were also the days for big family outings. The options were usually the beaches to the north, on the outskirts of Casablanca on the road to Rabat, or a forested area to set up a picnic for a few hours in the afternoon. Most Sundays during the summer months, the family would get organized to spend the whole day at the beach, together with cousins, neighbors, and family friends. All our family packed in the Simca and headed toward either Fedala or Pont Blondin. We had a large canvas tent that my father set up on the beach. Pont Blondin was a nice, isolated beach away from the big city crowds of the local Casablanca beaches. It had a beautiful protected cove and great clear water. We usually met some other families or relatives and spent the day playing on the beach, many times unfortunately getting sunburned as back then we really did not take preventive measures to protect us from too much sun exposure.

Our parents gathered with cousins and friends to barbeque under the shade of the old canvas tent. My dad sometimes liked to play volleyball, and he very much enjoyed swimming. Occasionally he would bring a fishing pole and try his luck for a while from a spot on a bluff over the opening of the small cove. The strong currents in the Atlantic were quite treacherous, and we always had to be careful not to get too far from shore due to the strong undertow prevailing all along the Atlantic coast.

Fishing With Father

At the beach: My father on the left, my mother left front, Cousin David Benayoun at front right holding baby Samy, circa 1940s

Sunday picnic at the beach, mid-1970s

At the beach, Pont Blondin, 1968

22 Rue Berthelot

Our big move was from the old traditional Jewish and Arab quarters on the edge of the medina, near to the port of Casablanca, to the heart of the modern French quarters with the large avenues and beautiful, modern, multi-story buildings. Rue Berthelot is a street located off the Boulevard de la Gare, the main avenue that connects la Place de France with le Marché Central, the modern fruit and vegetable covered market centrally located on the big boulevard. The Boulevard de la Gare was a four-lane, divided avenue lined with a variety of small businesses and shops with large glass windows displaying clothing, appliances, furniture, and books. There were several terrace cafés and the famous movie theatres very popular at the time, like L'Empire, Le Ritz, and Le Rialto.

The Boulevard de la Gare, like most major avenues built by the French, was lined with tall, beautiful palm trees. The trees and architecture of the French buildings reflected the popular style of that time. Most of the buildings were built during the boom years around the 1920s and 1930s when the French were establishing and building all of the city infrastructure.

The city of Casablanca, the economic capital of Morocco, was constantly growing and expanding due to the influx of newcomers from the rural parts of inland Morocco. A great number of the white buildings lining the Boulevard de la Gare were in the style of French Art Deco of the mid-1920s. Only recently, after years of neglect, have the Moroccan authorities decided to create a foundation to preserve and restore some of these beautiful buildings.

My father found us an apartment on the first floor of a nice, white, three-story building on la Rue Berthelot. Our building was a typical French modern building located in the midpoint of la Rue Berthelot and probably built in the early 1920s. It had a big open terrace on top with a small apartment for the Arab family who took care of the building maintenance. The spacious rooftop was commonly used by all the tenants to hang laundry to dry. On the rooftop as well were six storage rooms, one for each of the six apartments.

Each floor had two apartments and one studio that we commonly called *la garçonniére*. The entrance to our building was through a massive wrought iron portal leading into a large rectangular hall with marble floors. This hall was a gathering place and a small ball court for basketball and volleyball games of the neighborhood kids. The white marble stairs leading to the three floors were lined with a heavy wrought iron balustrade topped with a nicely polished, rounded wood runner. Very often as a kid, I would ride it like on a horse and slide down the last straight segment from halfway from our first

Main entrance, stepping in from the street, 2010

floor down to the entrance hall. Each apartment entrance had massive wooden double doors. All six apartments had the exact same floor plan.

22 Rue Berthelot, our apartment on the first floor, behind the sign

Simon, Robert, and Armand on a visit to the old apartment in 2007, at our front door

Our apartment opened to a long, straight hall. On the left side was the living room, connected through a nice arch to the dining room. On the right side of the hall were two bedrooms for the kids who still lived at home. At the end of the hall was the large master bedroom — our parents' bedroom — separated from the big kitchen by a small room we called *le debarras*, a storage room. Early on, it was used as sleeping quarters for a live-in maid. Between the master bedroom and le debarras, sitting on a wooden shelf in the corner was the latest modern gadget that came with the new apartment — our new black landline telephone. The phone number as I recall was 657-94. Also toward the end of the hall, adjoining the kitchen, was a small powder room, and separately a large bathroom to accommodate the whole household.

The front rooms facing the street all had large balconies. The master bedroom had a double balcony. The back room, bathroom, and kitchen faced the back of the building and an inner courtyard. A portion of the inner courtyard was actually the corrugated fiberglass roof of a local motorcycle dealership on the ground floor, adjoining our building entrance. I remember the motorcycle brand was Jawa. This small rooftop and inner courtyard we commonly called *la petite terrasse*, to differentiate from *la grande terrasse* on the top floor of the building.

La petite terrace became my private playground where I would venture to explore and discover the hidden corners leading to many small alleyways that connected several buildings on our street as well as adjoining buildings on our block. It was also the private roaming grounds and domain of street cats and city pigeons. Often from our window, we witnessed the careful, slow-motion moves of cats trying to ambush birds. The most vivid memories of my childhood in

Casablanca are associated with la Rue Berthelot, since I was about eight years old around 1963 when we moved from la Rue de Tanger.

On the same floor, sharing the same landing in our building, was the Amzallag family. On the second floor were the Ganancia and the Dahan families. On the third floor, the Sasportas and the Creuniers. Across the street lived the Sultans. On the rooftop of our building, living in the small apartment, was an Arab family, and the wife was our concierge in charge of maintenance and cleaning the common area of our building. They were a Muslim couple, Khattab and his wife, the parents of Mohammed. The wife was in charge of cleaning the stairs and keeping us kids from being a nuisance when we gathered and played ball at the entrance of the building. Khattab worked as a doorman at the bank at the corner of Rue Berthelot and Boulevard de la Gare.

Across from our building was le passage du Cinema Ritz, and nearby was la Cremerie Moreno, a tiny corner shop that was mostly a long counter to accommodate four or five customers. It served café crème, espresso, and some pastries. Mr. Moreno was the owner of this shop, and I will always remember that there I tasted for the first time one of my favorite French pastries to this day, the delicious napoleon, or mille-feuille, that is layers of puff pastry and custard cream.

Not long after we settled into our new neighborhood, we were quite an attraction, being such a large family and more religious with my father being a synagogue leader. The first year, after the sukkah was built on la petite terrasse for Sukkot, all our building neighbors could hear the Benayoun family chanting in the sukkah. During the eight days of the holiday as we gathered each night around a beautiful table, richly decorated, joining our father in reciting and chanting the Kiddush, or wine blessing, our voices rose through the thin green cane roof of the sukkah and filled the inner apartment building courtyard. We probably brought a little nostalgia to our Jewish neighbors, much more assimilated into French culture than we were, probably reminding them of some forgotten old traditional religious Jewish customs.

Most of our new Jewish neighbors in Rue Berthelot were less observant Jews, not attending synagogue as much as we did, and more French assimilated. Some of them originally came from Algeria or Spanish Morocco. Most of the neighborhood kids attended the more renown and secular French high school, the Lycee Lyautey. My father would not approve of sending us there, mainly because Saturday, our Shabbat, was a regular school day there.

My older brother Prosper, I guess more easily influenced by my father, was attending a small religious high school called Lycee Yeshivah. When my turn came, I was able to convince my father to let me attend the Cours Complementaire located on Rue d'Indochine, which was the main secular Jewish high school from the Alliance Israelite in Casablanca, located right across from Lycee Lyautey.

After learning that the Benayouns were more traditional and frequent synagogue attendants, and that my father was leading prayer and services at a local synagogue, on special Jewish holidays several of our neighbors in our building started to ask to attend the Kiddush wine blessings around our holiday dining room table. We became very close with the Amzallag family from the apartment adjoining ours and sharing the same landing. They had five boys—Victor, Lucien, Hayme (Jimmy), Lilo, and Dede. Most of them were already grown up. My mother and Madame Alice Amzallag became very close friends. Dede, the younger son, was closer in age to me and my brothers Prosper and Armand. We became very close as Dede would hang out most of the time in our house, often sharing meals with us, enjoying my mother's cooking.

On the second floor, Madame Dahan was living with her teenage son, Robert, and her elder mother. She was originally from Algeria and had some Spanish background. Madame Dahan, the younger one, was a single mother raising her only son. She was very elegant with beautiful long hair and a brown birthmark right below her right eye. She seemed to be attracted to and in admiration of my father. The mother and daughter Dahan became known as the "control tower," or *les corbeaux*, meaning "the crows," of our street, spending most of their time on their second-story balcony watching the ins and outs of all the foot and car traffic on the whole street.

The Dahan son, Robert, whom we called Coco, played in a band and had a big privilege to have his own garçonniére on the second floor, adjacent to his mother's apartment, where he could rehearse playing his music. His one-bedroom studio became the main hangout of all the teenagers of our building. One Friday night, most of the building neighbors were invited to gather around the Dahan's famous family TV set and watch proudly the live broadcast of our Rue Berthelot musician star, Coco Dahan, and his band play on Moroccan national TV.

The Dahans were the first family in our building to get the latest electronic gadget at the time—a brand new black and white television. We kids would be occasionally invited to come and watch soccer games and sometimes movies on the condition that we would restrict ourselves not to sit on the rug or on the sofa. I still have some vivid memories of my experiences watching soccer games from the Spanish league broadcast on Moroccan TV, usually on Sundays.

On the second floor with the Dahans was the Ganancia family with their two boys, Daniel and Robert. Robert was friends with my older siblings Jacqueline and Armand. The Ganancias were also from Algeria. The father, Edmond, in his younger years was in the French military in Algeria as a Zouave, a soldier of the light infantry corp. On the third floor was the Sasportas family. One of the sons, named Doudou, together with my older brothers Armand and Prosper belonged to the young group of Jewish teenagers on our street. On the third floor, as well, was the only non-Jewish couple in our building, the older couple Mr. and Mrs. Creunier who were both French. He was a correspondent for the French newspaper *Paris-Presse L'Intransigeant*. I was to learn much later that they had a daughter who was brutally murdered in the mid-1950s while traveling in rural Morocco.

Most of the teenagers when not in school would gather downstairs in the hall. At the entrance of our building, they played volleyball or basketball while keeping an eye out for the concierge coming down the stairs yelling to scare us so that we would scatter and run for cover before formal complaints to our parents. A few years later, a small coffee shop called le Tafraout opened across from our building and it became a gathering place for the neighborhood. No alcohol was served, but two large pinball machines there became the big local attraction.

At one end of our street was the traditional, small neighborhood grocery store, owned by and run, like most similar small stores across town, by a Berber Moroccan family. The grocery store was where we usually got most of our candies and snacks and last-minute needs for the house. The grocery store also supplied us with propane tank replacements for the kitchen. The delivery boy, a young boy we and most of our neighbors commonly called "Elmucho" was probably related to the store owner and was in charge of replacing the cooking gas tanks for all the neighbors' stoves.

Once a year during the Christmas period at the end of December, a big event took place on the Boulevard de la Gare. The long, four-laned boulevard was closed to traffic for one night, and a bike race was held on the road. All the best sport bike clubs and local athletes joined the race, among them the Moroccan bike champion at the time, El Gourch. The night race involved laps and dozens of kilometers around the long boulevard. The whole family would gather on the balcony and get a glimpse of this *peloton* when it passed by the nearby street corner.

Another family that moved from the old districts by the port at the same time as we did was the Edery family. Nissim and Rachel Edery had six kids — two sons and four daughters. Gisele, one of the daughters, was my age and close to my sister Evelyne. One of the boys, Loulou (Elie), was the same age and closer to my brother Armand and later became his partner in crime. Daniel was about my age or slightly older and was in my class in high school at the Cours Complementaire. The Edery family had moved to the area several months before us to a modern multi-story building up the street from Rue Berthelot and across from le Passage Sumica on Rue Nationale. They lived right above the famous café and brasserie la Chope. Their building was on a corner of la Rue Blaise Pascal, the street that was to become the main drag and pedestrian street. Their building was new, much more modern than ours, and had two entrances and two elevators. The main entrance was for the tenants and public access, and a second entrance was for the house cleaners, suppliers, and maintenance.

The Edery and Benayoun families had a very close relationship. Rachel and my mother enjoyed spending time together. Nissim Edery, the husband, was originally from the Spanish zone of northern Morocco outside Tetouan and spoke Spanish fluently. The family frequently went back for visits to the northern coast of Morocco around Arzilla and Tetouan where his family was from.

The BB Gun

At the Cours Complementaire a few students were from Muslim families, and in my class I became friends with one of them. His name was Chems-Eddine Youssef. One day, Youssef invited me to come play with him at his house. I had to ride the bus to a neighborhood of single homes and villas called L'Oasis, on the outskirts of town in an area where I had never ventured before. He met me at the bus station, and we walked together to his family villa, which was a very nice villa shaded by large trees and with a beautiful backyard. His family had two large German shepherd dogs in the yard. After we played in the yard for a while, I was welcomed by his mother to come inside the home into a beautiful room furnished and decorated in the Moroccan style, what I came to learn later was commonly called *salon Arab*. There were low sofas and some benches made of beautifully carved wood, with large cushions and decorated pillows. Most of the Jewish homes I was familiar with, including our own, were all decorated and furnished in a modern European or French style, so this was definitely different, and I liked it. We were treated to a nice snack by the maid of a typical mint tea and a large selection of cookies and sweets. I remembered for the first time feeling like I was being treated like an adult guest.

Youssef's father was at the time the president of a big Moroccan workers union called Rajah, and also the president of a big soccer team in the national league by the same name. Youssef told me about his different trips out of Morocco with his family, and one particularly left an impression on me. His recent trip was to Russia, visiting the Red Kremlin in Moscow and particularly the Lenin mausoleum, where he saw on display the glass coffin with the well-preserved body of the father of the communist Bolshevik revolution, Vladimir Lenin.

Later on, Youssef showed me his BB gun, which captivated my attention. At the end of that afternoon, I was able to convince Youssef to lend me his BB gun to take home. That was my first introduction to guns as a young boy. I first had to find the courage to get a supply of BB pellets. I had to locate a store where to buy them, but I knew of a sportsman gun shop not far from our street, near the Cinema Lux. Every time I walked by that store, I loved spending time glued to the large glass window, admiring the different hunting guns displayed.

Once I had the money and made up my mind, doubting seriously if at my young age I could legally purchase the necessary ammunition, I had to gather the courage to push the door open and go inside to get the sales clerk behind the counter to sell me a box of small BB pellets which were in the shape of tiny mushrooms. My brother Simon agreed to come along with me on this special mission. After several minutes standing in the street across from the store trying to convince Simon to buy the pellets for me, I realized he would not, so I gathered my courage and finally stepped inside. Trying to appear sure of myself, I casually requested a box of pellets, paid for it, and walked away as fast as I could before the clerk could change his mind.

My idea was to use the gun and try to ambush and practice some shots on the wild street cats roaming la petite terrasse. These cats were a big nuisance, frequently raiding our kitchen, often through our large kitchen window, for fresh fish or other meats in the sink waiting to be cleaned for cooking. Ever since the now-famous fish raid, where a large cat got away with one of my father's biggest fresh fish catches, I felt it was my duty to retaliate. These cats were practically wild, totally on their own, and were not too impressed by our vocal shouts to keep them away.

My younger brother Simon helped me set some small targets across the terrace and I got familiar with the rifle, taking practice shots from the bedroom window of our house, toward the backyard. One afternoon I set myself up to try to ambush the big tomcat. The culprit, known to us and spotted many times escaping with stolen food from our kitchen, finally ventured into my field of vision. I was ready for him and took my best shot, hitting him on his back thigh, causing him to jump high off the ground. Once back on his feet, he escaped, running not to be seen again in the same area.

A few days later while practicing some shots with Simon and having him run back and forth to set up the target across the yard, we got into a small argument about how many times he should get the privilege to fire the gun. As we argued, I made the mistake of threatening to use the gun on him to scare him off. I must have fired one BB on the ground not too far from where he stood, and that got him so scared that sure enough he ran to tell our mother the whole story of the gun. Our parents, of course, never suspected or imagined I had a borrowed weapon in the house. Once my father discovered it and after giving me a severe physical correction, the gun went straight back to its owner, my classmate Youssef.

Summer Camp Immouzer

I do not recall if any of my brothers or sisters attended any summer camps, except for Samy who was very active in the Jewish Boy Scouts. *Les Scouts Israelite de France* had a whole organization in Casablanca, and Samy became very involved as a Boy Scout counselor. One summer in the mid-1960s, my parents decided to send me to a summer Jewish camp located in the Atlas Mountains, on the outskirts of the city of Fes, in the town of Imouzzer du Kandar.

The opportunity presented itself when a cousin or a family friend, working in one of the Jewish programs' offices in town, offered a spot for me at a substantially discounted price to attend the summer sleep-away camp for two or three weeks. I packed a heavy suitcase and was driven to the Casablanca train station to join the group of young Jewish city boys and girls. Once on the train—my first ever train ride—I had quite a discovery leaving the big city and getting to see large open fields and pastures, valleys, rivers, and *douars*, which are the small Moroccan traditional villages, as the train made its way to the hills and mountains of northeast Morocco and the area of Immouzer.

Robert at summer camp Imouzzer, 1967

My memories of that summer camp were very strong in the sense that it was another powerful and very meaningful introduction and exposure to nature and the outdoors, an attraction that was to become a true passion for me in the years to come. In camp, our group of boys was named la Troupe de Jaguars, and each day we had different outdoor activities. We would march on hikes to interesting natural sites, like a local park with water springs and small streams. A favored hike I have a strong memory of was to la Cascade Imouzzer. We hiked into a small valley leading to a canyon, and at the end was a waterfall cascading from a small stream up on the rock wall of the canyon. Surrounding the small pools of water at the foot of the waterfall were several fig trees, and their particular pungent smell was to remain with me for a long time. While on a hike or in camp, our team sang a song still fresh in my memory.

"Jaguar toujours vaillant des patrouilles,
La route, les champs t'attendent,
Prend ton fanion et marches devant
Vers les terres lointaines:
Jaguar toujours!
Vaillant et fort!"

[Jaguars always valiant patrol; The road, the fields are waiting for you; Take your pennant and march ahead; To the distant lands; Jaguars always! (leader calls); Valiant and strong!" (group response)]

The whole experience of those few weeks at summer camp outside the big city influenced me so strongly in many ways, with the daily nature activities and the interactions with a completely new group of friends, sharing meals, playing games, constantly on the move in the big outdoors.

The camp itself was located on an isolated hill in the countryside and may have been an old French army barracks. The sleeping quarters for the boys were in a large room with two rows of bunk beds on each side separated by one long sink with multiple water faucets. The girls were on the other side of the building with the same set up, and in the middle as a buffer were the counselors' rooms and sleeping quarters. The dining area where we had our meals was a long, covered patio opened on three sides and with long tables. Little did I know that this type of living arrangement would be a forerunner and preparation for things to come later in my life. In Israel, I lived my last three years of high school in a kibbutz lifestyle in Aloney Itshak, a Kfar Noar, or youth village, starting in the summer of 1969.

Hiloula Rabbi Yehya Lekhdar

My first introduction to the outdoors and open spaces away from the big city had to do with the yearly festive ritual of pilgrimage to the sacred grave of our regional *tsadik*, or holy man. These festivals are better known by the Jews of North Africa as *hiloula*.

This tradition of praying at the gravesites of Jewish holy men evidently grew out of similar practices carried out by Moroccan Muslims. It is likely that the Berbers, the local native tribes of North Africa before the coming of Islam in the sixth century, were the original source of this practice in Morocco. Throughout the country, one sees rounded white domes housing the graves of *marabouts*, the Muslim saints. Pilgrimages to marabouts are celebrated with festivals known as *moussem*. During a moussem, Muslims light candles and pray at the tombs, just as the Jews do during a hiloula.

Camping and picnic at the Hiloula Rabbi Yehya Lekhdar. From left: My father, Jacqueline, my mother, Samy, Cousin Allegria holding our baby brother Simon, circa 1950s

Camping out at Hiloula Rabbi Yehya Lekhdar, circa late 1940s. In front of the tent is Uncle Armand Suissa sitting on a live lamb wearing a hat. The little boy is my brother Armand.

Hiloula Rabbi Yehya Lekhdar, circa late 1950s. Cousin Allegria and my mother, with my baby brother Simon on a donkey.

Hiloula Rabbi Yehya Lekhdar

Hiloula Rabbi Yehya Lekhdar. My mother and Cousin Allegria posing in front of our tent

Hiloula Rabbi Yehya Lekhdar, circa mid-1960s. Me riding on a donkey, my brother Simon on the right.

The main religious purpose of a hiloula is to pray for a good life and the resolution of problems. At the tomb of the saint, Jews light candles, touch the memorial stone, and pray. By performing these actions, many Jews believe that these prayers will have more power than those performed in their synagogue or at home.

Many of these Jewish holy men have been dead for over two hundred years. After the death of a learned and pious Jew, the local community would honor his memory by choosing to bury him in a special location. Some of these wise Rabbis were born in the land of Israel and possibly came to Morocco to settle or collect money and raise funds for Religious institutions. Others were wise, educated men who were sources of inspiration and guidance for members of the community during their lifetime. These rabbis were, in most cases, traditionally buried in small mausoleums outside their towns or villages, close to a natural feature such as a small valley near a stream, water spring, or similar.

Each town or Jewish community developed a kind of allegiance or traditional religious connection to the gravesite of their local rabbi or holy man who left a deep impact on that community either by his devoutness or by performing some great deeds. Each year around late spring, these small gravesites became the festive gathering places of hundreds of Jewish families coming to pray and celebrate the traditional hiloula.

A hiloula is a happy event, celebrated with lots of food, drink, and music. For some of the larger hiloula, families rent rooms and gather with friends to feast and celebrate the memory of their holy man. Sometimes a few participants would bring musical instruments, like a lute or a darbuka drum to play Andalusian music. Participants with their families partake in these joyous gatherings involving music and drinks like wine and

Hiloula Rabbi Yehya Lekhdar

homemade *mahia*, a fig liqueur flavored with anise, as they sing Hebrew songs and trade stories.

My family tradition, probably due to my father's connection to his hometown of Settat, was to attend the yearly pilgrimage to the gravesite of Rabbi Yehya Lekhdar. This was located near a small Arab douar, or village, called Benahmed, about ninety kilometers inland, east of Settat and southeast of Casablanca. We would spend one weekend there camping, celebrating and praying.

My first recollection as a child of a late spring hiloula event was one day walking home after a session at Rabbi Eliahou's Hebrew prayers study at la Rue Fayolle. The synagogue was located near the busy main street of Darb el Englize, also called la Rue des Anglais, which was the main thoroughfare crossing the heart of the old Jewish quarter during the mid-1940s until the 1960s. Jewish homes, businesses, cemeteries, and numerous synagogues were lined along la Rue des Anglais. The street led as well to the large municipal food markets of Bab Marrakech, with its numerous stalls of vegetables and fruits, live poultry, fish, and meat. As I made my way walking home, I noticed a big gathering of Jewish families with a lot of household gear like pots, pans, rugs, and blankets in the process of loading all these onto the roof of a large bus, while joyfully chanting and singing. Some of them were wearing the traditional garb common to the Jewish Moroccan population before the arrival of the French colonizers around 1912. For the men, that was comprised of the black djellaba with tarbouche hat and the babouche slippers. The gathering of several families with men, women, and young children were all clapping hands and chanting:

"Haway jah, Haway jah Edawinah"

[Here he comes, here he comes, the holy man to heal us.]

It took me awhile to finally understand that this was a point of departure from the Jewish quarter to the hiloula. Large trucks and buses were chartered for the occasion probably by the Jewish community leadership in order to accommodate the demands of the large local Jewish population wanting to attend the annual pilgrimage to the hiloula of the rabbi.

For my family, when the time came for the special weekend of the year, we all piled in our family car, the famous black Simca Aronde, with so much gear and luggage. Blankets, pots and pans, tents, and rugs were packed in the trunk and on the roof of the car. Once every inch of the old vehicle was crammed with food and camping gear, we all piled in for an exciting one-hundred-kilometer road journey toward Benahmed and the holy tomb of Rabbi Yehya Lekhdar, or Victor le Vert as we kids loosely translated his name in French, for a weekend of camping, prayers, and celebrations with friends and family in the outdoors. We drove away from the coast, going through the outskirts of town and then through the countryside with large open fields, some of them covered at this time of the year, late spring, with wildflowers, particularly the red coquelicot poppies blooming everywhere. My father, driving with his left arm resting on the edge of the car window, would occasionally point toward the fields and mention the names of the different crops he identified growing there.

I recall on one occasion we had car trouble. The car was overheating, and my father was concerned, watching carefully the heat gauge. We had to stop numerous times by the side of the road to let the engine cool off. One time, a local Arab farmer checked on us and offered kindly to fetch some water for us. We handed him our *kafteerah*, or water pot, from the trunk of the car. He filled it from his nearby water well and we refilled the Simca's radiator.

My father realized later that a small water leak from the car radiator was causing the engine to overheat. After several similar stops along the way, we finally made it to our destination.

On an elevated hill, a few white buildings were around a big open area enclosed by a white wall, the largest building being the synagogue. In the center was the actual burial site, with a large, flat esplanade area for the crowd to gather on. The small compound was by a green valley with a small creek meandering through it. This was the main campground, with dozens of tents of the many Jewish families already set up and celebrating. Once our campsites were chosen and our tents set up, we all gathered to pray in the small synagogue and around the gravesite of the rabbi. Each of us made special prayers or expressed silent wishes as we threw small white candles into the big fire that was kept burning the whole time.

The local Arab farmers from the surrounding small douars, knowing the tradition of this big annual gathering of the Jews from the city, made their way from the farms and villages on horseback, mules, or donkeys, bringing with them herds of sheep and cattle to sell for the occasion. They also brought donkeys for hire, for us to take short rides from the campground to the nearby water springs.

As in every big, joyous hiloula in Morocco, a big mitzvah is to slaughter a lamb or young calf, not only in praise and to honor the memory of the tsadik rabbi, but to partake in some great *mechoui* barbecue. Sometimes several families would share the purchase of a lamb or calf and have it slaughtered on the spot by one of the numerous shohet present there for the occasion.

The strong wax smell of hundreds of candles melting away dominated the air. There was the noise and smell of the sheep and cattle, the braying of donkeys, the sight of animals being sold, slaughtered, skinned, and processed upside down hanging from a tree or tripod. Tents of many different colors were scattered among the trees in the green pastures. Columns of smoke rose in the air and there was a strong smell of grilled meats from the many barbecue fires. People sang and played musical instruments. All around the campground was the sound of drumbeats of the darbukas, accompanied by the playing of the oud, which is the traditional lute.

Most of the weekend was spent outside running among the tents with friends. One of the favorite local activities was riding on donkeys and mules and, for the most daring of us, a real horse. For a small fee paid to the local Arabs boys, you could hire a ride, and we played cowboys while taking a short ride upstream to the source of the small creek, a freshwater artesian spring called El Kebibat, a local natural feature, one of the most scenic spots in the valley.

The scenes in my memories from these festive gatherings, with the colorful, traditional, folkloric, and spiritual aspects could easily be compared to a native tribe's annual get together. These annual weekends of my early childhood will always remain for me my first true exposure to the outdoors, with the odor of animal dung strongly associated with the open pastures and fields of Morocco.

In much later years, as the Jewish community shrank substantially, the annual hiloula evolved into a more subdued event. Most of the visitors stayed in newly built lodgings and rooms, as several small buildings were built on-site for the visiting crowds that still chose to spend a night or two to visit and pray.

Jewish Holidays

Pessah

Pessah, the Passover, has always been the biggest holiday celebration of my childhood. It has been the grandest family get-together and the one holiday that required major preparation. For Pessah, which falls generally around April each year, the preparation started almost a full month before.

Pessah was also the big spring clean-up. To this day, I associate the smell of fresh paint with the Pessah preparation. The whole house had to be completely and thoroughly cleaned. Furniture was moved and area carpets and rugs, curtains, sheets, and blankets washed and aired. Silver and brass housewares were cleaned and polished. Two or sometimes three workers—Ali, Hmed, and Bouazza from my dad's office—would be at our home for several days helping with the housecleaning tasks. Our parents bought us new shoes and dressy clothes for the occasion, and even new pajamas. This was done in anticipation of all the elaborate, traditional dishes to be cooked for this celebration lasting eight days, with the Mimouna, the after-Passover festival, on the eighth day.

When I was younger and we were still living at Rue de Tanger, it was nothing unusual for my father to buy a live male lamb from a local farm and have it brought to the house. In this case we had access to a spacious rooftop. My father getting a lamb slaughtered for Pessah fulfilled in his eyes the mitzvah of the Paschal lamb. A lamb shank had to be on the Seder plate to symbolize as in the Bible where the Hebrews had to use the lamb's blood to mark their front door so death would pass over their houses and not take their firstborn sons. Also, we needed plenty of fresh lamb, the preferred meat, for the numerous meals and tagines to be had during the eight days of celebration.

Once ritually slaughtered by the shohet and he deemed it kosher, the lamb was skinned and dressed properly. Every part of the animal would go to make a wonderful, amazing, juicy Moroccan tagine cooked by my mother. While we still lived in our old neighborhood, the Muslims all around us celebrated their big holiday, Aid el-Kebir, also called Aid al-Adha, and had to buy and slaughter a whole lamb per each family, so this was a common practice.

Once we moved to Rue Berthelot, the whole lamb affair the days before Pessah became slightly complicated. My father nevertheless insisted on keeping the old tradition of buying a live male lamb to be butchered at home. This was slightly more challenging in part due to our modern French neighborhood. We did not have a private rooftop to park the lamb, waiting for the shohet and the proper help to be present. Therefore, when the lamb was brought to the apartment, we had to keep him overnight in the bathroom. The lambs for Pessah are not little babies, but big young sheep. My younger siblings and I were totally fascinated by the large, fluffy ram with a set of horns. One of his front legs was tied to one of the supports of our large metal bathtub. We kept peeking inside the room from behind the door, observing and checking on the ram. We were so impressed by it but made sure not to get too close. We were impressed as well by our Arab housemaid who was probably originally from the countryside and used to being around farm animals. She went in and out of the room as if the live ram was non-existent.

With the bathroom window open, some of the neighbors must have heard the sheep bleating. Later, when my mother was coming back from an errand and going up the stairs, she ran into Madame Creunier, our only non-Jewish neighbor, coming down from the third floor. After the usual greetings, Madame Creunier mentioned that she could have sworn she heard a sheep bleating from somewhere around the building. My mother was, of course, too embarrassed and never admitted that we were the culprits keeping a live sheep in our apartment overnight.

The next day, my dad and two of his loyal employees, the familiar faces around our household of Ali and Hmed, accompanied by the shohet ritual slaughterer stepped into the roomy bathroom. I remember watching as "the Slaughterer" sharpened his special knife, making sure the blade didn't have the slightest nick on it as required by kosher law. He checked it by running the blade along his thumbnail, and once ready he gave the okay to Ali and Hmed to hold the lamb down while the special Hebrew blessing was recited. Then the shohet slaughtered the lamb with one quick motion to cut his throat.

What I did not know at the time was that for my father, a little suspense was still in the air regarding his investment on the purchase of the whole lamb. With all the special requirements, there was no guarantee that the animal, even properly dispatched by the shohet, was indeed kosher. Ali and Hmed, starting the butchering process, hung the lamb upside down in the center of a big frame ladder, cut it open, and let the shohet check the insides, to make sure it was a healthy animal. The shohet proceeded to check some of the organs, mainly the lining around the lungs, before making the final pronouncement.

I could see my father slightly nervous about the final diagnosis. After a few minutes, finally came the voice of the shohet in the typical Judeo-Arabic dialect... *Msio Dabid had el Houleh Meziane ou kasher le mehadrin.* "Mr. David, this lamb is perfectly good and suitable to our kosher requirements." This brought a big smile to everyone's faces and the general mood relaxed, celebrating the happy results. If the lamb had been deemed non-kosher, my father would have had to discard it at a total financial loss.

I remember Ali and Hmed cutting a small opening on the back leg, putting their mouths on it and blowing air through the opening. For many years I didn't know the purpose, until much later after I became a deer hunter in Texas and had to skin a deer. In North Africa, a common practice is to blow air in to help separate the skin from the body, to make it easier to pull the skin off.

Once the skin was off and all the internal organs were removed, including lungs, heart, liver, stomach, and intestines, the head was split open and the brains and any meat from the cheeks and skull saved. The lamb's skin with its fluffy wool fur would be sent out to be processed and come back a few weeks later all nice and soft to be used as a small rug around the house.

Each and every part of the lamb was destined for a traditional Moroccan dish or tagine stew. The special dishes used for Pessah, the plates and pots usually stored away the rest of the year, were brought out. The stomach, once thoroughly washed and cleaned, would go to make a dish called *douwarah*, or *douara*, which is like a stew with onions and spices. The long intestines were washed and left to dry in the sun. The carcass was quartered, taking care not to cut any bones. Some of the meat, like the back legs, had to be cleaned from any blood and blood vessels and salted for hours in order to be deemed kosher. The best meat, like the ribs and the backstrap, would be featured in my mother's most famous holiday dinner dish of the first Pessah night, *el ghalmi bel terfass*, the Moroccan tagine of spiced lamb cooked with white truffles. Some of the organs, like the lungs, heart, and liver, would be lightly sautéed, chopped, and stuffed inside a portion of the large intestine to produce a *tehane*, a Moroccan large stuffed saucisse that was barbecued or broiled before serving. The brains would be cooked separately to make its own brain dish.

Before Pessah, all the *hametz* had to be discarded or stored away for the eight days duration since no leavened foods were allowed. On the last night before the holiday, the tradition was to take a few breadcrumbs and scatter them symbolically in each room. Then we turned off all the house lights. My father would hold in his hands a burning candle and a chicken feather while reciting some special prayers, and us kids followed him around as he visited each room. With only candlelight to guide us, we would use the feather to gather the breadcrumbs onto a special plate as a symbol that the whole house was now cleansed, with any bread or other flour products or other foods deemed hametz totally out of the entire house.

The next morning, the breadcrumbs collected the previous night would be burned in a small charcoal fire in the kitchen. Later that day, the whole household would get ready for the first night of Pessah, taking turns bathing or showering and putting on our brand new, dressy outfits before joining my father to make our way to evening prayer services at the local synagogue.

Coming back home from the synagogue was one of the greatest moments as our apartment was all decked out, lights brightly shining in every room, with the walls freshly painted, brightly colored rugs laid out everywhere, and the fragrant smell of fresh cut flowers decorating the table and the big buffet. Above the buffet, the large mirror made of elegant rosewood reflected the joyous mood. The long dining table was magnificent, decorated and covered with a mosaic assortment of colorful dishes and salads.

The large varieties of salads included a whole selection of traditional cold small dishes, like salade de tomates fraîches, salade de tomate cuite, betteraves en rondelle, radis, artichaut crus, artichaut bouilli, carotte râpée, salade oranges et olives noires, fenouils, poivron grillés vert et rouge, fèves et amande grillées, différentes sorte d'olives. That is, tomato salads, beets, radishes, artichokes, carrot salad, salad of oranges and black olives, fennel, grilled green and red peppers, grilled fava beans with almonds, and olives.

We all changed from our synagogue clothes into pajamas, or when we got older into *gandoura*, the long, traditional robes with embroidery fronts. Then everyone took their places around the illuminated dining table. My mother would be very nicely made up, dressed in a brand new, brightly colored kaftan. She looked radiant, but she was probably exhausted after the long weeks of preparation, cleaning and cooking, culminating with this special moment of the whole family gathered around this holiday dinner.

My father changed from his formal three-piece suit and felt hat of Borsalino style, which is like a fedora, into new white cotton pajamas and his white babouche slippers. He would take his place in the middle of the table, never at the head of the table. The two chairs on both sides of my father were in high demand — premium sitting spots — leading many times to small bickering among my siblings for having the privilege to be seated on either side of our father.

For Shabbat dinners and holidays, my siblings and I would greet our father by kissing the back of his hand, both cheeks, and his forehead to wish him Shabbat Shalom or *Chag Sameach* on a holiday, as a mark of love and respect. Strangely enough, in my memory as a young boy, these were the only occasions I was able to actually touch and kiss my dad, to show or display a mark of love and affection toward him.

Together, standing up, we all chanted loudly the festive Pessah Kiddush, (wine blessing) right after that my father lifted above our heads the big brass platter containing all of the Pessah Seder food symbols covered with a richly decorated fabric. Standing up, we all joined in raising our voices chanting the *Beevheelo* theme song of Pessah, and even giggling at times as my father would hover and circle the large platter around each head. My mother would make the typical festive ululation sound from her mouth several times as we all kept chanting, singing and repeating the Pessah blessing of *Beevheelo yatsanu mimitsrayim halahma anya b'nai horin*, which means "In a great rush we came out of Egypt with our unleavened bread, free at last."

This old Judeo-Moroccan tradition symbolizes that even after so many centuries have passed since the Lord delivered our ancestors from slavery in Egypt, we, the Jewish people as their living descendants, should feel as if we were there with them, benefiting from this big miracle and salvation. Once the big platter passed a full round, lightly touching the head of every participant around the table, one of my older brothers would hold the Seder platter above our father's head.

After that, once seated around the big table, we began the reciting and chanting of the whole Haggadah, the story of the Exodus from Egypt and the traditional songs for the Seder. We sang and chanted the specific different tunes to each chapter. At the proper moment while chanting the Haggadah, my mother or one of my sisters would bring to my father a large bowl and a water jug in order to mark the reciting of the ten plagues brought on the Egyptians. Water from the jug and wine from the Kiddush cup would be simultaneously poured in the bowl while each of the ten plagues was chanted. From all my childhood memories, I have never seen my father as happy and totally in bliss as on these Pessah dinners, surrounded by all his family—his wife, sons, and daughters celebrating one of the most cherished Jewish holidays, marking the rebirth of the Jewish people and their delivery from slavery to freedom more than three thousand years ago.

After the many salads and cold dishes came the traditional first course—a soup of green fava beans with lamb. That was followed by a spicy fish tagine, then the plat de resistance, *the ghalmi bel terfass*, a tender lamb ribeye served with white Moroccan truffles. Once the dinner was completed and most of the required four glasses of wine were drunk by the adults as specified, then came the second part of the Haggadah, the Sefokh. Usually by this time only a few of us boys were still able to stay awake and be motivated enough to continue to accompany my dad, chanting with him the second half of the Seder, culminating with reciting the Shir Hashirim, the Song of Songs attributed to King Solomon. In conclusion of the Pessah Seder, the last song was the chanting of "Had Gadya," a fun song about one little goat which is sung in the Judeo-Arabic dialect, and a kind of fable to symbolize the unique and unequal power of God.

I have an anecdote about my father's last Pessah in Casablanca in 1980, before he passed away at the young age of sixty. Present were our parents, Samy, Armand, Evelyne and her baby son Nathan (who was about one year old), Simon, and Nanou. Many years later, while living in Texas, I received by regular mail from France an audio cassette sent to my brother Michel and me from our brother Samy. Samy had the great initiative to make an audio tape and record the whole Seder night with all the prayers and chanting since we were not able to be present. I enjoyed listening to it, and in a way I felt included in our father's last Pessah.

Three or four decades later, I came across that same old audio cassette again, and as with all our family videos, I decided to digitize once more the audio track and convert it to an MP3 file to be able to listen to it on a digital player. While in the process of converting the audio track,this time around with a better more advanced technology, I discovered an extra thirty minutes of prayer chanting and blessings that I never knew existed after the first digital conversion. The most touching part in those recovered minutes was my father's voice at the end of the taping reciting two special Hebrew blessings intended each for my brother Michel and me. My father,who was fluent in Hebrew, was using the conventional Hebrew version for a traditional rabbi's blessing,addressing directly my brother and me, emphasizing and repeating his strong wishes, to see us both keep our vibrant Jewish legacy , strong and alive for the future generation. The whole experience of discovering my father's voice blessing us individually with such an intense, well-meaning, loving prayer, almost forty years after his passing was very emotional for me and brought me to tears on the spot while listening to his voice and this somewhat buried message .

The Pessah holiday culminates with the last day celebrating the Mimouna, marking the end of the eight days of abstaining from eating any bread or leavened products. During the day preceding Mimouna night, some of my father's Muslim clients and business connections, knowing our Jewish traditions of the Pessah holiday, would mark the occasion by coming for a visit to our home bringing with them fresh produce from their country villages. What I remember is mainly a goatskin full of buttermilk — el rayb. Since buttermilk is fermented milk, and we cannot drink fermented or leavened foods during Passover, the arrival of buttermilk marked the end of Passover dietary restrictions.

I have strong memories of the particular taste of the buttermilk coming out of the *shikwa*, or goat skin. It usually filled several jugs to be refrigerated, and we drank it for many days. Some of the buttermilk we kept in the goatskin, and our house maid, who was familiar with the old process would make fresh butter from it. She would hang the goatskin on a door frame and shake for hours the contents until it produced large chunks of fresh white butter that we would enjoy for days after, spread on our French baguettes for breakfast.

To celebrate the end of Pessah, it is a widely known tradition for the Jews of North Africa, particularly we Moroccan Jews, to follow the customs of the Mimouna. A large table is set with a wide selection of sweets and cookies, the buttermilk and couscous porridge called *berkoukes*, and special Moroccan crepes called *moufletah*. At night on that last Pessah day, after the big dining table covered with sweets is set, all Jewish homes celebrated an open-door invitation to neighbors, friends, and family. We visited each others' homes to be greeted by singing and tasting the numerous sweets offered on a generous table display for all to partake. It was a joyful occasion to mark the end of the Pessah holiday with its rules and dietary restrictions. I also recall that on the next morning after the Mimouna night, I would accompany my mother to the old Jewish cemetery not far from Bab Marrakech to visit her father's gravesite, my maternal grandfather Messoud Suissa, whom I never knew to commemorate the anniversary of his death.

Hanukkah

The Feast of Dedication is an eight-day Jewish holiday that commemorates the rededication of the Holy Temple — the Second Temple — in Jerusalem after the time of the successful Maccabean Revolt against the Seleucid Empire of the second century BCE. The Jews found not much oil left to light the Temple's menorah, but it lasted eight days by a miracle.

My memories of the Festival of Lights, or Hanukkah, are of a minor holiday. My mother made special fluffy, sugary doughnuts fried in oil. We hung on the wall in one corner of the hall our old metal menorah that we called *hanoukia* in Hebrew. Each night for eight nights we gathered, standing across from it as my father lit a homemade cotton wick that my mother had carefully rolled and prepared in advance. He would first fill with olive oil the small compartment of the hanoukia where there were eight aligned slots on the bottom and one higher in the center, that one being the *shamash*. We would light the shamash first. Then every night one more wick was lighted until the last night all eight plus the shamash were lighted. The whole family gathered, reciting and chanting the blessings as each wick was lit, to celebrate and commemorate the famous miracle.

Purim

Purim is a Jewish holiday that commemorates the saving of the Jewish people from a conspiracy to destroy them. This took place in the ancient Persian Empire. The story is recorded in the Biblical Book of Esther, called *Megilat Esther* in Hebrew.

Like Hanukkah, Purim was traditionally a minor festival, but elevated to a major holiday because of the Jewish historical experience. Haman, the king's advisor who wanted to kill the Jews, became the symbol of every anti-Semite in every land where Jews were oppressed. The Purim holiday has become a thankful and joyous celebration of Jewish survival against all odds.

We celebrated Purim with a special synagogue service. The whole congregation chanted the reading of the Book of Esther, which many congregants read from a parchment scroll. We all stomped our feet on the floor to make noise each time the name of Haman was mentioned. My mother made special Purim *berkoukes*, which is large couscous steamed and then served with milk and butter. She also baked a round bread loaf with two eggs in the center. When all the family was seated around the table for the Purim meal, after the ritual blessing of the bread we used a fork to perforate the eggs, to symbolize piercing Haman's eyes. Different families in Casablanca would cook slightly different dishes for Purim depending on the region and their own family customs.

To fulfill the mitzvah, the traditional *mishloach manot* gifts of food or drink are sent to family, friends, and others on Purim day. "Mishloach manot" means literally "sending of portions." The mitzvah of giving mishloach manot derives from the Book of Esther. It is meant to ensure that everyone has enough food for the Purim feast and to increase love and friendship among Jews as a counter to Haman's assertion that the Jewish people are characterized by strife and disunity. During Purim, my mother would send us out with samples of her home-cooked dishes to deliver to our cousins, neighbors, and friends in the neighborhood, who in turn would reward us with a small monetary gift.

Sukkot

Not long after we moved to Rue Berthelot, la petite terrasse became the ideal spot for my father to build the yearly sukkah to celebrate the fall holiday of Sukkot. This festival reminds us of how the Israelites wandered in the desert and had to make shelters. Ali, my father's worker, was in charge and had always been the dedicated sukkah builder, sometimes with the assistance of another worker and, of course, us kids trying to join in the excitement of erecting this magical structure.

First, fresh cut cane had to be obtained and delivered to the house. The cane was always readily available in certain areas of the town as the locals knew that the Jewish tradition required us to build this square hut made of fresh green branches each year during the fall season. During the September and October months, Moroccan vendors and farmers would haul loads of cane to town for the Jewish population to buy and take home to build their booths.

Ali made sure the cane was delivered to the right spot on la petite terrasse where he would be setting up. He used a long knife to remove the leaves and peel the branches to expose the naked, smooth, green sticks of cane. Using thin rope, he created a crisscross lattice wall with the long cane sticks, setting up four wall panels and one roof panel. After the panels were securely connected and the structure was free standing, the roof was then covered with green branches from palm trees, while very long palm branches were posted upright in each of the four corners of the new structure.

Once the sukkah was up, my mother would give Ali some tapestry and special decorated rugs to cover the four walls and the floor. An electric light was threaded through the roof to hang from the center of the ceiling. My mother would have us kids help to make some colorful garland from scratch, cutting different colors of paper in long strips and then gluing them into chains using a flour and water paste. Once the sukkah was finished, the whole family spent the next eight days having our meals in it, with all the logistics involved in hauling and passing from the window all plates, silverware, and large tagines of hot food from the kitchen all the way to the sukkah. By adding a small wooden ladder from Samy's room, we could easily go out through his large window and climb down to the terrace and enter the sukkah.

During the Sukkot holiday, we always had a great feeling of excitement. It was like a festive outdoor picnic gathering each evening. We enjoyed sitting under the freshly cut green foliage roof, feeling the cool autumn breeze of the night while having dinner and celebrating this ancient fall harvest holiday.

Monsieur Elie Bittoun

On our street was a small framing shop for pictures and mirrors. La Miroiterie Bittoun was owned by Elie Bittoun. Monsieur Bittoun, like my father, was born in Settat, and he grew up attending school with my father. Elie and his wife, Tata Fifine, were very close with my parents and were our great family friends. They had two grownup sons traveling or living outside the country. One of them lived in Sidney, Australia. Many years later, my brother Michel got in touch with him and paid him a visit during his trip to Australia in the mid-1980s.

Elie Bittoun, being a childhood friend, got along very well with my father, even though he was one of the rare friends who was not at all religious, rarely attending prayer services, and always enjoyed a drink or two. He was a chain smoker and full of life, always ready to celebrate and enjoy company. After closing his store for the day, making his way home Elie would frequently come up to our apartment for a social visit and an aperitif. We could hear his loud, cheerful voice as he made his way into our living room raising his glass with toasts in Arabic.

Lahh ekhelinah aishiin tan mouto!
Ndarbou el tassa!
Allalah Mimouna!
Mah kein gher el tattouuse!

My father was a hard-working man totally dedicated to his work, his family, and the study of Torah. He did not drink or smoke except maybe on special occasions, like at festive gatherings or celebrations. Elie Bittoun was the total opposite, always ready to party — smoking, drinking, singing. My father probably liked him for his joie de vivre, his good jovial spirit. He was often seen at his regular spot at the brasserie and café next to his store on the Boulevard de la Gare, having his daily aperitif, enjoying the food under no dietary kosher restrictions, always joking around, and often flirting with the local French ladies, some of them customers of his store.

When he was at our house, Elie was always served a good drink accompanied with the usual *cardoons* that are called *kharchouf* in Arabic along with raw hearts of artichokes, olives, radishes, almonds, etcetera. There was always a lively exchange of stories and laughs between my father and him.

Early on, I took a great liking to Elie Bittoun and developed a special bond with him. One summer as I was looking to earn some extra money, Elie needing some help around his shop, offered me my first summer job at his store. I gladly accepted and became his assistant and errand boy, supervising his three Arab workers who were in charge of all the labor involving cutting glass for mirrors and custom framing as well as being on call for helping with glass repairs in private homes and offices around town. He also wanted my help to keep an eye on the cash register and answer the phone when he was away from the store. This was my first summer job as a teenager earning some pocket money.

One day Elie needed to go to Marrakech for a business meeting and offered me the opportunity to join him on a day road trip to discover this colorful, scenic town. After getting approval from my parents, we got on the road very early, driving in his French-made Simca vehicle. I had never been to a large city outside of Casablanca. Once in Marrakech, after his meeting in town, Elie wanted to surprise me. Leaving Marrakech behind, we drove toward the snowy peaks of the Atlas Mountains in the far background, several kilometers from Marrakech. As we left the valley where the red-ochre city of Marrakech lay and gained altitude driving on the mountain road, we got to L'Oukaimeden, a ski resort, the only one in the Atlas mountains. This was my first exposure to snow.

Elie drove to the local French *auberge* within the ski resort where the owner of the restaurant, a French lady behind the counter at the inn, was very happy to see Elie. After taking a short walk and playing in the snow for a while, we had a late lunch at the inn, and soon got back on the road to return to Casablanca, getting home after dark.

Many years later, coming back from Israel in 1977 when I was twenty-four years old and on my first visit back to my parents in Casablanca since leaving them in 1969 as a fifteen-year-old, I stopped by Uncle Elie Bittoun's shop for a surprise visit. I tried to act like a regular customer to see if I could pull a joke on him. He did not have any idea it was me until I finally told him. We got a good laugh. He was very surprised and happy to see me. He invited me to join him for a drink, so we went to the local brasserie around the corner for a good beer and to catch up on my years in Israel. I saw Elie Bittoun one last time in December of 1980, during the shiva for my father. He was devastated by the sudden loss of his childhood friend. He always had great admiration and great respect for my father's many achievements and his Jewish religious values.

Samy, Jacqueline, and Armand

Samy

My oldest brother, Samy, was born in November of 1945, the year after my mother lost her first-born child due to a complication during the delivery at home under the care of a midwife. Samy was born in a private clinic. His Hebrew name is Shlomo. He was named after our father's deceased older brother. Samy being the first male child was probably very cherished and pampered. By the time of his bar mitzvah in 1958, my father seemed to have developed big plans for his son's future, mainly giving him a good religious education.

My father was probably under the strong assumption of the late 1950s that a French religious Jewish institution, away from home and loving parents, would do a better job educating and teaching his first-born son. The plan was that after his bar mitzvah, the young boy would be joining a boarding school in a yeshiva in France. Therefore, Samy, at the age of almost thirteen, found himself in France in the small town of Le Pin, some twenty-five kilometers outside Paris, in a religious Jewish boarding school, coping with a new set of rules and religious practices. The experience did not go too well, especially after an accident involving him and some of his friends chasing each other, where he fell and hurt himself and had to be hospitalized for several weeks.

Samy came back home after two years and continued his schooling at a couple other schools and programs in Casablanca and in France. He was also active in the local chapter of the Jewish Boy Scouts as a counselor, and later at the age of seventeen or eighteen hitchhiked with a backpack all over Europe. Samy was also considering making Aliyah to Israel, and he later joined a special program based in France that trained and taught basic farming skills to small groups of Jewish youngsters before eventually sending them to live and work in a kibbutz community in Israel. In the final stages of the training period, deciding to not continue on to Israel, Samy opted out of his group while still in France and ended up living in London for a few years before finally

Samy, Casablanca, 1950

Samy, Casablanca, 1962

Samy, Venice, 2018

settling in Paris, France, with his new French wife, Genevieve. A few years later their daughter, France-Yael, was born in France.

Years later, after getting separated from Genevieve, Samy met and got married to Aline Mouyal, originally from Rabat. They have two children, Audrey and Benjamin. In 2019 they celebrated their thirty-fifth wedding anniversary.

Jacqueline

My oldest sister, Jacqueline, was born in 1948. Her Hebrew name was Esther. She was always helping around the house, and she played a big role helping my mother raise me and my younger brothers and sisters. After graduating from high school with good grades, she strongly refused attempts by my parents to marry her off the old-fashioned way. She refused to let our parents meddle in her private life or introduce her to some established older Jewish man to whom she was not attracted to at all. With my father's concerns and Jacqueline's own encouragement, it was decided that it would be best for her to continue her studies in Israel in a special study program offered by the local underground emissaries of the Israeli Jewish Agency.

The special study program in Israel allowed young Jewish students recently graduated from a French high school in North Africa, Europe, or Turkey to move to Israel and spend the first year studying and gradually transitioning from French to Hebrew in order to be later accepted into a regular university study program. The program and the boarding school were in the city of Netanya on the Mediterranean coast of Israel. Jacqueline left Casablanca in the late 1960s to spend the year in Netanya. She later was accepted to study at Mount Scopus University in Jerusalem, where she met her future husband, Sylvain Marciano, who came from the town of Oujda in eastern Morocco.

When I moved to Israel in 1969, I was able to visit Jacqueline occasionally while she was a student in Jerusalem. Sometime in the early 1970s, Jacqueline and her boyfriend, Sylvain, decided to leave Israel to establish a new life together in Paris, France. They got married in Paris and raised a family. She was a hardworking, loving mother who was dedicated to her two boys and husband. Michael and Lionel were both born and raised in Paris. As a well-paid executive within her company, she was

Jacqueline, Casablanca, 1950

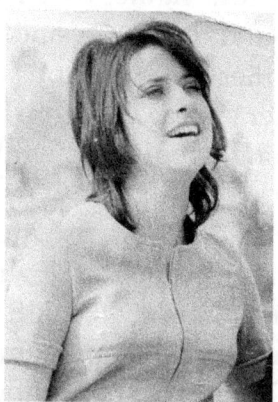
Jacqueline, Israel, 1970

Jacqueline, Paris, 2000

able to combine a professional career and a traditional Jewish home, always finding the time and energy for cooking and organizing to invite friends and family into her home and around her table.

Jacqueline played a big role while my father was hospitalized in Paris in 1978, and later was essential in taking care of our mother in Paris and our brother Prosper in Casablanca. Around the end of 2008, Jacqueline was diagnosed with an acute case of leukemia, and after a hard fight against the disease, she passed away during the fall of 2010 at the young age of sixty-two.

Armand

Born in December of 1949, Armand was the third child and second boy. His Hebrew name is Amram, after our paternal grandfather. For some reason, he was the only one born at home, with the help of a midwife.

One day in 1967, after the Six-Day War in June, we were sitting around the table for lunch and Armand, who was about seventeen years old, made a surprise announcement. He told our father that plans were made for him to leave home to immigrate to Israel, with or without my father's blessings or his passport, which was held by my father in the house safe. Armand would be leaving the following week. Everyone was shocked, trying to digest this latest news.

Apparently, Armand in the last few months was active in a small underground Zionist group for Jewish teenagers. The very militant Dror group was meeting secretly around town, and the young teenagers participating were being strongly motivated to emmigrate, being offered the opportunity to leave Morocco and join the Israeli military. Everything was arranged ahead of time, including airline tickets and a kibbutz that would welcome them once in Israel. They would live, work, and study Hebrew in the kibbutz for the first few months. Apparently, parental permission in certain cases was not necessary or required for anyone aged seventeen or older, at least that is how my father was confronted with this ultimatum by his son. With Armand's decision and in light of his rocky past and frequent troubles, my father after a few days realized his lack of options and decided to go along with his plans to move to Israel. He helped Armand prepare for the big departure.

Armand, after getting to Israel and spending six months living and working at a kibbutz and learning Hebrew, enlisted in the military shortly after and served his full three years. After being discharged, he worked for a period as a bus driver in Haifa and Jerusalem for the big Israeli bus co-op Egged. Armand left Israel in 1972 to live in Paris and then Montreal, coming back several times to live and work in Israel for three or four months at a time, never able to really establish himself living full time in the country. In the late 1970s he decided to go back home to Casablanca and lived for a couple years with our parents.

To be able to get back into Morocco was not an easy task, since the only passport Armand was holding at the time was an Israeli passport. That would not let him back in the country, and to try to renew or apply for a new Moroccan passport was going to be complicated, a long process with no guarantees while living in Europe illegally. The only alternative was to be smuggled across the border, from the Spanish enclave of Ceuta in northern Morocco.

With the help of relatives and family friends in Casablanca, my parents were able to bribe a Moroccan border officer in a village close to the border. Once all arrangements were made in advance, my mother left Casablanca on the train to go and spend one night with the family of the border control agent. Armand travelled from France and made his way along the Spanish side to the vicinity of the border crossing in the mountains. With the help of a paid smuggler, he was able to cross at night from a remote area into Morocco and was brought to the home of the border agent where he was reunited with our mother. She was terrified during the whole process. A few years later, Armand returned to Paris, getting married there and starting a family and having a very successful career with the Xerox company.

Armand and his wife, Fabienne, moved to the south of France in the mid-1980s, living in San Rafael and later Aix-en-Provence where they had two kids, Sarah and Arik. Armand and Fabienne later divorced.

Now with Samy, Jacqueline, and Armand gone to either Israel or France, we were in 1968, about a year after the big 1967 Six-Day War took place between Israel, Egypt, Jordan, and Syria—a war that made a big wave with the resounding military defeat of these three big Arab armies by the tiny state of Israel. A surge of tremendous pride and admiration was felt by most of the world's Jews, particularly the Jewish communities like ours living in an Arab country.

During the war, access to news and media, especially foreign and the more objective French newspapers and magazines, was very limited and tightly restricted by the Moroccan government. No French magazines or newspaper dailies came into the country during the conflict due to strong government censorship. The local radio broadcast in French was reporting a completely different story, the same big lies coming from most of the Arab countries in the Middle East, mainly that Israel and all its military were being wiped out and the Egyptian army was a few kilometers away from taking over Tel Aviv.

Armand, Casablanca, 1971

Armand, Israel, 1971

Armand, Aix-en-Provence, France, 2012

At night my father would play with the dials on our bulky TSF radio presiding in one corner of our dining room until he was able to get the right shortwave frequency to hear the news report broadcast every night in French from Israel. As all of us gathered around him, we listened carefully to the daily news report. We felt so relieved to learn that actually the Israeli forces were in a much better position on all three fronts, facing the Egyptians, Jordanians, and Syrians, after having practically destroyed most of their enemies' air forces. At services in the synagogue, some of the congregants secretly exchanged recent editions of French news magazines like *Paris Match* or *Nouvel Observateur* that had been smuggled in by travelers recently coming into Morocco. The magazines featured articles and full-size pictures from the battlefield, portraying the victorious army of Tsahal in the Sinai, Golan Heights, and the West Bank of the Jordan River.

These heroic pictures of the Jewish army in the battlefield gave a tremendous boost in our pride and reinforced our strong connection to the Jewish state fighting for its own survival. All these encouraging articles were later to play a role in my mind and strongly influenced my decision to move to Israel.

Haim Douck and the Decision to Leave Home

Haim Douck was one of my best friends during the days of high school. He lived a few blocks from us, on the Boulevard de la Gare next to the Marché Central. His father had a business of freight forwarding and was a custom broker. He drove a nice American car, a Dodge Rambler.

Haim's parents would usually go out on Saturday nights, so Haim would often invite me to spend Saturday night at his house. We would hang out together and play with his two brothers, Eddie and Michel, as well as with a very attractive blonde neighbor slightly older than us, Claire Chriqui, that both of us flirted with. We started experimenting in secret with smoking cigarettes, and on my way to Haim's apartment on a Saturday evening, I would stop at the corner tobacco shop to get a pack of local cigarettes, Casa Sports or Olympic brand.

In 1968, attending my second year at the high school Cours Complementaire, I was about fifteen years old in the eighth grade and enjoying a great friendship with my best friend Haim. He and I were in the same class, sharing the same student desk. We spent a lot of time together developing a great camaraderie—attending our first teen dance parties, trying to get to know girls our age, making our first moves on the dance floor, dancing the trendy Le Twist and Le Jerk. We tried hard to get the girls' attention and be lucky enough to get a slow dance with one of them. Haim was very outgoing and would not hesitate to approach any girl at a party to ask for a dance. Being turned down often did not affect his confidence. He kept going forward to try with the next one until obtaining satisfaction. I envied him, but did not dare to imitate him, afraid of being turned down or losing face. I was shy and much more reserved.

Like typical teenage boys, we talked about girls, cigarettes, dance parties, and school gossip. Sometimes the topic of Israel would come up, and the general trend for many local Jewish families during the 1960s, including some of our classmates, was of leaving Casablanca and moving to Israel, France, or Canada. I clearly remember him mentioning that neither he nor his parents, so well-established and owning a business, would ever consider such a move. It was mostly me sharing with him my idea of one day maybe following the path of my sister Jacqueline and my brother Armand and moving to Israel. So I was totally surprised and unprepared when one day at school Haim told me that he would be leaving very soon, at the end of the school year, to go to Israel on his own to continue his high school studies there. His parents and siblings would remain in Casablanca. This was so unexpected. I was very surprised and not at all prepared.

Within a couple of months, at the end of the school year of 1968, my friend Haim left Casablanca to start his ninth grade in Israel. When school resumed in the fall, I found myself sitting alone in class without my desk partner. We had been such a great team, studying and doing homework together, attending our first dancing parties, trying to get attention from girls, spending weekends at each other's homes. We both felt so comfortable with each other's family members.

Finding myself somewhat isolated and slightly depressed, I got into my mind the idea of convincing my parents to let me go to Israel as well. With the help of my brother Prosper, who was a year and a half older than me, we started putting pressure on our parents. We came up with a plan to threaten to quit attending school unless they gave in to our demand to let us go to Israel. My parents, having already three of their children living outside of Morocco—Jacqueline and Armand in Israel, Samy in France—would not even give it any consideration.

Together, Prosper and I were totally committed to our goal of leaving Morocco for Israel. I started looking into options of how to best get my school to contact my parents. One day, I decided to get the teacher's attention and try to get him to expel me from class and send me to the principal's office. Then my parents would be aware of my strong commitment, to really try to achieve my goal and be allowed to move to Israel.

To get in trouble at school, I chose the most boring class on my schedule, which was the Hebrew class. My first move was not to wear the *kippah*, the little cap worn by Jewish men and boys. This was a requirement only during Hebrew class. The teacher finally noticed me and ask me politely to comply. When I refused, he asked me to read my homework. When I responded that I didn't do it, he gave me an assignment for the next Hebrew class. I responded, "Monsieur, don't bother giving me any assignment because I will not do it." Everyone in class, including myself, was so surprised by this exchange. Until that moment, I had been an average-to-good student, not very extroverted in class, mostly keeping to myself, doing my assignments, and getting average grades. The teacher had to respond to my blatant provocation and asked me to leave and go wait for him at the principal's office.

My school, the Cours Complementaire, was the main Jewish high school from the Alliance Israelite Francaise in Casablanca, located on Rue d'Indochine across the street from the bigger Lycee Lyautey high school campus. The Lycee Lyautey was the biggest main French high school in town, with the full French curriculum and mostly French staff. Madame Ifrah was the assistant principal of my school and in charge of discipline. She was widely known and feared by the student population for maintaining student discipline and order in and around the school campus. She was known for the occasional strong backhand slap to the face of any student who got out of line. She was very athletic, always wearing workout outfits like sweat suits and tennis shoes.

Confronted by my Hebrew teacher explaining to her my latest behavior, Mrs. Ifrah's verdict was an immediate two-day expulsion from school, accompanied by a letter to my parents and a meeting in her office with at least one of my parents present before I could rejoin my classes. As you can imagine, that didn't go over very well at home. On the day of the scheduled meeting, my father, being so angry and frustrated by my behavior, had to promise and swear not to hit me if I was to be present at the meeting.

Mrs. Ifrah apparently knew my father, as her husband and my father were acquainted with each other from the same line of work. Mrs. Ifrah, after going over my grades and past records, looked me in the eyes and very gently inquired what was the matter with me and why this sudden change of behavior. I responded honestly by telling her that my sincere wish was to be able to go to Israel and that my family wouldn't hear of it. She realized this was a much more complicated problem than a regular school disciplinary issue. She told me that she herself, like many others, sometimes felt like she wanted to leave everything behind for another place but had to compromise and make the effort to stay committed to continuing her job assignment within the Jewish educational world.

At the end of her talk, she made it clear to my father that there was not much she could do to help in this situation. The options were simple—either get back to school the next day as if nothing had happened, all would be forgotten and I could continue my school year with a clean slate, or if I was still obstinate, to simply return my school books the next morning and she would wish me luck on my new path.

I could see on my father's face his anger and embarrassment when I responded that I wanted to go to Israel. That brought the meeting to an end. Leaving the school office, I made a quick escape. With the anger and frustration I had caused my dad, I did not want to get into the car and face him alone. I thought it would be better to make my own way home, so I walked back.

My father made it clear that if I didn't go back to school, I would not be able to continue living under the same roof with my family since I would be setting a bad example to my younger siblings. To show him my determination, I looked at different options for temporary lodgings at night. I was able to arrange to sleep over at different friends' homes under the pretext of studying for exams, showing up at my home during the day when my father was at work to get a fresh change of clothes, clean up, and grab a meal generously fed to me by my mother. My mother was not the disciplinarian and was probably feeling helpless in dealing with this situation.

One of my close classmates, Daniel Mechaly, was aware of my situation and willing to help me achieve my goal. He had a great idea of how to help me. On the roof of their apartment building they had access to a storage room where old furniture not in use was kept. He was able to obtain a key to the room. We were able to rearrange the storage area and put in an old, small bed and mattress not being used. Daniel smuggled sheets and blankets from his house without getting the attention of his mom. In the evenings, knowing the usual time my father came home, I made my way to the storage room at my friend's building and waited patiently for him to sneak up to visit me and bring me some leftover food from their kitchen.

One day my mother convinced me to stay and wait for my father, explaining that he had something important to communicate to me. She guaranteed he would not physically try to punish me, so I agreed to stay. When my father showed up, he was accompanied by a tall, mustached man whom I had never seen before, but I could tell he was not part of the Jewish community. He was introduced to me as Monsieur le Commissaire de Police, the chief detective of police. He led me into one of the rooms of our house and explained that if I didn't obey my parents and give up this idea of wanting to go to Israel and resume going back to school, it would be in his power and obligation as a Moroccan police officer to take me away to some kind of incarceration, with the approval and legal authorization of my parents. Somehow, I could tell the man was bluffing, and that probably my father was running out of options and had staged this whole setup to try to put fear in me and make me change my mind. I played along and once the meeting was over, I was able to sneak out of the house and get back to my cozy rooftop storage room for another night on my own away from home.

Within a few days, my brother Prosper told me that after a long debate and discussion with my parents, he had agreed under certain compromise conditions to return to school and resume his classes. My father, overwhelmed by this united rebellious behavior of two of his teenage boys at home, also setting bad examples for the younger siblings, convinced Prosper that if he went back to school and finished the regular school year, he would let both Prosper and me leave for Israel if that was still our strong wish.

I continued to hold off for a few more days, spending nights out of our home, until one evening I was hanging out at the local Tafraout Café across the street from our building entrance. The café was a neighborhood hangout where we frequently played the pinball machine. My father walked in and cornered me in front of the regular crowd and made me understand that I had to follow him home right away. He assured me that he just wanted to have another talk. I was relieved to leave the café and follow him and not be embarrassed by being slapped in front of everybody.

Once at home seated across from each other in our dining room, my father told me he had finally made a decision for lack of alternatives. He would agree to let me go to Israel, but only with my brother Prosper at the end of the school year, five months away, in the summer of 1969. He wanted me to move back into the house, but knowing my determination not to return to school until my departure for Israel, in light of my rebellious attitude and his total disapproval of it, he asked me to take my meals separately in my room and not be seated at the same table with him during family dinners for the next few months.

Since I was no longer attending school, I had my own schedule at home, mostly staying up late and sleeping late. I was still very much in touch with my classmates Daniel Edery, Daniel Mechaly, and Bebert Abitbol. They seemed to be impressed with my dedication and commitment to fight to convince my parents to send me to Israel, to leave for my own vision or idealism I had created in my mind. As a fifteen-year-old teenager who had not travelled much, I somehow felt strongly connected to Israel, dreaming of a new life away from Morocco and in the Jewish homeland. I wanted to contribute to the Zionist dream in Israel.

One morning after I got up late and was walking around the house, Madame Ganancia, our second-floor neighbor, came by to chat with my mother. Noticing me at home on a school day, she asked my mother if I was sick or indisposed for missing school. When my mother explained my special status of waiting to go to Israel within the next few months, Madame Ganancia mentioned that if I was interested, her brother, who owned two stores around the corner from our street, would gladly offer me a job. That is how I was hired as an errand boy by Mireille Ganancia's brother, Mr. Achache, the owner of two fancy, fashionable menswear stores. This was my second job, after la Miroiterie Bittoun.

The Achaches and Ganancias belonged to the groups of Jewish families and entrepreneurs that had originally moved from Algeria to Morocco the following years after 1912, after the takeover of Morocco by France. They were looking for new business opportunities and to invest in the booming expansion of the new city of Casablanca. Algeria had been declared French territory already in the mid-1800s, and the Jewish population there was able to take advantage of French education many years before the Moroccan Jews could. As a result, they were more French assimilated, better educated, and slightly better off financially to take advantage of new opportunities created by all the recent growth.

The two stores were located one at the entrance of the passage Sumica, the other a block away and across from the café called la Chope. My job as an errand boy involved assisting with menial tasks in the stores, from sweeping to folding up garments that had been tried on to running between the stores to fetch inventory. My new job allowed me to finally earn some pocket money, which was welcomed as my regular allowance had been suspended by my father—another repercussion of me refusing to go back to school.

I do recall the two stores were connected by an old field telephone, like in World War II movies. After picking up the handset and giving a few quick turns to the handle to make it ring on the other end, you could talk and check inventory or have a regular phone conversation. Many years later, I ran into one of the Achache sons while visiting Paris and we reminisced about the old days. He explained to me how the World War II field telephone's cable was run underground through a series of existing old tunnels and passageways connecting the stores.

During the time I was working at the clothing stores, I was contacted by Madame Douck, the mother of my friend Haim. She insisted for me to stop by her house for a visit and to pick up a letter from her son addressed to me. Postal mail could not travel officially from Israel to Morocco but usually had to transit through some family members living in France or elsewhere in Europe before being re-mailed to Morocco.

Madame Douck was so happy to see me and to share with me her concerns about news from her son. Haim related in his letters about how unhappy he was ever since he left home and about his difficulties adapting to his new life in the boarding school in Israel. He wanted to make sure I didn't make the same mistake and to warn me not to follow in his path to join him in Israel.

I carefully read Haim's letter addressed to me. He described how he found himself in a new country unable to understand and communicate in the Hebrew language and how he had to share a room with two other immigrant boys from another country. He had to get up early to study half the day and work the other half. He wrote about the heat, the mosquitoes, the basic lodging facilities, and the food. He begged me to stay put and not join him as he and his parents were starting to explore the options of getting him back from Israel to Casablanca.

I have to admit, I was a bit surprised, but at this late stage of the game I had already caused so much trouble and had fought so hard to get my way, and my father had already given his approval, for me to leave. I also felt very strongly that for other reasons I was much more committed than Haim ever was concerning moving to Israel. Not really able to comprehend the complications and obstacles that Haim must have been confronted with, I was disappointed that my friend was not adapting well, yet I remained convinced my only option was to forge ahead with my decision and continue toward my goal of leaving Casablanca to start my new Israeli adventure.

As the summer of 1969 approached, we needed to start the process involving the different steps for my brother Prosper and I to depart for Israel. Morocco, being an Arab state, did not have diplomatic relations with Israel, nor mail or telephone connections. Most of the waves of Jewish families immigrating to Israel starting in the '50s and '60s, after the creation of Israel in 1948, were very discreet and kept out of the public eye from the Moroccan population at large.

When a Jewish family wanted to leave for Israel, they got in touch with a Jewish neighbor or colleague or someone at the synagogue to let them know they were interested. The message got transferred and within a short time a contact was made, followed by a home visit. The first step for Prosper and me was for our parents to start the application for a passport, and in Morocco that could be a long and somewhat costly process. Having a passport was considered a luxury status. My parents were able to complete that first step, and soon thereafter we received a visit at home by two underground Jewish agency representatives. The *chlihim*, or special envoy, came to interview Prosper and me and present the different options to my father for our future lives in Israel.

After inquiring about our school levels and grades and asking a few questions, they explained to our parents that Prosper, being a junior in high school, could join a special French study program created in Jerusalem for Jewish students from North Africa and France. This program was the same as the one our sister Jacqueline was in. It offered the option to study and complete the senior year and then take the Baccalaureate in French, the same as in any French high school. He could continue on to a transition *mehina* year, a university prep year, in order to be accepted to an Israeli university.

In my case, since I was just finishing ninth grade, my only option was to be sent to a *mossad*, a Kfar Noar youth village boarding school that is similar to a kibbutz, located usually in the countryside. Students from sixth to twelfth grades lived and worked on-site accompanied by teams of teachers, counselors, and staff. I would have to take accelerated courses in Hebrew or go to an *ulpan*, an intense immersion program, for the first few months in order to make the transition from French-speaking to Hebrew, to complete my remaining three high school grades all in Hebrew. The Jewish agency, or more specifically one of the departments within the agency called Aliyat Hanoar, would cover all expenses and charges, as customary, for our continued education and schooling in Israel, including paying for airline tickets to get us there.

One of the questions my father was asked by the visiting emissaries was about which choice of village boarding school was best suited for me, either religious or secular. My father and I were a bit surprised as we imagined that in Israel there was no option to choose. With my background of having religious Hebrew studies with Rabbi Eliahou imposed on me for several years, together with regular synagogue attendance and prayers imposed by my father, I was not too eager to choose the religious option. My father, though, kept insisting on at least some minimal or middle-of-the-road compromise, which I reluctantly agreed to. In Israel, I would find out to my great disappointment that the religious option had been selected for me. I will explain later.

After a few weeks, the emissaries contacted us and gave specific instructions about the date, time, and location to be packed and ready to leave. After several months of working at the retail clothing stores, I had to let Mr. Achache and his brother-in-law, Monsieur Ganancia, know that it was time for me to leave and pursue my goal to continue my education in Israel. The owner was very surprised and tried to convince me to give up my plans and continue working for the store. He was willing to give me a substantial raise to entice me to consider a future career and advancement in the retail business working for him. I was almost offended by his offer, for underestimating me. My vision, my goals for the future, were so much higher than his perception of me wanting to serve his own interests. Once Monsieur Achache realized my deep conviction and Zionist vision to pursue my goal, almost in admiration he wished me the best of luck as we parted on very good terms.

Haim Douck and the Decision to Leave Home

When the final day came in that early summer of 1969, after having packed and said goodbyes to school friends, we parted from our younger brothers and sisters at home. Evelyne was thirteen, Simon was twelve, Michel was nine, and Nanou was eight. I did not see them for several years after that. The instructions were for us to leave our suitcases at home with our parents and to walk several blocks to a meeting in the lobby of a small hotel near Cinema Triomphe, located near the popular bar hangout called Igloo. Once at the hotel, a small group of us got in a van for a ride to the Casablanca airport. After checking in our luggage, we had one last opportunity to spend time with our parents saying our goodbyes. Officially, we were on a school trip to Marseilles, France, which was actually our first stopover on the way to Israel.

For most of us kids, this was our first time getting on an airplane, a very exciting experience. As we took off flying over the city and countryside, my face was glued against the window of the plane and I discovered to my big surprise the variety of colors of the fields below, the different shades of brown, green, yellow, grey, and black. I thought that green would be the dominant color for most of the open fields and pastures.

My brother and I soon realized that we were part of a large group of young Jewish boys and girls of different ages coming from the major cities of Morocco. The majority were from Casablanca like us, but others were from Marrakech, Fes, or Meknes. Their ages varied from twelve or thirteen all the way to seventeen or eighteen. Within a few minutes of the flight, I could feel the general excitement of our young group beginning a new adventure, of starting a new life in the true Jewish homeland of Israel.

After landing in Marseilles in the middle of the night, we were driven to a compound on the edge of town where we would stay for a few days to get all paperwork and logistics processed before completing the second half of our journey. The compound was several small buildings scattered among big eucalyptus trees. An old hospital had been converted to welcome and temporarily house Jewish immigrants from North Africa on their way to Israel. During the days of our paperwork being processed, we got to know each other and became friends. We organized social activities for ourselves.

Prosper was born in February 1952 and was about a year and a half older than me. He was a gentle, soft-spoken, and sweet boy. He looked up to our brother Armand who was about two years older. He did very well in school, had good grades, was popular with girls, and was a great dancer. Already in Marseilles, Prosper began dating a good-looking, tall, blonde girl named Orly Berdugo from Meknes. On my end, and for the first time in my adolescent years, I found myself dating a girl as well. She was from Marrakech and one year older than I. She was more experienced, which was perfect for an inexperienced boy like me, so things were off to a very good start.

After we landed in Israel with big excitement and strong emotions of reaching our long-coveted destination, we were driven to a youth village boarding school in the northern part of the country. Ramat Hadassah was a couple kilometers outside the small town of Kiryat Tivon and beautifully located in rolling hills. It was more like a summer camp. The grounds were nicely landscaped, with green lawns, shrubs, and trees surrounding the well-maintained compound. Several activities were organized for our group, some involving social dances and campfires. Daily meals were served in the common dining hall. Our group really got to bond together. We were free to get around and walk to the scenic town of Kiryat Tivon and its small shops and local movie theater. Within a few days, more boys and girls landed in Israel to join our group that had left Casablanca together.

During my stay in those few weeks in Ramat Hadassah, I was able to connect with my friend Haim and arranged for us to meet. By then he had been living in his boarding school in Israel for a little over a year. Haim wore the military uniform of a high school navy cadet, since he had signed up to be in specialty courses taught by the Israeli navy to prepare and train future high school graduates for service. Wearing a military uniform in Israel comes with several benefits, and advantages among them free trains rides. Also, for hitchhiking it was customary for Israeli drivers to offer rides to soldiers in uniform standing at a major road junction.

Haim came all the way to Ramat Hadassah to visit. We were so happy to meet and share stories from within the last year since we parted ways in Casablanca. Listening to his stories and adventures in Israel, I realized the many challenges and difficulties he had experienced. He was now trying to convince the same organization that brought him to Israel to consider sending him back to his family in Casablanca. Haim explained that he was practically on the run from his boarding school, staying with different relatives temporarily and desperately trying to get his passport back from the Jewish agency in order to leave Israel. I was surprised at the turn of events and his disillusionment in Israel and was sad for him.

That was the last time we saw each other until many years later in 2007. Haim, who later took the name of Harry, ended up going back to his parents in Morocco and then moved to France for many years. He returned with his French wife to settle back in Casablanca to take over his father's business. In 2007, while I was visiting my dying brother Prosper in Casa and by pure coincidence ran into Harry, he invited me to his home to meet his wife, Colette, and share some old memories of our childhood.

While in Ramat Hadassah, our brother Armand came to visit us in his military uniform, carrying his Uzi machine gun. Armand, after leaving Morocco in late 1967, had gone to live on a kibbutz for six months, working there and studying Hebrew before enlisting in Tsahal, the Israel Defense Forces, and volunteering for a combat unit of a paratrooper battalion.

The initial all-volunteer training in the paratrooper battalion was known to be very arduous and demanding and could be as long as six to eight months. After completing the first few months of intense training, Armand had decided to scale down his commitment and was transferred to a logistics unit to serve the remaining time of his three-year mandatory service. I was very happy to see my brother and very proud of his green military uniform with the reddish military boots. I was especially interested in his Uzi machine gun. Armand let me handle it and proudly showed me how to take it apart and put it back together.

Besides my friend Haim and my brother Armand, three of my father's sisters were living in Israel. They made Aliyah from Morocco in the early 1950s, settling in Migdal Haemek. They came as well to visit Prosper and me and invited us to visit them for a weekend. I had never met them before since they had departed Casablanca with their families when I was just born, but I recognized them from the pictures I had seen at home.

One of the first official trips I decided to take from Ramat Hadassah was to see my grandmother, Meme Hninah, the mother of Mamie Suzanne. Meme Hninah made Aliyah in 1955, a couple years after I was born. Through my mother and her sister, my aunt Tata Simy, I had heard many stories about her and pictures of her were displayed around our home. My mother and Tata Simy undertook together in the mid-1960s a month-long trip by boat from France to Israel to visit their mother.

After inquiring about bus schedules and getting the proper directions, I started my journey to the small town of Tirat Hacarmel at the foot of Mount Carmel, on the outskirts of Haifa. Meme Hninah was living in a small, modest, two-room apartment in the old part of town, where the old Arab village center used to be. Once I finally located her address and rang the doorbell, to my surprise my brother Armand opened the door. He had the weekend off from army duty and was visiting as well for Shabbat. Meme Hninah was a petite woman, soft-spoken and with a big smile. She was one of the most generous and giving people. Armand introduced me and she was happy and very flattered by my visit.

Meme Hninah, who was widowed in her early thirties with six young kids to raise on her own, had always been a hard-working person, trying to make a living and support the children. After moving to Israel with her two boys, Raphael and Armand, she settled in the town of Tirat Hacarmel and worked as a cleaning lady for well-off families living in the luxurious district of the Carmel neighborhood of Haifa.

After a few weeks, the time came for our group of new immigrants, to be dispersed to different schools, each of us assigned to a particular study program or school depending on age and grade. Ramat Hadassah was only a temporary base and sorting point. First, most of the older students, including Prosper, left for their boarding school and the French study program located in Jerusalem in the Moshava Germanit neighborhood. The majority of the others soon followed, leaving me and a few others to be sent last to Kfar Hassidim, a large agricultural youth village located a few kilometers southeast of Haifa.

After I got checked in by a counselor and went into the dining hall for my first meal, I realized right away that this was a big mistake and a very bad choice for me. The large student population was religious, wearing the head cover and chanting blessings loudly before the food was served. Growing up in Casablanca, our father wanted us so badly to follow in his path regarding daily religious Jewish practice, forcing me and my brothers to attend intensive religious Hebrew sessions on a daily basis after regular school. Study sessions taught by very old-fashioned rabbis from little backward villages in the Atlas Mountains in the interior of Morocco did not sit well with me. I have to admit now, though, they taught me good skills in reading and in chanting the daily prayers as well as the chanting of the Torah and haftarah portion from the Prophets.

My bar mitzvah was celebrated at the age of fourteen, after waiting for Simon to turn twelve so my father could have one big celebration for both of us. This same thing happened for my two older brothers, Armand and Prosper, an accepted and common tradition among large families like ours with many sons. Soon after, I began acting like a typical teenager rebelling against certain religious demands and practices, mainly the regular attendance at prayer services. So now, finding myself on my own, far away from home at the age of fifteen and a half, the last thing I wanted was to be coerced into daily religious prayers or services of any kind.

After lunch that first day, I made my decision. I immediately requested a meeting with the school management to try to explain the whole misunderstanding of finding myself in a religious boarding school. After locating someone who was fluent in French among the school staff and able to translate for me to convey my disappointment and frustration, I was told that the decision had been made by my parents back home in Casablanca. At this stage I had no choice but to comply since I was younger than sixteen and my parents were so far away. When I kept insisting, they sent me to the school principal. He tried to talk me into accepting the fact that there was little that could be done. Seeing how upset I was, he mentioned that perhaps an adult family member living in Israel and speaking on behalf of my parents could physically come to his office and sign a special request for me to be transferred to a secular boarding school.

  I was assigned a bed in a room to be shared with two other students who had not yet showed up. I spent my first night there totally depressed and thinking very hard about my options and solutions. Banging on the door woke me up around 5:00 a.m. as the counselors were making the rounds to wake all the students to gather for the morning Shacharit prayer service. I locked my door so to not let anyone in. After a few hours in my room, I decided to sneak out of the village and make my way to Tirat Hacarmel to pay a visit to my mother's brother, Uncle Armand Suissa. Past the village I started walking on the main road away from the school and toward the closest road junction to catch a bus ride to Haifa.

  Uncle Armand was a bit surprised to find me at his doorstep, especially during a weekday, but I explained to him the reason for my sudden visit. I wanted him to come back with me the next day to the boarding school and explain to the principal that a mistake had been made. He could sign a document on behalf of my father requesting for me to be transferred to another boarding school village that was not as religious. Uncle Armand would not hear of it on the assumption that without proper consultation first, my father would be very displeased with the change in my choice of school. After trying very hard to convince him without much result, I threatened that if he didn't help me, I would not only refuse to go back to school but I might even commit suicide...an empty threat on my side. That, he took seriously.

The next day, sitting in the office of the school principal, Armand Suissa, as our adult family representative, assured the principal that a mistake had been made and I should be transferred to a non-religious school. He agreed to sign his name to the change, and before long I was on my way with my suitcase to a new school called Aloney Itshak, located in the hills in the center of the country, between Tel Aviv and Haifa.

Aloney Itshak

The Aloney Itshak youth village, located in a nature reserve in the central part of the country, ten kilometers from Caesarea, was founded in 1948. In the early days of its development, Aloney Itshak absorbed children from Europe who had been rescued from the Holocaust and who came in large numbers to the new state of Israel through the Youth Aliyah organization. Throughout the years, Aloney Itshak absorbed children of different *aliyot*, or immigrations. There was the mass immigration of the 1950s when children arrived from North Africa and as far away as India. In the 1960s came the immigrants from Eastern Europe as well as North Africa. Towards the end of the 1960s, there were the children from North America, South America, and Turkey. In the early 1970s came the Russian children, children of the Prisoners of Zion — Jews who were imprisoned for practicing their beliefs. Many of these children were in their final years of high school.

Aloney Itshak was where I was finally sent and where I would be spending the next two and a half years. After a stop at the offices near the main entrance, I went to the small building where the laundry was located, to drop off my suitcase so all my personal clothing could be properly labeled with my name. Rahel, the lady in charge, welcomed me and inquired about my country of origin. She asked a young student to show me to my assigned room. To my great joy and relief, I soon discovered that most of the group that came with me from Casablanca were already here. We were very happy to be reunited, especially Orly Berdugo from Meknes who was Prosper's girlfriend from the last few weeks since we left Morocco. Orly and her brother Joe were together in the original group. Joe was in the same French program as Prosper. I was glad to be reconnected with others, girls like Simone Lallouz and Lison from the same group that left Morocco together.

I was assigned a room with two other boys my age recently arrived from Istanbul, Turkey. Neither Albert Arditi nor Danny Biret spoke French so the only way to communicate among us was using the little basic spoken Hebrew we knew or were starting to learn in school. Albert and I were to become close friends for many years to come, up until this day.

Our boys' dorm room was in a one-story building with a red tiled roof, shaded by oak trees. A dozen rooms faced a long, open corridor. In a separate smaller building were the common showers and bathroom. Not far behind our building was the girls' dorm with about the same disposition. The Aloney Itshak campus was located in the heart of a thirty-one-acre nature reserve, among beautiful oaks and surrounded by woods.

Our class of about thirty-five boys and girls newly arrived from mostly Turkey or Morocco started ulpan, the intensive Hebrew language classes, under our teacher, Carmela. She was a young, good-looking, enthusiastic, and dynamic brunette from the nearby little village of Givat Ada. For the rest of the summer and until the official school year started, while the rest of the student population of the village was away on summer break, the groups of new immigrants would take the ulpan. The classes went very well for me, thanks to my religious background and fluent knowledge of Hebrew prayers and all the reading acquired during the long after-school Hebrew studies as a young child in Casablanca. The lessons focused mainly on learning Hebrew, making progress and improving our speaking skills while adapting to our new life in communal living in our small rural village.

It was during that time that my brother Samy and his new French wife, Genevieve, living and working in London, England, drove all the way to Greece in their brand new Volkswagen Beetle and from there boarded a ship with their car to sail to Israel to tour the country. Samy and Genevieve showed up at the main office of our village to see me and I was taken by surprise. I was delighted to see Samy and be introduced to his new wife. With my counselor's approval, I was granted a few days leave to accompany them, and so I left the school to join them on our first expedition to discover the country of Israel.

Samy had been teaching French and living in London, where he met Genevieve. Genevieve was born and raised in France and came from Tulles, a small town in south central France located in the province of la Correze. They fell in love and decided to get married. They tied the knot in a civil ceremony in London, with my mother making a special trip from Casablanca in order to be present. After Genevieve went through an official conversion to Judaism, with my father's blessing their Jewish marriage was celebrated in our home in Casablanca at la Rue Berthelot.

Samy and Genevieve were experienced travelers and had all the proper Michelin guidebooks, allowing the three of us to really discover and learn the history of Israel as we toured the whole country in their new compact car. We first headed to Caesarea, located on the Mediterranean coast and a short distance from my school. We explored the imposing ruins of this once-famous, ancient Roman port city and its harbor, amphitheatre, and extensive aqueduct built by King Herod to honor his patron Julius Caesar. We continued on to Jerusalem, my first visit to this amazing, historical city that I was to live in a few years later and become so enamored and fascinated with. Samy, as he was called then before he decided to shorten his name to Sam, was very thorough in his travels, making sure he covered all that was to be seen and reading up on the history of each site.

I vividly remember joining him on a walking tour on the crest of the imposing and famous fortified walls surrounding the old city of Jerusalem. We hiked a full circle on top of the walls with some incredible views of all the historical sites around. We crossed the Armenian quarters, the Arab neighborhoods, the Christian churches, and the old Jewish quarter abandoned in 1948. This was my first visit to Jerusalem, the cradle of three religions, recently and finally unified as one city after the 1967 Six-Day War, only two years previously. The city was unified under Israeli control, allowing all pilgrims from all affiliations, including all Jews, to pray at the Western Wall, the last remaining vestige of the Temple.

First visit to Jerusalem with brother Samy, summer 1969

Jerusalem, summer 1969

From Jerusalem we continued on our journey to the Dead Sea and the ancient fortress of Masada, where after taking a swim, or rather a float, and bathing in the Dead Sea, we checked into an adjoining youth hostel at the foot of Masada. We got up the next day at 3:00 a.m. to start our arduous hike to the summit to watch the sunrise from this remote desert fortress built by King Herod. Masada is famous in Israel as a national historic monument and one of the country's symbols of its courageous struggle for survival. During the first Jewish revolt against the Romans (A.D. 66-73), it became a place of refuge for people fleeing the Roman army. It was the last rebel stronghold to hold out and was taken in A.D.73 after the Romans legions penetrated its walls after a long siege

We continued all the way south, crossing the Arava desert along the border with the neighboring country of Jordan, all the way to the city of Eilat on the shores of the Red Sea. I recall not being able to find a room at the local youth hostel there, so we decided to spend a windy night on the beach. I do not remember much after that. I am sure Samy brought me back to my school and then continued his summer travels. The next time we saw each other was four years later during the spring of 1974, in Paris after the Yom Kippur War, details mentioned in my chapter as a soldier in the IDF. (Israel Defense Forces)

By early September the whole student population returned and the village was at full capacity with grades from sixth or seventh to twelfth. My class, *Kitah Youd*, or Grade Ten, was made up of four classes. I was part of a class with my group of recently arrived immigrants. Our class had a special Hebrew study curriculum taking in consideration our previous backgrounds of studies in another language. We had a lighter load of Hebrew studies, like Hebrew literature and Bible studies, allowing us to integrate all and have a chance to graduate. The second tenth grade class was made of immigrants as well, but they had been in Israel for several years and were more advanced in Hebrew than we were. The third tenth grade class was mostly made up of Israeli-born or students that came to Israel at a very young age and grew up in the country. It was their Israeli parents' choices to send them to a boarding school, for economic or family reasons. The fourth tenth grade class was made up completely of American boys and girls who were in Israel on a special study program from the US for a full year. They had their own study program and curriculum in English, with their own set of special English-speaking teachers and counselors.

When the new school year started, my lodging arrangement changed. I was now sharing a slightly bigger room with three others — my friend Albert from Istanbul, Rami from Tel Aviv, and Jay from Connecticut. The new schedule in the village was attending classes for half a day at the school and the other half working physically within the village for the general maintenance and upkeep of the whole campus. Each morning after breakfast we would each get our work assignment for the day. The choices were:

-Dining hall kitchen crew to cook the meals, serve, and clean the *hadar haokhel*;

-Maintenance and repairs, to help with general maintenance of the buildings and dorms around the village;

-Landscaping crew to maintain the grounds, lawn, trees, and shrubs on campus;

-The laundry room crew to launder all the students' bed linens and personal clothing and sort and put them back into each student's individual compartment for them to retrieve;

-The *loul* crew to take care of the chicken coop where several hundred chickens were maintained and fed daily to supply the kitchen with most of the eggs needed for the village;

-Vegetable fields crew to take care of the fields where the village grew a selection of vegetables like green bell peppers, onions, and cucumbers.

Each one of these departments was headed by a professional, paid, adult staff worker, and the students were assigned to work for him and assist him. We were each distributed work clothing including a hat and work boots.

My first work assignment was not the easiest. I was dispatched to the big fields to work in the heat and tend a large field of green peppers, under the supervision of Menahem, the main caretaker of the crops, from the nearby kibbutz. Before heading out to the field, located a short distance down in a valley on the outskirts of the village, my new work group was first introduced to the big old mule parked in the barn. Menahem showed us how to first take her to water before harnessing her gently to a big four-wheeled cart loaded with empty plastic crates. We threw our tools into the back and off we went, piling ourselves on the back of the cart heading out into the fields.

For the next few weeks as I was assigned to the fields, I became used to the routine of pruning and harvesting, and even delivering the full crates of fresh vegetables to the kitchen, proudly taking charge of driving, sometimes on my own, the mule and the loaded cart all the way from the fields to the big dining hall kitchen in the center of the village campus. Strangely enough, one morning the mule refused to get up, and once Menahem was alerted and by her side, he realized that she was too weak and too old and probably didn't have long to live. From that day on, we had to rely on the big village tractor to shuttle our tools to and from the fields.

After working short stints in the kitchen and at landscaping, I was assigned to the loul, or chicken house, where I quickly learned how to take care of the chickens under the supervision of David, a farmer from the adjoining village of Givat Ada. His house was halfway between our village and the small town. When hiking on the main road from our school to the town we would pass his house and often see him working in his own fields. David, who probably came as a young boy from Eastern Europe, had his own crop fields around his house where he grew mostly grapes and some vegetables.

David was a hard-working man in charge of the whole chicken operation. Inside two large metal buildings, the chickens were kept in long rows of metal cages about three feet from the ground. Each cage held two or three white chickens. The floor of the cage was slightly slanted down toward the front, to allow freshly laid eggs to roll gently to the front of the cage and out through a small gap, ready to be collected every morning.

The eggs had to be cleaned, washed, and stacked up properly in the egg trays. We watered and fed the chickens and occasionally cleaned the floor below the cages. The beaks of the chickens had to be melted against a special very hot plate, to trim the beak to prevent injury to other chickens, and this was mostly David's job. On the roof of the buildings was a sprinkler system to turn the water on in order to cool off the building when the summer temperatures got too high, so that the chickens would not get overheated.

During the first few days on my new assignment, I noticed a few chickens roaming freely around the building, among them a big rooster. At first, I did not pay too much attention, until one day doing my routine collection, with my hands full holding an egg tray, the big rooster rushed me at full speed, charging my legs and causing me to drop my tray. I was totally taken by surprise. Apparently, the big rooster must have felt threatened by my tall rubber boots and was protecting his territory. I decided to be ready for the next assault with a big shovel in the vicinity. After several confrontations and a few whacks with the shovel, Mr. Rooster understood his place and kept clear of me while I was doing my rounds.

I started feeling very comfortable doing my work routine and assignment at the chicken compound. I liked working with David and requested to remain on the loul assignment for a while. Since it wasn't really a popular job, there was no problem granting my request.

As the school year progressed, I started to make friends. The majority of my class were boys and girls from Turkey who came from well-off urban Jewish families, mainly from Istanbul but a few from Izmir and Bursa. Most of the students coming from Istanbul had attended either private French schools or Alliance Francaise establishments. Most spoke French fluently, which was very comforting and created a great social ambiance for new friendships, especially between me and the girls in our Kitah Youd group. There was Orly, Simone, Lison, and Evelyn who came with me from Casablanca; Suzette, Shelly, Sarah, Odette, Vicky, Jenny, and Fanny from Istanbul; and Yonah from Argentina. Regarding boys, there was Itshak, Dany, Nisso and my roommate, Albert Arditi, who was my new accomplice and partner in crime. He did not speak French but learned quickly and ended up getting married to his French high school girlfriend, Nathalie.

In our extended Kitah Youd, I became friends with other students originally from Morocco that had already been living and attending the school for several years. There was Alain Zenou and his brothers Albert and Maxime in the junior and senior classes above us, and Meyer Benayoun and his cousin Yaakov and his sister. Among the whole group of tenth graders, not counting the Americans, there were students from Turkey, Morocco, Argentina, Brazil, France, Iran, and Mexico as well as several native Israelis.

In my room, Aloney Itshak, 1969

With roommate Albert Arditi, Aloney Itshak, 1969

Every day we would wake up to the voice of Devorah, our building supervisor "mother," making her rounds, knocking on our doors and calling our names to make sure we were getting up, getting cleaned up and dressed, and organizing our rooms. After the beds were made, we were off to the dining hall for breakfast. Once or twice a week we were required to do the *spoonja*, where a bucket of soapy water was dumped in the center of the room and we mopped the water out to every corner of the room to clean it.

After breakfast, we walked the short distance from our rooms to the school campus and our classrooms if that week's schedule was school in the morning and work in the afternoon. For work we had to put on our special work clothes and wait for Mansour, our designated group's student representative friend in charge of distributing the various assignments. After classes we either went back to our rooms or hung out in the main plaza by the dining hall to wait for the doors to open. If we were in our rooms, we listened for one of the kitchen staff banging on a tall, hollow metal pole acting as a bell to signal to the student population that lunch or dinner was being served.

In October of 1969 I turned sixteen, and to my total surprise a spontaneous celebration was organized by friends waiting for me in my room. That same year, as I recall, was the big event of the landing on the moon.

After a few months my mother came to visit me, traveling all the way from Casablanca. She came to Israel to visit her mother, my grandmother, Meme Hninah, and her two brothers, she wanted to see with her own eyes where and under what conditions I was living. When I showed her my room, she didn't appear to be too impressed by the very basic comfort and conveyed to me that my father would be more than happy to arrange for me to go back home to Casablanca. I didn't take her seriously, besides the fact that after all the trouble I had caused to get my parents to agree to send me, I was too proud and in no way I was going to turn back.

As in every Israeli high school, our tenth grade class had to participate in the Gadna military youth training program. Once a month, young military instructors from the Gadna core of Tsahal would show up at the school to teach and train us. We had full days of different activities, some involving long hikes around our area.

Our first serious Gadna training outing was to the Golan Heights. Dressed in boots and special Gadna uniforms, our whole class was transported by *tiyoulit*, which is an Israeli original hybrid creation of a mix between a bus and a truck, to the upper Galilee and the Golan Heights. We camped for a couple of days and slept in small tents. We took long hikes around the valleys and canyons and visited the old Syrian military positions and trenches dominating the old border between Syria and Israel before the Six-Day War of 1967. We checked out abandoned Syrian tanks scattered throughout the area.

Eilat Mountains, Aloney Itshak first Gadna trip, 1970

*Old Syrian tank, Golan Heights.
From left, Robert, Mickie, Albert and a friend*

A few months later our whole Kitah Youd was off for a weeklong camping and military training in far southern Israel, a few miles north of Eilat, in the Arava desert. Beer Orah, the military camp compound, was a large Gadna training facility where most Israeli high school students came to be prepared for our mandatory upcoming three-year military service after our senior year in high school.

Our whole class group camped in several large tents. After being taught how to use them, each of us received an old World War II military rifle vintage made in Czechoslovakia, hence the name "Tchekhi." These guns were the most basic single-shot, bolt-action military rifles and were very popular in the Israeli army in the early years, starting in the late 1940s. We carried them around and cleaned and oiled them every day, to be inspected every morning by our commander. These guns were real and functional, except as we learned later the guns were all missing the firing pin so to avoid any misuse or accidents. We each also got military harnesses to strap on, with pouches and water canteens attached. Most days, if not at the firing ranges or on some campground maintenance duty, our squadron under the command of a young Israeli army officer would march out of the camp into the surrounding hills for long hikes and exercises, sometimes during the night as well.

The whole experience was demanding but exhilarating. We had opportunities to discover and explore the area near Timnah, better known as King Solomon's Mines, and hike into colorful canyons and find local water springs.

Gadna military training, Beer Orah, 1970

Kitah Youd in Gadna training, Beer Orah, near Eilat

After several months at the school and well into the school year of 1969-70, while not working or studying, I was hanging out at the girls' dorm, mainly with my friends Orly and Simone. All of us were a bit homesick, comforting each other by sharing letters and recent news from our families and friends we left behind in Morocco. For our Israeli teachers, counselors, and staff around the school village, as in most of Israel, the notion of boys and girls developing relationships and going steady with each other was commonly accepted, which was not at all the case from where we came from. Therefore, as we were living, studying, and sharing meals together, couples were slowly starting to emerge, mostly in the junior and senior classes.

In our class, my friend Orly from Morocco was sharing her room with two girls from Istanbul, Shelly and Suzette. Like most other Turkish girls having attended Catholic French schools back in Turkey, they spoke French fluently, and like most Jews from Turkey, they as well spoke Spanish Ladino, a language that Jewish communities throughout Turkey inherited from their ancestors expelled from Spain after 1492. They were able to preserve and practice that language to this day. Shelly was an attractive brunette and seemed to be the center of attraction for boys from the junior and senior classes as well as for boys from our own grade. Since the majority of our immigrant group were Turkish, when we would hang out together during school, work, and after, we listened and became familiar with their Turkish language as they spoke it among themselves and even learned a few basic words and phrases.

While in high school in Istanbul, Shelly fell madly in love with a slightly older Turkish but non-Jewish young man. Her traditional Jewish parents, concerned about the romance and where it might lead, decided to send her away to continue her studies in Israel. At our occasional Friday night social dances, boys from our school tried hard to compete for her attention, but for the first few months she was still focused on her previous romance with even a small picture of her old Turkish boyfriend nailed on the wall next to her bed. Since I was frequently hanging out in her room visiting my good friend Orly, I was aware of her previous romance, and knowing the attention she was getting from the local boys in our school, I never imagined I stood a chance with her. Therefore, when it did actually happen, it was a big unexpected and very pleasant surprise.

One early evening after school while waiting for the dinner call, Orly, Suzette, Shelly, and I were playing a game of Monopoly. When the bell from the dining hall sounded and as everyone made their way to dinner, Shelly decided to skip dinner and just stay in the room. I decided to stay as well and skip dinner to keep her company, never anticipating that as a result we would officially start going out together.

With Shelly at Gadna in Golan Heights, early 1970

Shelly, Aloney Itshak, 1969

Within a few days the big news was out and everyone knew. We became an item, one of the first couples to go steady in our class. My status at school changed as I suddenly became better known as Shelly's boyfriend, and for the envious Turkish boys, I was "the Moroccan boyfriend."

The attitude from the school staff regarding boyfriend-girlfriend couples was supportive, and I even started to attend and enjoy our once-a-month Friday night social dance party held at school. The dance was usually held in one of the classrooms or in the local *miklat*, the village underground bomb shelter. My roommate, Albert, was also going steady, with his second or third girlfriend as he was quite popular in school and not particularly picky about his girlfriend selections. For me, having my first serious relationship with a steady girlfriend made a big difference socially, allowing me to better acclimate and motivating me to really adapt to my new life in Israel.

During the school year, on special weekends about once a month, I was able to visit my relatives and spend Shabbat in different places like Migdal Haemek, Ramat Eliyahu, and Tirat Hacarmel. Most of the time I favored visiting my grandmother, Meme Hninah, in her small two-bedroom apartment where she happily welcomed not only me, but my two brothers Armand and Prosper and my sister Jacqueline, all at different times, always with open arms and great home-cooked food. Meme Hninah was a very loving woman, generously sharing whatever she had, always making me feel so comfortable and at ease in her simple and very modest home.

One night, Armand, while still a soldier, paid me a surprise visit at school by showing up driving a big heavy military truck and asked me to join him on a long drive to Jerusalem to pay a surprise visit to Prosper and Jacqueline, both living and studying there. Armand by then had switched assignments in the military and was now driving large military trucks all over the country, while being based out of Tirat Hacarmel near the port city of Haifa. Occasionally my brother Prosper studying in Jerusalem and I in Aloney Itshak were able to coordinate in advance so we could meet and spend Shabbat weekend together, visiting either our aunt or grandmother and sharing stories about our schools and studies.

By the summer of 1970, as the school year was coming to an end, I had to decide how and where I was to spend the summer. Most students went back home to their parents. Most of my Turkish friends whose parents still lived in Turkey arranged to fly back home for the summer. My options were either to stay in the village on my own with a few other students in my situation or find a family relative to stay with. I opted to stay in the village and even get paid some wages to continue taking care of the chickens.

In the summer months, as the school emptied itself of its student population for the school break, most of the teachers, counselors, and school staff lived on the premises in individual small-family cottages scattered throughout the campus grounds. As in a conventional kibbutz, everybody gathered daily for meals served in the large dining hall. Since most of our dorm buildings were vacant during the summer, I chose to share with a senior student a small *tsriff*, or tiny one-bedroom wood bungalow among the trees. These were usually reserved during the regular school year for senior students.

During the summer, my job every morning consisted of feeding, watering, and attending to my couple hundred chickens, collecting daily the fresh-laid eggs. As I settled into my work routine, one day while dressed in my typical kibbutz khaki work outfit with my rubber boots, I came to deliver the filled egg trays to the kitchen while riding on the school tractor. As I approached the dining hall kitchen, I was surprised to hear French spoken by a group of freshly arrived girls my age. From the conversation I overheard, they seem to be impressed as they were watching me. This was probably their first introduction to a typical kibbutz scene, with an Israeli farm boy in the midst of his labor. We started talking and I found out that their group of boys and girls from France had just arrived during the night to start a four-week summer program to tour Israel. Their program was using some of our village's facilities, like the dorms and dining hall, as a base for a couple weeks while taking daily outings to discover the country.

I was excited and happy to learn that I would be having company for a while in the village. As it turned out, they were delighted to have somebody "local" like me to explain and arrange things. The first thing I was able to arrange for them was a record player and a set of records to help them put together a dance party for their group—after hours, of course, and away from their counselors. Also, most importantly for them, I was able to point them to where to buy alcohol in the small town nearby.

Aloney Itshak, in front of my summer bungalow, 1970

Hitchhiking to town, summer 1970

The summer of 1970 took a fun and unexpected turn with the presence of the visiting French group. That summer was also the first time that I experimented with drinking hard liquor. During one of the late-night get-togethers, dancing and listening to music with the French group, I did not realize the need to pace myself and I got very drunk from cheap Israeli brandy. I ended up very sick in bed for a couple days, not able to attend to my duties at the chicken compound and almost losing the good trust of my boss, David, who depended on me for the care and management of the chicken house. Recovering in bed the next day, I obviously could not attend to my chickens. On that particular very hot summer day, I forgot to turn on the special water sprinkler located on the metal roofs of the loul to cool the building and relieve the hundreds of chickens from the heat and the danger of dying. Luckily for me, somebody from the staff passing by realized the heat and took the initiative to turn on the sprinklers, saving the chickens and me from a big disaster.

During that summer, my brother Armand, on a weekend leave from the army, came to visit me at the school. An Israeli soldier toting around his Uzi was a big hit with one of the French girls of the group and Armand started dating her.

As the new school year was soon to be started, everybody was returning to the campus. My class was starting our junior high grade eleven, or Kitah Youd Aleph. One could sense all the excitement of the different classes, everyone getting back to school and sharing stories and experiences from the summer, checking out the allocated new dorms and new roommates. I was still sharing a room with Albert, and this time, apparently due to a new policy, also with an American boy from New York, David Maliniak.

Albert's parents had moved to Tel Aviv from Istanbul and lived in an apartment in a high-rise building in Yafo, also called Jaffa, the oldest part of Tel Aviv. His father owned a Volkswagen Beetle, recently acquired in Israel. During the school year, Albert would invite me to spend the weekend with him at his parents' place, which was a great opportunity for me to discover Tel Aviv and hook up with other schoolmates around that area. Albert was about the same age as me and could not wait to get a driver's license by any means. He was, like me, under the legal age of eighteen to get a license in Israel. With his father's approval and help, Albert came up with an incredible scheme. With a little bribing and some local special connections to Istanbul, he was able to obtain a Turkish driving license with a birthdate showing he was eighteen years old. Based on the Turkish-issued drivers licence, he got an international driver's license allowing him to drive in Israel.

Tel Aviv, 1971, From left: Michel Wartowski (Belgium), Shelley Benshusan (Turkey), me, Vicky Levy (Turkey) a friend, Albert Arditi (Turkey)

Albert became one of the first "legal" drivers in our class. He was able to borrow his dad's car, a fact that made him even more popular in school and made our weekend getaways and social agenda in Tel Aviv definitely more exciting for us and our friends.

Dressed as hippies for a Purim school play, with Albert Arditi, 1971

42 years later posing together in Estepona

Alain Zenou, who was in my school grade, was also from Morocco and we became close friends. Alain and his two older brothers, Albert and Maxime, were known as the Zenou brothers on campus, all three attending the same school. The family came originally from the town of Oujda in eastern Morocco, on the border with Algeria, and had settled in Israel around the mid-1960s. Alain was part of my school grade but not in my new-immigrant class since he was much more advanced in his Hebrew level, but he enjoyed hanging out with our French-Turkish-speaking class group. Alain invited me several times to spend a weekend at his family home in Or Yehuda, a city in the Tel Aviv District, giving me a chance to meet his whole family. They reminded me so much of my own family and I took great pleasure enjoying not only the great ambiance around the Shabbat table, but the delicious Moroccan home cooking by his mother. The three brothers graduated from the pre-military course in Aloney Itshak, and all three completed their military service in the army intelligence unit. To this day I am still in contact with Albert Zenou who is living and working in the New York area and with Alain in the Tel Aviv area.

Alain Katz, me, Alain Zenou, 1971

As mentioned before, our high school had a separate English study program for American Jewish boys and girls. Aloney Itshak had the privilege of being one of the few boarding schools in Israel to host the American high school study program. Boys and girls from different Jewish communities in the US came as a group to study for a year in Israel and tour the country. The regular American high school curriculum was taught to them by special English teachers. This program gave them the opportunity to live the kibbutz lifestyle within our village. Some of the American boys and girls were assigned to share our dorm rooms, and that way they were motivated to interact more with the general student population.

The American student program in general had their own separate activities with their own counselors due to the big differences in cultures and mentality between them and the rest of the students. At first it was not always easy to connect and bond with individuals from the group as they always hung out together playing ball, either baseball or American football which none of us knew much about or even understood the rules. We envied some of their cool clothes and American gadgets. We liked their t-shirts, hats, and jeans as well as their loud music. We did not always understand each other as their knowledge of Hebrew was limited and they did not seem to be very motivated to communicate in any language besides English.

The year of 1969 was the year of Woodstock and the love revolution in the States. The American students had brought the popular music with them, from bands like Led Zeppelin, The Who, Santana, Jimmy Hendrix, Jethro Tull, Creedence Clearwater, Pink Floyd, The Doors, Deep Purple. Most of my exposure to American music of the '60s I owe to these kids that we were trying to emulate.

Also, as typical of those late 1960s to early 1970s, drug use, mostly of marijuana and hashish, was rampant among the American students. With their more advantageous backgrounds and financial means, locating and buying drugs became favorite activities while on outings in the big Israeli cities around the country. Hashish and marijuana were probably so much cheaper on the streets of Israel than in the urban cities of the US. At one time during the school year, the drug situation became a real problem among the American students, and the school staff and the local police had to get involved, causing a good many of them to be expelled from the program and sent back home to their parents.

Albert and I got along with very well with our American roommate during our junior year of 1970 to 1971. David, from the state of New York, was a very nice guy. One particular evening, David invited us to a special event with some of his buddies from the American group. After dinner we snuck out from our building and Albert and I followed David in the dark as we made our way toward the vegetable fields on the outskirts of the school village. I did not have a clue where we were heading, but soon we were hiking on a small path up a hill until we reached what looked in the dark like a cave entrance. As my roommate and I stepped inside, I saw in the flickering lights of burning candles a few people sitting around. Music came from a small portable cassette player. We were welcomed in English by the American boys and girls there sitting on blankets and foam mattresses inside the cramped space of the cave. As my eyes adjusted, the only other person I recognized who was not American was Albert Zenou, my friend Alain's brother who was from Morocco and from the senior class. I knew he had an American girlfriend, and she was there as well.

After we found a place to sit, they initiated us to drinking directly from a bottle that was passed around, followed by a fat hashish-filled pipe. I was so taken aback and so impressed by the whole setup it didn't even cross my mind to refuse. After a while the hard liquor and the smoke started to take effect on me. I had never before experimented with smoking pot, and with the combination of liquor and hashish, I began to drift into a torpor, lying on my back spreading myself on the ground in that dark and musty cave.

After a while, as we were lying around, we started to itch and scratch. Some of the participants who were more aware realized that we were being bitten by some kind of crawling insects, like ticks or spiders, and decided to get everybody to leave the cave at once to head back to our dorms. The problem was, I was in no shape to get on my feet to hike back. In some way or another they helped me make it back to the vicinity of my dorm building where they alerted some of the girls from my class to come take me to my room.

Yaakov Begas (Turkey), David Maliniak (USA), Alain Zenou (Morocco), with me standing behind

The following morning, I could not get out of bed and had to miss school. Fortunately, with the complicity of my roommate David, who was the main instigator of this idea to initiate us into drugs, and my friend Alain, who was probably briefed by his brother Albert about my whereabouts on that night, we were able not to attract too much attention from our group counselor. The incident went unnoticed by the school staff, even though it took me a couple of days to sober up, with my arms, legs, and torso covered with itchy red bite marks from that night.

Sometime in early 1971, my father came to Israel from Morocco to visit his three sons and his daughter—Armand, Prosper, me, Jacqueline—as well as his four sisters and his mother all living in Israel. He came to the school and wanted to see how I was adapting to my new life. I was very happy to see him and proudly gave him a walking tour around the village grounds.

My father wanted to meet one of my school counselors, so we went to the cottage of my counselor Tovah. She was a soldier assigned to our school and in charge of helping and tutoring new-immigrant student groups like mine. She kindly invited us in to have a cup of coffee and tried to answer some of my dad's questions about my grades and general progress in my new life in Israel. My father was knowledgeable in Hebrew and could understand and hold a conversation in that language, but it was more the ancient Hebrew from the Old Testament and prayer books rather than modern Israeli Hebrew. I facilitated the exchange by translating questions and answers between his French and Tovah's Hebrew to be more expedient. After a while, the doorbell rang. My girlfriend, Shelly, was at the door supposedly to ask something from Tovah while peeking behind Tovah's back knowing that I was there with my father. Shelly and

I exchanged a complicit look and big smiles before she left, and my father clearly couldn't have missed the whole interaction.

Later that day as I walked with my father to the little town for him to get a cab or a bus to get back to where he was staying with family, he asked questions about the girl at the door. He had understood the existing relationship. Morocco was more traditional and such relationships were not common at this young of age. He wanted to know where she was from, her parents' professions, etcetera. I had never before talked with my dad about girlfriends and I was embarrassed to elaborate.

The following weekend I went to visit my father and have Shabbat with him at my aunt Tata Sol's house, his sister living on the outskirts of Rishon Letzion which is just southeast of Tel Aviv. I got there on a Friday afternoon. My father related to me an interesting story about a documentary film he had just watched on Israeli TV the previous night. It was about the Jews of Morocco, broadcasted on the main — and at the time, only — Israeli TV channel. To his big surprise, he recognized me and my brother Simon at a younger age appearing in the film in a Casablanca synagogue. I was a little surprised and amused as I was convinced that he must have been mistaken, confusing me with somebody else. The chances were practically nil that I could have appeared on the Israeli national channel.

Many years later, sometime in the early 1980s, finding myself in Tel Aviv, I visited the newly inaugurated Beit Hatfutsot, the Museum of the Diaspora, an incredible museum dedicated to the Jewish diaspora and displaying the history and cultures of the various Jewish communities of the world. I enjoyed the exhibitions and decided to check the video section where one can choose any country and view the archives of videos and documentaries for that Jewish community.

From Morocco three movies were available to view. I started to watch one about the Jewish community of my city, Casablanca. After some minutes of different scenes showing the vibrant activities and Jewish life taking place there, to my total surprise I recognized our teacher Rabbi Eliahou from our Hebrew school and the small group of kids reciting prayers. As the camera panned the front row, there I was at the age of seven or eight with my brother Simon holding a prayer book open and reading. Suddenly it all came together and made sense when my father, years earlier during a visit to Israel, told me that he recognized me and my brother on TV. It was an unusual coincidence that he happened to be in the country at the time and watching this particular documentary being shown on the national Israeli TV channel.

Come to think of it, I did have a recollection of when the actual event took place. It must have been a morning when my brother and I were dropped off at the little synagogue on Rue Fayolle for our regular Sunday morning session of Hebrew prayer studies. I remember a group of English-speaking visitors equipped with video or film cameras came into the synagogue while we were studying that day. After a short conversation with our rabbi, our small group was relocated from the back rows, where we usually were assigned, to the very front, near the Aron Hakodesh, the wooden ark where the Torah scrolls were kept. The film crew could then have an overall view of the class and the surroundings. Even though I recalled the events of that day and the visiting foreign film crew, I never thought that one day many years later in faraway Israel my father first, and then I, would have the opportunity to view the footage shot that day with me and Simon as young kids.

A few years after I moved to Texas, I got in touch with the offices of the Museum of the Diaspora and explained the whole story and kindly requested a copy of the video for my own records, which they gladly consented to. They agreed to have a copy made for me to be picked up by one of my good friends living in Israel, and he would mail the video cassette to me in Texas. Today that documentary can be found on YouTube under the *Spielberg Jewish Film Archive: Edge of the West*, where after about fifteen minutes my brother Simon and I are seen.

It was during my junior year, 1970 to 1971, that I was to learn very perturbing news about my brother Prosper. He was also in his second year in Israel, preparing his French Baccalaureate and living in Upper Nazareth with his French student group. I had visited him and stayed with him a couple times in his shared apartment and could see that he was very popular and well liked among his classmates. Prosper was a good-looking young man and a great dancer on the dance floor. He loved dancing the jitterbug and loved to play hand drums. He was very popular among the girls in his group.

Orly, who dated Prosper for several weeks during our transit from Casablanca to Marseilles and Israel, had an older brother, Joe, who was in the same French group as Prosper. Through her brother she knew the latest about Prosper. One day Orly took me aside at school to let me know that Prosper had tried to commit suicide and was removed temporarily from school. I was not supposed to know. I was unprepared to learn such devastating news and completely shocked. The events were already a few days old and I didn't have any idea of his whereabouts or what I could do to be of any help. Armand and my sister Jacqueline who were older than I were notified, but I was not.

Several months later I was told one version of the events leading to Prosper's behavior. He had become enamored with a tall, good-looking brunette recently arrived in his group, and after dating for some time and being a popular couple, they had a fallout and broke up the relationship. Prosper didn't take it well and was trying very hard to get back with her. Realizing he was not very successful, he tried to get her attention by staging a suicide attempt. He slit his wrist while in his dorm. He was rushed to a local hospital where he was treated, but unfortunately being a minor and not having his parents living in Israel, he couldn't be released. He had to be transferred to a special hospital for mental patients and kept under observation for several days to make sure he was mentally stable and that he would not try to hurt himself again. Armand and Jacqueline, being the older siblings, were contacted and came to check on him. After several weeks and some counseling, Prosper was finally released to rejoin his class and finish the school year. I can only imagine how this completely traumatizing episode in his life must have affected him.

As I started my second year at Aloney Itshak in Youd Aleph, Junior year in Hi School , I applied and got accepted easily to a special pre-military program within our school. If a student was accepted to attend this, instead of regular days being divided half day in high school and the other half working in the village, he was then exempt from partaking in any work within the village and released to attend instead the classes of the military course. The course was taught by military officers from the Intelligence Corp of the Israeli army. Major Obadiah was in charge, assisted by two captains. Graduates from the high school and the two-year pre-military training program would be assigned to serve in the Israeli Intelligence Corp during their three-year mandatory army service.

The main curriculum study program of the pre-military class and the training we received was basically developing our skills in understanding and writing Arabic as well as learning to decipher transmissions of signals in Morse code. The classes were held in a separate small building on the edge of the school campus. The Israeli Defense Force Intelligence Corp tries with their best technologies to eavesdrop and monitor communications of the surrounding Arab militaries, therefore they required a pool of soldiers fluent in the Arabic language. The Corp was always teaching and training soldiers for the task, preferring to select candidates who were either native speakers born in Arab countries or already familiar with some basic knowledge of Arabic.

The classes improved our skills in the Arabic language and specifically focused on military jargon used

Pre-military intelligence training class in high school, me in uniform standing behind Mr. Stone, a visiting donor to our school. Seated next to him is Major Obadiah, commander of our program

commonly by air force, navy, and ground forces from Egypt, Jordan, and Syria. We were taught mostly to listen and transcribe quickly in writing what we heard. This was achieved by a lot of dictation, at first at a very slow pace, but as we progressed the speed was increased. In class all our desks were wired and connected so that with our headphones on we could listen to the different Arabic dictations as well as Morse code signals broadcast from our instructor's desk. We had to decipher and transcribe by writing by hand.

As an added benefit of being enrolled in this pre-military program, even though we were still civilians we qualified to wear the Israeli Defense Force military uniform, if we chose to, when travelling outside our school. The IDF uniform came with certain privileges, like travelling for free on the trains through Israel and being able to hitchhike to get anywhere. In those days it was common and widely supported that vehicle drivers in Israel would give a free ride to any Israeli soldier

Visiting my grandmother Meme Hninah, on her balcony. Pre-military classes in Aloney Itshak, 1971

standing on the roadside. I took advantage of the uniform while traveling to visit friends and family, saving quite a bit on bus fares. With my long hair, I did stand out among the other soldiers while waiting for a ride or riding the train, as most soldiers in mandatory service conventionally had to wear their hair short by army regulation.

During my junior year of 1970 to 1971, I witnessed the passing of my paternal grandmother, Mama Mryem, at the home of her daughter, my aunt Tata Sol in Rishon Letzion. My father made the trip once more from Morocco to be present at his mother's bedside in her last days. I joined him there and was present as well when she passed away. I stayed by the side of my father for a few days during the following mourning period of Shiva.

During a Jewish holiday school break in that year, I was invited to a friend's house in a *moshav*, a type of shared agricultural community. Dany Itshaky was one of the few Israeli students in our grade in the regular Hebrew-level class. His family lived on Moshav Ein Ayalah on the coastline, south of Haifa. Dany had arranged for both of us to work for a few days during our school break at a large gas station on a highway on the outskirts of Haifa to earn some extra money pumping gas and checking engine fluids for car drivers.

On another school break during that same year, I partnered with my friend Odette Saban to pack our sleeping bags and hitchhike our way south to the town of Eilat and camp out for several days on the beautiful beaches of the Red Sea, a very popular hangout in those years for Israeli youngsters with limited budgets. Once we got there, we decided like a lot of other beach campers to earn some extra cash by being hired for a few days as dishwashers in the big hotels in the area. The hotels were always looking for cheap, temporary labor supplied by the town's visiting teenagers camping on the local beaches. One big advantage of the job, besides the pay, was the great meals we were fed before and after our shifts.

With my extra cash and the end of the school year in sight, plans were made with my two French friends, Michel Wartowski from Brussels and Alain Katz from Paris, to spend a few weeks that summer sharing a room at a friend's mother's boarding house in Tel Aviv. It was on Gordon Street, right across from the beautiful Tel Aviv beach and what was to become in later years the Tayelet, the beach promenade. My friend and roommate Albert Arditi, already in Tel Aviv and having access to his parents' car, was going to join us. We would all spend time together enjoying the summer school break.

Our new friend Alain Katz, who had only recently moved from Paris to join our school, was a people person, very outspoken, with a wide network of friends and acquaintances. Within a few days in Tel Aviv we were invited to socialize with a group of visiting French boys and girls about our ages sent by their families in France to spend their summer in Tel Aviv. Most of them had relatives in the area. We started hanging out with this French crowd, meeting at the beach and at some of the hotel swimming pools in Tel Aviv and Herzliya. Dizengoff Street, with its many restaurants and coffee shops only a block from our boarding house, became our daily meeting and gathering place.

One night we were invited to a party in a private home in Tel Aviv. It was mostly a French-speaking gathering. I noticed a tall, very attractive, blonde French girl across the room. I was too shy to approach her, but we exchanged looks during the whole evening. The next day as my friend and I were seated in a coffee shop on Dizengoff, I recognized the girl walking by. She was with a brunette girl who turned out to be her sister. We invited Patricia and her sister, Micheline, to join us, and they gladly accepted.

Once we were better acquainted, we made plans for later that day to go out on a date. That night we ended up at Tiffany's, one of the most exclusive and famous nightclubs at the time. It was along the Tel Aviv seashore. Albert was also getting involved with a nice French girl from the group. That summer of 1971, both of us were totally enamored. I was completely captivated by what was to be one of my biggest love stories as a young man, one of my most romantic and intense experiences as I was turning eighteen years old that year.

All good things have to end, and as the summer break was wrapping up, we had to get back to our school. It was not easy for me to part from Patricia after such a great time and intense new romance. We had difficulties saying our goodbyes and promised to stay in touch and write to each other. The French school year started a little later than ours did, so Patricia and her sister still had a few more days of vacation left in Tel Aviv. That made it even harder to leave, but with a heavy heart and great sadness I got back to Aloney Itshak to begin my senior year.

Sometime around 1971, my roommate Albert and I were to meet and become friendly with a new student recently arrived from Paris. Nathalie was a very attractive French girl and seemed to be flirting with both of us. Plans were made for a weekend get-together and to attend a rock concert while staying at Albert's parent's home in Tel Aviv. By the end of that weekend, Albert was the lucky one to be seduced by Nathalie and they were in love. This created at first a little tension between the two of us, but we soon got over it. I realized Albert and Nathalie were seriously considering not only leaving school but also living together.

They lived together for a couple of years in Tel Aviv, ending up getting married in 1973. At the wedding ceremony, at a very nice hotel near the Tel Aviv beach, I was Albert's best man, dressed in my army uniform and holding one of the four poles of their *chuppah* canopy. The three of us stayed up the whole night in their hotel honeymoon suite drinking, smoking, and talking about our future plans and dreams. I helped Albert and Nathalie sort through the wedding gifts, mainly counting all the cash and checks from the guests.

Not long after their wedding, Albert and Nathalie decided to move to the US, and after settling in New York City they started raising a family. A few years later, in 1979, I moved to Texas and we visited each other and reconnected. Albert and Nathalie made a special trip to Austin to be present when my first son, David, was born and the circumcision took place in January of 1982. Albert was also present at David's bar mitzvah in Austin in 1995.

The senior year in our school, being the last year before the compulsory three years of military service, was a little special as far as general school rules and discipline for the class. The regular schedule for all the grades was that at night in the dorm rooms everybody was supposed to be in bed with lights out by ten-thirty. Each night our group counselor came by making his rounds to check on us and to remind us to put our lights out. The senior class was granted an exemption from the lights-out rule for homework and study sessions. Another privilege was the option for the boys to let their hair grow long or to grow beards as that was popular for youngsters like us during those years.

During the night, a man from the nearby village acted as a security guard. He was in charge of patrolling the grounds, riding on the back of a mule and guarding the premises to make sure none of the students were roaming around outside their rooms or buildings. The night watchman, an older man, was not very good at his job, though. The junior and senior boys quickly learned how to skirt his patrol path, moving rapidly in the dark areas between buildings to join our girlfriends in their rooms after hours or meet in the surrounding woods.

As the school year got underway, we were made aware that some school staff changes had taken place. David Braha, who was our junior-year counselor, had been promoted to the new chief counselor in charge of all school rules and discipline regulations. In his new position, Mr. Braha introduced some big changes, mainly affecting our upcoming senior class, specifically about the rules of the lights out in the dorms. Also, no more long hair. I and most of my class group did not like at all the new changes because we were looking forward to our senior year privileges. We were prepared to argue our case.

Other new facts became known for our senior class of mostly recent newcomers trying to graduate and pass the *Bagrut* exam, or baccalaureate. Successfully passing the Bagrut was a requirement in order to pursue any college studies in Israel. We soon learned that our school, trying to keep its national statistics level comparatively high versus other institutions, would be limiting the number of students allowed to participate in taking the national exam. Doing so, the school would be practically eliminating the chance to go to college for a large percentage of students.

Odette, our classmate who investigated and researched this topic, found out that some of us could do better by applying separately on our own as freelancers to take the test. If you were an independent candidate and a recent immigrant, you could even select which two other credits on top of the four credits required and stand a better chance to pass the test and get the coveted Bagrut certificate. Odette and a few others soon made up their minds to move out from the Aloney Itshak village and study and try to apply as freelancers for the twelfth grade graduation exam.

In light of these recent changes, I started having a new attitude with the school, and soon enough, one day David Braha confronted me. After noticing me in the dining hall wearing my hair long from the summer, he kindly asked me to go get a haircut. A few days later, seeing that I had not complied, he reiterated his demand. I let him know that as a member of the senior class I really did not have to comply with the recent rule change. David, realizing he was being confronted, was forced to take action against me to set an example for the rest of my group.

One option was to expel me from school, but because of my status as an immigrant student under the care of the Jewish Agency and the Youth Aliyah and without my parents living in Israel, this was complex. He couldn't just expel me from school, he had to follow a certain procedure, which was basically to send me with a letter to the main offices of the Jewish Agency in Tel Aviv to be seen by a social worker for juveniles. The agency would have to recommend the proper solution or compromise for dealing with my attitude.

After several trips to the Tel Aviv offices of the Young Aliyah department of the Jewish Agency and taking some psychological tests and having several interviews, I was briefed on how best to graduate from high school. I was offered the option to leave the boarding school and move to Haifa where the Agency would arrange for me to live with an Israeli family as a boarder.

They would also arrange to register me for classes at a local private school in Haifa for adults, so I could try to complete my high school requirements to graduate.

Haifa and Jerusalem

Within a few weeks after moving out of Aloney Itshak, it was arranged for me to move to Haifa to have room and board at the home of a middle-aged Israeli couple in the Carmel neighborhood. I shared a room with their twelve-year-old son who, thinking back, I am sure due to their older age must have been adopted. While in Haifa, I had a monthly meeting with a social worker who kept track of my class work and progress.

Since I was no longer subject to regular school hours and managed my work and study schedule on my own, I visited more often my grandmother, Meme Hninah, who lived on the outskirts of Haifa. As well, I tried to more frequently see my brothers Armand and Prosper. Armand by then had finished his military service and had become a bus driver in Haifa for the Egged company. His goal was to ultimately be able to buy a share into this huge cooperative transportation company that controlled most of the public buses throughout Israel. As a cooperative, Egged is completely owned by its partners, the bus drivers themselves.

Finding myself with extra time and living in a large city, I got a job with the Haifa postal service to become a mail carrier, delivering mail daily on my regular routes of about two long streets. I would ride the bus every morning to the big post office downtown, sort my mail in the proper order at my assigned station, stuff all in a big leather satchel, grab my official mail carrier hat, and ride the bus again to start my route.

Before relocating to Haifa, one weekend I visited my grandmother with Armand. He and I attended a dance on Friday night held on the campus of Haifa University. At the dance, mostly for the college students, we met two Israeli girls and went out with them the rest of the weekend. After moving to Haifa, I reconnected with Ilana. She was born and grew up in a select, upper-middle-class neighborhood in Haifa, and she was also a senior in high school and studying for the twelfth grade exam. We spent the weekends together studying either at her parents' place or sometimes I would join her when she would babysit for a family in her neighborhood. In April of 1972 I took my exams on four subjects and was able to pass them successfully, leaving two more required exams scheduled for later that year.

Armand and Prosper, both being immigrants to Israel and under the law of return, were entitled to certain rights and benefits like all newcomers to Israel. Mainly, they each had the right to obtain from the Jewish Agency a fifty percent share into an apartment with government-subsidized rent, with the option to purchase that apartment with very favorable government financing. Armand, having recently completed his duty as a soldier, decided with Prosper to apply and try to get one apartment, combining both their new-immigrant entitlements. After several interviews and availability checks, they decided to request an apartment in the Jerusalem area. Armand for professional reasons was considering moving to the capital city of Jerusalem, hoping he would stand a better chance of achieving his goal of investing in a share ownership in the Egged bus co-op. Prosper was studying at the Hebrew University of Jerusalem at the Mount Scopus campus.

In early 1972, Armand and Prosper moved into a nice two-bedroom, one-bath apartment that was located on Rehov Naftali in the Baka neighborhood of Jerusalem. This was near the German Colony neighborhood, called Moshava Germanit, and a couple blocks from the old Jerusalem train station. On a visit to spend a weekend with my two brothers, as we were sitting down for a Shabbat dinner and I was feeling a bit homesick, they suggested for me to look into the possibility of moving in with them. I brought up the subject at the next monthly meeting with my counselor and social worker, and after several back and forth interviews in Haifa and at the Jerusalem office of the Jewish agency, I was granted approval to join Armand and Prosper in their apartment in Jerusalem.

We three brothers were finally able to reunite and live under the same roof. The apartment was furnished with the bare minimum, but we didn't mind. We enjoyed spending time together, exploring the incredible, historic city of Jerusalem with all its multifaceted culture, particularly the old Arab city with its narrow streets and colorful *souk*, which is an open-air bazaar, and large crowds of local and international visitors. Out of the three of us, Prosper was the most familiar with the city. When he first came from Morocco, he had spent his first year living in Jerusalem. His old school and dorm were about two blocks from our apartment.

Armand was driving his bus around Jerusalem and Prosper was attending classes at the Mount Scopus campus. Within a short time, through the help of a neighbor we recently met, I was able to get a regular full-time office job as a clerk in the State Treasury Office, in the Department of Government Workers payroll. The neighbor, Moshe Revah, was a long-time employee there. His family came from Morocco in the late 1940s and he was born in Jerusalem. He was very kind and invited us many times to his parents' home for Shabbat.

Robert, a few months before enlisting in the military, 1972

Before moving to Jerusalem, I had been notified by the military draft office that a date had been set for me to enlist and start my three years of mandatory military service. Mid-May of 1972 was the date I was supposed to present myself at the local military branch. I still had not completed the second part of my graduation exams requiring me to take a test on two more subjects, and most importantly for me, I wanted to spend the summer with my French girlfriend, Patricia, who was coming back to spend two whole months in Israel. I decided to request a few months' postponement for starting my army service. I applied and wrote a long letter to the drafting board requesting a deferment of six months. After a few intense weeks of waiting, it was granted.

As I was settling into my new life in the apartment with my brothers and getting used to my new job, I started making some big plans for the upcoming summer visit with Patricia. She and I had been staying in touch by exchanging letters, frequently writing to each other since we last parted at the end of the previous summer. Unexpectedly, just a couple months before the summer, I received a letter from her basically letting me know that she had met and fallen in love with a new boyfriend. She was still coming with her sister, Micheline, to spend the summer in Israel at her aunt's place in Tel Aviv and she was looking forward very much to seeing me, but it would be solely as friends.

French sisters Micheline on the left, Patricia on the right, in Jerusalem, summer 1972, few weeks before enlisting

At first I was devastated. It took me a while to digest the news. The previous summer's romance had made me fall in love like never before. Both of us had been looking forward to a repeat of the same. Feeling deeply hurt in my heart and in my pride and very disappointed, I looked at my options and resigned myself to the facts. I decided to just enjoy the upcoming visit, but knowing that I needed to get on with my life, I decided to write again to the draft board, to ask them to rescind the six-month postponement. I was ready to move on and proceed with my three years of service by mid-summer.

Patricia and her sister came as planned to spend their summer vacation in Israel. We were happy to be reunited and acted as if nothing had changed. They came to stay with me in Jerusalem and I gave them a big tour of the city. I made plans with my friend Moshe, who owned a nice vehicle of his own, for us to go on a road trip for a few days to the Dead Sea and the Sea of Galilee in the north, where we camped one night on the shore of the Kinneret Sea.

My new date to enlist in Tsahal, the Israel Defense Forces, was set for early August 1972. I spent my last weekend as a civilian with Patricia in Tel Aviv. I let her know of my change of plans as we parted that last night. Accompanying her in a cab back to her aunt's house, we had big hugs and a few tears. We were both very sad knowing that our lives were going separate ways.
The next day in Jerusalem, Armand accompanied me to the local military enlistment office. A large group of young men my age , surrounded by their families and friends gathered for the occasion to say their goodbyes and give last-minute recommendations before our group of enlisted men boarded the big bus. Armand, having gone through the experience a few years earlier, was probably somewhat melancholy knowing how difficult the first few months of my induction could be. After a big hug and some awkward jokes, I got on the bus and it drove off with us waving from the windows to the parents, friends, and families standing on the curbside.

Israel Military Service (Tsahal), 1972–1975

The Bakum Tzrifin was a big military compound in central Israel where all new inductees got processed. Bakum is the acronym for "Reception and Sorting Base" in Hebrew. As we got off the bus, we were immediately welcomed by one of the most notorious NCO (Non-commissioned Officer) in all of Israel. He had a big mustache. He barked a short speech letting us know a few basic rules.

After being registered, medically checked, photographed, and vaccinated, we each received our basic personal gear that included boots, belts, hats, several sets of uniforms, and a large, heavy, green canvas duffle bag called—even in Hebrew—a kitbag. We had to stuff everything in the kitbag, lock it with a small padlock, and keep a close eye on it. We started the old military dance of "hurry up, hurry up ... and wait."

The Israeli army had two major periods in the year for taking in new draftees. One was during the month of May and nicknamed the promotion of *maw maw*, meaning a rough crowd, which referred to the eighteen-year-old guys with less high school education who were probably already working at jobs. The second one was during August for mostly the freshly graduated high school students, commonly nicknamed the *hokhmologim*, or smart asses.

For the next few days we waited to be individually interviewed and assigned to our units. We would gather every morning and march to the open space in the center of the base, nicknamed "the slave market," and wait for the day's work assignments. Most soldiers were assigned to do menial cleaning around the base, but each day more and more of us were being dispatched to our new units to start boot camp.

While waiting for our selection, some instructors from special combat units, like the paratrooper brigade or infantry ranger unit, would come among us to ask if anyone was willing to volunteer and try out for their fighting units. The ones showing an interest would be invited to join them with kitbag on shoulder for a few hours of intense workout around the compound, just to test their commitment.

During my short interview, the officer noticed that I had some pre-military training with the intelligence program at my old high school, but since I did not officially graduate from that program, there were no specific details in my file. I decided to apply to join the Israeli Navy and be sent to the prestigious navy officer course, which is considered very exclusive and hard to get into. If you are lucky enough to be accepted, you have to agree to serve an extra two years, added to the mandatory three-year service requirement. The Navy is relatively much smaller than the other two main branches of the military, the Air Force and the Land Forces, or Infantry. The training and the studies for the navy officer course can be as long as two years. The first step I had to go through was a long series of written exams for general evaluation, and from a pool of several hundred applicants, fifty individuals would be selected. I was happy to be counted among them, and that was the first hurdle. We were put on a bus and dispatched to the main Navy base and headquarters near the port city of Haifa.

Israel Military Service (Tsahal), 1972-1975

We were told that we would be spending the next week in intense training on land and sea. In military lingo this was called a *guibouch*, meaning to create a cohesive core of soldiers learning to bond with each other while being carefully observed and monitored by the training staff. After the sixth day of this training, only thirty candidates out of our group of fifty would be officially invited to start the eighteen-month navy officer course.

We were each given a numbered tag to be displayed on our hat so that the staff observing us could easily keep track of us and our behavior under the strained situations. The first activity was on the water in the port of Haifa, where after being split into smaller groups we boarded large, wooden rowing boats with heavy wood paddles. We were to head out to the open sea and wait for further instructions. As my group started rowing, we soon realized we needed to get better synchronized if we wanted to get anywhere. We appointed someone to handle the rudder and give us instructions for better steering and better rowing synchronization in order to gather speed and direction. I realized that I needed to be more proactive and not just wait for orders but also to take some initiative under the watchful eyes of our staff observers, who were totally silent once the task was given to us.

On another day we were given backpacks with extra weight to simulate regular soldiers' gear. We were also given machine guns, but fake ones since we were not yet properly trained to handle real ones. We were transported to a forested area in the surrounding Carmel Mountains and started a long day of intense hiking with our extra weight, through canyons and creeks all the way to the coast and then hiking in and out of the water along the shoreline. I was trying to keep up and keep a positive attitude, but I could tell that my companions were trying much harder as we were all in competition for the coveted thirty open spots.

The worst day for me was when we boarded a small commercial cargo ship owned by the Navy and used for training young recruits. We left Haifa and headed out to the open sea. Once past the calm water of the harbor marina and onto high seas, our group was invited to attend lectures in a classroom down below the bridge, in the lowest part of the boat. While we attended these classes about safety and fire drills on board, I suspected the boat was purposefully being rocked sideways. I imagined the real drill was to make the whole class seasick.

Sure enough, most of the class got sick that day, which was anticipated, but more importantly we were being observed by the staff to see how we handled ourselves under those conditions. I could barely stand up or function. After a while we were allowed to go up on deck for some fresh air and to start a series of drills, running from one end of the boat to the other with specific tasks and assignments. I did my best to drag myself along, barely able to stand and constantly having to lean overboard to throw up.

One of the final drills I recall on that day was jumping overboard into the water from the edge of the boat, a height of about thirty to forty feet, dressed in our regular army uniforms and wearing the army-issued, heavy military boots and life jackets. Once in the water, floating awkwardly and heavily burdened by our boots and clothing, we had to push large, floating metal oil barrels away from the boat hull, then swim around a raft.

Our instructions were to gather around the raft and push away from the ship as far as we could, as if maybe simulating a fire escape and distancing ourselves from the ship. The big challenge at the end of the drill was getting back on board the ship by climbing a wide rope ladder hanging off the side of the ship. Between the weight of heavily soaked clothing and leather boots and the constant rolling waves slamming us against the side of the ship, the task was arduous.

By the time we got back to base after this grueling and exhausting long day, I knew in my mind that I did not stand a chance to make it as one of the thirty finalists. I was depressed and deeply disappointed knowing that this was one of my childhood dreams from the days of fishing with my father in the Casablanca harbor and watching the maritime boat traffic. I had dreamed of one day becoming a merchant marine officer. My plan was to serve in the Navy as an officer in order to get trained, get skills, and get a professional long-term education, acquiring at the same time a trade that I could later use after the military.

Friday morning as the list of names of the final thirty candidates was announced, some of the guys that had labored so hard but were not on the list were totally dismayed, some even in tears. I had anticipated the results and was not surprised. I didn't really expect to be selected seeing how the competition among us was fierce and how I had discovered that seasickness affected me so badly. I had resigned myself that I stood very little chance to be one of the finalists, but nevertheless I felt very sad and deeply disappointed after all the effort and expectations of the last couple weeks.

Back at the Bakum, or triage center, after another brief interview I was offered to be trained as a transmission and communications specialist. I was still a little disoriented and under the shock of my recent failure at the Navy training experience. I reluctantly accepted, but first I was to join the Golani Brigade combat unit of the Infantry to do my classes and the basic training called boot camp. I would first train as a combat soldier before being dispatched to the special communications school.

The next day at the regular "slave market" gathering, my name was called up as part of a large group and we climbed into the back of a big military truck heading north. Some of the guys with me had not been told their exact unit assignment. Once realizing the direction we were headed, they decided they didn't want to be trained as combat soldiers and grabbed their bags and jumped out while the truck was stopped at a traffic light. The military training base of Schraga, located on the outskirts of the northern coastal town of Nahariya, near Moshav Shavei Zion, was the base for the Golani Brigade where I would be spending the next four to five months training.

The first few days were a rude awakening. I don't know what I was expecting, but this was a rough introduction not only to military training and discipline but also to a particular language, culture, and Israeli mentality I had not been thoroughly exposed to yet since I first landed in Israel as a fifteen-year-old teenager. During the first two and a half years in Aloney Itshak, while living within the village boarding school in the countryside, I felt somewhat sheltered and isolated from mainstream Israel. The last six months before enlisting, living and working in two major cities like Haifa and Jerusalem gave me a slightly better exposure to Israeli society.

In my new platoon and company, I really had to concentrate and make a big effort to comprehend and react quickly to instructions and orders, some in a special Hebrew slang being barked at us constantly. No excuses, no time or special consideration for my slow comprehension of instructions or orders. I tried to imitate the other soldiers and react as fast as I could, trying to keep up the pace and not attract any unnecessary attention.

Israel Military Service (Tsahal), 1972-1975

*Golani boot camp,
August 1972*

*Robert, second from the right, Golani infantry training in
northern Galilee, 1972*

After being fitted with our new helmets, special vests, water canteens, and folding shovels, the intense daily training got under way. After a few days, our battalion started on a long march culminating in a swearing-in ceremony at the Golani Interchange in northern Galilee. A monument there is dedicated to this famous brigade and its fallen troops, and battalion official ceremonies traditionally are held there. After a few speeches by the top brass and a solemn ceremony, we were each issued our own rifle and a small Hebrew Bible. The idea of getting both at the same time, the Bible and a weapon, symbolized our Jewish history and our commitment to defend our homeland. The rifle each soldier got was at the time widely used within infantry combat units. It was the Belgian-made FN-FAL with wooden stock.

In my platoon, I was able to befriend the only other new immigrant like myself, Lionel Serfaty, who was also from Morocco. I learned later that he was the son of the principal of my old high school in Casablanca. Lionel and I soon started sticking together, speaking French while commiserating and trying our best to manage and keep up with the intensity of the early days of training.

We trained and learned about weaponry from daybreak until late at night. The sleeping hours were limited to about four or five hours in best cases. At night we also had guard duty around the perimeter of our building. We slept in large rooms with about twenty of us, ten on each side on single metal cots with thin foam mattresses, rough army-issued brown blankets, no sheets, no pillows. Most of us stuffed our military boots under our foam mattresses for two reasons—for an elevated headrest to compensate for lack of a pillow, but mostly not to get our boots stolen, as I was to find out one early morning, after not having done so. I was

Israel Military Service (Tsahal), 1972-1975

terrified to find them gone, realizing the consequences could be grave and involve some serious disciplinary measures. I wore my extra pair, and soon, with the help of a couple soldiers from my platoon, I recovered my missing pair from the building next door in the same way mine were raided . . . *a la guerre comme a la guerre* . . . .

My brother Prosper one day showed up looking for me—a surprise visit—by coming to the gate of my base. Since as a civilian he could not come in past the entrance, somebody went to fetch me. I was so happy to see him even for only a few minutes. We had a good visit, exchanging stories while standing by the side of the road outside the main gate entrance.

While in boot camp, weekend leaves off the base were scarce, maybe once a month, if lucky, and when it did happen, it was quite a complicated ordeal before earning that privilege. First there was the long, demanding preparation for weekly inspection by our commanding officer. It took hours of preparation to clean our general gear and dorm room. Only after successfully passing our officer inspection could we proceed to the next step, which was packing all personal gear and weapons to be hauled on our backs and stored at the main headquarters of the base. All personal gear had to be stored with properly signed receipts for each item listed, another very long process. By the time I could get clearance, get out of the base, and arrive at either my grandmother's or my aunt's house, I would be so exhausted that I would just sleep most of the weekend, and then it was time to head back on Sunday morning.

Most of the soldiers in the unit, being native Israelis, had a support network of family, friends, classmates, and girlfriends waiting for them at home and pampering them during their short visits. A network of support was essential for boosting morale and encouragement and certainly contributed to a positive attitude. Most young Israeli soldiers while growing up at home were very familiar with the whole military service and the training process, having had older siblings, other family members, neighbors, schoolmates, etcetera, come home sharing the experiences they went through.

Thinking back on those early days of training, that was one thing I was missing. I really did not have a support network around me to back me up. Many years later, when our two boys, David and Daniel, each decided to go to Israel and serve in the IDF, I made sure that they first belonged to a social group of peers from similar background for a few months before enlisting, to create a strong bonding experience before joining the military. For myself I had to try to create one on my own. I drew a lot of comfort from letters, mostly from my parents, my brother Samy, and, most importantly, from Patricia writing me on a regular basis from France. Letters from my parents in Morocco could not come directly to Israel and had to transit through France, mostly through Samy in Paris.

A picture I carried with me during boot camp training, from summer of 1972, a few days before enlisting.

Israel Military Service (Tsahal), 1972-1975

Patricia and I kept in touch writing to each other even though she was dating a new boyfriend in Paris. I kept and cherished a picture of her in my front shirt pocket, next to my standard military-issued, emergency first aid battle dressing and drew some comfort from the memories of the last two summers in her company.

In the early years of the Israeli army, during the first few months of training at any military camp, a certain tradition among the training staff was still somewhat prevalent and tolerated. This was called *tirtour*, or basically extra training time as a collective punishment for a platoon or squad. If the platoon sergeant for any reason was not satisfied with our performances, he would wait until the training day was officially over late at night and then instead of dispersing us to our barracks to get some valuable, ever-shrinking few hours of sleep, he would initiate an extra set of exercises. In the worst-case scenario, he would initiate the ultimate, dreaded stretcher exercise. One soldier would lie on a stretcher and a team of four soldiers took turns carrying the heavy stretcher on their shoulders while hiking at a fast pace in the dark, sometimes on uneven surfaces like across a freshly plowed field.

A few months into our training our whole company went, as we often did, on field maneuvers in the hills of northern Israel. We set up camp, two men to each small tent, in a remote area in northern Galilee to practice field exercises in the surrounding valleys and open fields, getting familiar with the terrain and learning how to set up positions and move as a military squad. One night after dinner, when we had a few minutes to lie down and relax in our small tents and get ready for the night exercises, most of us, being exhausted, must have fallen asleep and missed waking up on time to show up for night training.

Looking For Home

When our two corporals and our sergeant showed up to find many of us missing in the yard by the flagpole, they came by the tents to check on us. Finding us in deep slumber, they decided to play a trick on us, to rob as many rifles as they could by pulling them gently from control of their sleeping young trainees. Once they were done, they called on us to gather. By pure luck in my case, I had fallen asleep on top of my gun so they couldn't easily have taken it. As we lined up, some of the soldiers realized the disappearance of their personal rifles and were in total panic. They could not comprehend the dire situation of losing their guns, never suspecting for a minute the staff scheme.

The lineup was usually of three parallel rows facing the flagpole. Our platoon decided as a last-minute resort that in the dark, the ones without their weapons would be better hidden in the last row, as if we could delay for a few more minutes the terrible fact of the sudden disappearance of the guns. Sergeant Suissa, with a smirk on his face, confronted the soldiers, asking them about the whereabouts of their guns, wondering if they had "sold their guns to the Indians." Our platoon was too much in shock to even imagine what to think. After lecturing and threatening us with dire consequences, mainly that this was going to be a very long night, one that would be remembered for a long time, he finally asked the two corporals to fetch the missing rifles and redistribute them back to the soldiers.

Before we went out that night, the sergeant told us that once our regular night training was finished, instead of crashing in our tents to get some rest, we were to get back to the main square and go out for an extra-long group punishment. The tirtour took several hours, with us running around in the hills in the dark. We finally got

Israel Military Service (Tsahal), 1972-1975

back after 1:00 a.m., completely worn out and having lost some hours of valuable sleep time.

A few weeks later, during one weekend when we were on base, the whole battalion was invited to the dining hall for a short lecture by a visiting officer from Headquarters. While seated in the large, crowded hall, with my limited Hebrew skills I was barely able to follow and understand what was being said. At the end of the lecture, the officer asked if any soldiers had any complaints regarding staff abuse or extra hours of training. Somebody from our platoon rose to relate the chapter of the group punishment we had been subjected to on that particular night during field training maneuvers.

The matter was investigated by Headquarters, and as a result, Sergeant Suissa was put on trial, demoted, and sent to military prison for thirty days. The main reason, as I came to understand later, was that our sergeant, in his eagerness to inflict group punishment on our platoon, had later staged that night a mock weapons swearing-in ceremony. We were made to swear allegiance again and to promise never to sell our weapons to Indians. That was totally out of line and against all military rules. Not only was it a joke, but each soldier can only partake once during his early training in an official ceremony, to swear allegiance to the defense of his country and to his military unit, never to be repeated a second time even as a training exercise.

Our training for the first few weeks focused on teaching us the most basic skills of an infantry soldier and getting us familiar with weapons used in our battalion. We practiced with the rifle, the Uzi submachine gun, the FN and the big FN MAG, which is the special FN machine gun with bipod. We trained on the American bazooka and the Russian RPG anti-tank rocket launchers, the mortar, and armor-mounted big guns like the Browning .30 and .50 calibers. We learned to handle hand grenades and took turns throwing live ones under supervision.

Once we mastered individual skills and weapons, at the next level we were taught how to move in the terrain as a squadron within a platoon. We had to know how to read maps, read the terrain and its topographical features, and navigate. We learned night mobility versus day. New weapons were assigned within the platoon, with each soldier matched with a specific personal weapon and some group gear. I was given an Uzi and a pack of ammunition to carry on my back as part of the ammo needed to fire the mortar, which was assigned to another soldier. As we progressed in our training and maneuvers, we proceeded to learn how to operate within our company and later within the battalion.

During a training exercise one night, we were taught how to move around a defensive position. We had to cross over a barrier made of concertina wire. I was ordered to jump forward and lie across it with the whole length of my body, so my weight would lower the wire to the ground and acting almost like a bridge. I protected my face with my arms crossed in front of my body while still holding my gun. This allowed my squad to safely cross the wire by stepping on my back, or actually on the metal shovel I carried on my back like everyone else did. All went well, except when the staff corporal helped me back on my feet, I found I had a bleeding gash a couple inches long on my right knee from the barbed wire. I still had to finish the exercises with my squad before being able to clean up and dress the cut. To this day, after all these years, that scar is still apparent on my knee.

I remember one particularly nice person in my platoon, an Israeli-born soldier from a small village in the countryside. He was not particularly athletic and was

Israel Military Service (Tsahal), 1972-1975

about the same size and build as me, with a very strong determination and an outgoing personality. I don't recall his name, but he was from a moshav and seemed to always have a positive attitude no matter how intense the training was or how exhausted we were. We sometimes talked, often sharing stories about our different backgrounds and our lives in general. He was very motivated and set on going to the officer course and becoming a leader. He had a big smile and was always ready to help others. On days when most soldiers were getting mail and small parcels from home that were full of sweets and home-baked goods, he would share some of his mother's cakes or cookies sent to him, knowing that I never received anything except an occasional letter from France. This was always much appreciated.

As we were getting toward the end of the training period, I hurt my foot during a practice jump out of a moving armored half-track. The next day my foot was so swollen I couldn't get my boot on, so I had to report my injury and was dispatched to the infirmary. After a brief visit at the local medical office, I was sent to the Rambam main municipal hospital in Haifa for a full set of x-rays and better diagnostics. A twisted ankle and a cracked bone in my foot was the final diagnosis. The military orthopedic doctor who was treating me asked me which unit I was in. When I responded I was in the Golani Brigade, he was surprised and showed me the x-ray of my foot, explaining that a mistake was probably made in my files due to the fact that I had a small deformity of bunions on both my feet. I should only be a 72.

Let me explain. Every young man before enlisting had to get a series of checkups by military physicians where we were graded and given a medical profile. The top grade was 97—why not 100? We used to joke that being circumcised was the reason, but probably a false assumption. Any medical issues could impact that grade. Combat soldiers had to be between 82 to 97. Below 82, you could only be assigned to a non-combat logistics unit or other less physically demanding unit. Apparently due to an oversight in my medical file, I had been graded at 97, but due to bunions on both feet, I should have been at 72. I honestly did not grasp the concept on the spot, and after getting my foot properly bandaged and wrapped, I was on my way back to base with special restrictions for a few days to let my foot heal.

Only much later I was to find out the impact of the new findings. After graduating from basic training and getting a little time off that definitely helped the healing process, I was to report for training as a transmission and communications specialist. The training was to last several weeks, and after graduating I would be assigned to another combat unit. One day while in class, I got called in to my commander's office and was told that due to recent changes in my medical profile, which was lowered to reflect my updated records, I would have to be discharged from transmission training and reassigned somewhere else.

After a couple interviews about my future options, it was decided that if I was interested and could be accepted, I would be a good candidate for a logistics officer course. The next course would start in six months. I would be detached to a logistics base to work there until the start of the course. One of my options within the logistics unit was transportation, which I figured would be a good opportunity to get a driver's license, paid for by the military. In the meantime, I would get experience driving large trucks.

Driving school lasted several weeks on a base in Kiryat Malachi, in the south. We were taught to drive big military trucks, and once I obtained my heavy-truck

Israel Military Service (Tsahal), 1972-1975

driver's license I was assigned to a large military transportation center in Tirat Hacarmel, on the outskirts of Haifa.

Now in early 1973, while I was slowly adjusting to my new soldier life in the IDF, I was trying to stay in touch with my family, mostly through letters since my brothers and sister were all back living in France. Samy was married to his first French wife, Genevieve, and was living in Paris. He was working as an executive and doing relatively well. He and his wife had recently bought their own nice apartment in the 14th arrondissement. Jacqueline, who had met Sylvain while studying in Israel, had also decided to leave Israel for Paris. After getting married, she and Sylvain were working hard and trying to get established, to create a new life for themselves.

My brothers Armand and Prosper each for his own reasons decided to leave Israel for Paris, to try their luck at starting a new life in France. I imagine that was not a very easy endeavor with little savings and no proper working visas to stay in France. With both of them gone from Israel, the apartment in Jerusalem was sublet, so I really did not have the option of going there anymore.

About that time, I learned about a special IDF program to match soldiers like me with no parents in Israel to be adopted by a kibbutz in order to give us a home and a place to go for weekend leaves from the army. Back in the early 1970s the status of "lonely soldiers" serving in the IDF was just starting to get a little attention. Many years later, by the time our two sons went to Israel to serve in the IDF in the early 2000s, a completely new concept and special logistics had been put in place to help young Jewish immigrants wanting to come to Israel by themselves to serve in the IDF. These young men could benefit from special assistance and support while serving as soldiers.

Taking advantage of the new program to assist me, I selected one kibbutz not too far from Haifa—Kibbutz Givat Oz, near the ruins of the historical ancient city of Megiddo. I decided one day to take my chances and just show up at the kibbutz with my small backpack and a letter from the military. The kibbutz staff in the main office was totally taken by surprise, and only after several phone calls realized that indeed there was such a hosting program between the IDF and several kibbutzim throughout the country to host and procure a home for soldiers like me.

I was shown to a room similar to those in my days at Aloney Itshak, with two beds and a wooden closet, quite bleak. The whole experience so far was not very encouraging and as I began to wonder if I should just give up, to my luck, within a few hours I was introduced to another soldier who was living full time on the kibbutz and in the same building as me. He welcomed me and invited me to have coffee. Max, who was born in Morocco, spoke fluent French and was serving in the Nahal Brigade.

Kibbutzim had a special program long in existence, since the early years of the creation of Israel. Originally to help create and strengthen new agricultural settlements, most kibbutzim were established on the borders of the country. Small groups of young soldiers from the Nahal Brigade who had farming backgrounds were organized and trained so that they could be posted to these frontier settlements. They helped not only to establish the settlements but also provided security. Max, within his Nahal military unit, was alternating his three years of military service with short periods of training on a regular military base and living and working full time on the kibbutz, taking part in the everyday life of the farming community of Givat Oz.

Israel Military Service (Tsahal), 1972-1975

Givat Oz, being located a couple of kilometers from the old border with Jordan and the West Bank, was considered until the 1967 War as a border agriculture community. As such, it would benefit from having a unit from the Nahal Brigade spend most of their regular service on-site, living there and working in all the different farming activities of the settlement. Max's room was so well equipped and furnished, with a small fridge, books, records, and stereo sound system, that I became envious. I discovered that this was the ideal way to combine military service while living onsite within a kibbutz community. I would be spending most of my visiting weekends at the kibbutz with Max, being introduced to his friends and after working hours mostly hanging out at the dorms of the foreign kibbutz volunteers. These volunteers were young men and women visiting from all over the world, temporarily working and living on the kibbutz, getting room and board in exchange for physical labor in the fields.

When not at the kibbutz, I mostly stayed at my grandmother's house and would meet with friends around the Haifa University student dorms. Through my high school friend Odette and her boyfriend, Simon Telby, who was a student at Haifa University, I was introduced to Moroccan girl students. Often while staying at my grandmother Meme Hninah's for the weekend on leave from the army, I would take a quick shower, switch to my civilian clothes, and catch a bus to the University of Haifa's campus to hang out with some of the girls. I enjoyed their company, sharing with them stories about activities and new experiences in my life as a soldier.

Being posted in the northern part of the country and being on the road a lot behind the wheel of my big Leyland military truck, I became familiar with the road networks of the whole Upper Galilee and Golan Heights regions as my driving skills improved. I got to know very well all the roads and the whole area, transporting every day a different load, such as food supplies, ammunitions, troop units, barrels of fuels, even Navy missiles being serviced when not mounted on missile boats. I became familiar with most of the army compounds, military bases, and border-fortified Israeli positions all around the Syrian, Golan Heights, and the Jordanian Valley borders.

One day, driving very close to the Lebanese border on a small, scenic, winding mountain road in a beautiful forested area in north Galilee, I came to the entrance of a military outpost. After presenting the proper documents at the gate, I drove inside looking for the officer I was supposed to present myself and my truck to. I was directed to a small dining hall.

Walking inside, I heard the soldiers around me speaking in Arabic while dressed in the same standard IDF-issued uniforms as mine. I started getting worried. As soon as I entered the dining room, I noticed a big, prominently displayed poster with two large swords painted with Arabic writings. The idea crossed my mind that maybe in a moment of inattention I had mistakenly crossed the border into Lebanon and was among Lebanese soldiers, but the officer came toward me and I soon realized I was in a military outpost of the special infantry combat unit called the Sword Battalion, Unit 300, an Arabic-speaking unit of Israeli soldiers of the Arab Druze minority. They traditionally served in the north of Israel, where most of their villages were located, and helped protect and patrol the Lebanese and Syrian borders.

Looking back at those years, I recall one specific long two-day drive I had to make without really understanding the purpose until a few years later. I was sent to a Navy base around Haifa to pick up a large truckload of

Israel Military Service (Tsahal), 1972-1975

life jackets. My assignment was to deliver these life jackets all the way south, deep into the Sinai desert, to a large force of armored tanks camped out in the middle of the arid desert. I was a little perplexed at the time about delivering life jackets to such a location, but it was not for me to question my orders.

A few months later, in the midst of the October War, also known as the Yom Kippur War, I got the answer to my question. An armored tank division under the command of General Arik Sharon was training in total secrecy on the possibility of building a floating bridge across the water of the Suez Canal, in case of a new military conflict with Egypt. Military maneuvers were taking place, practicing for the possibility that the IDF might one day have to send forces across to carry the fight to the west bank of the canal. Life jackets were required for all crews, of logistics soldiers and engineers working on or crossing the bridge. In early 1973, that whole scenario was only a remote military option that nevertheless had to be rehearsed and practiced secretly.

It was on that particular long drive south with my truckload of lifejackets that I was pulled aside by the military police for going over the speed limit on a major highway. They inspected my whole truck as well as the contents to match my paperwork. This was maybe one of the reasons I recall precisely what I was hauling that day. A few weeks later after a trial of less than two minutes, for that speeding ticket I was given an unusually harsh sentence of twenty-one days in a military jail.

Apparently, on the day of the speeding ticket trial, the base commander must have noticed in my file an existing record of a previously broken rule, more of a disciplinary nature, that took place during boot camp that I must have gotten a warning for. All I can imagine is the base commander, probably in a hurry to get home on that particular Friday afternoon and with the long line of waiting offenders to be processed, must have concluded that this was my second speeding ticket and quickly sentenced me to twenty-one days in jail, quite a harsh sentence for a small first-time traffic transgression.

The first few days of my sentence were spent in the small two-room lockup on base before being transferred to the main IDF jail compound in Tzrifin called Keleh 4. The IDF prison's soldier compound was one of two IDF jails in the country, where soldiers serve time from a couple weeks to several months for breaking military rules. I was assigned for the next three weeks to the privileged section of "light duty prisoners," for soldiers like me who had committed minor offenses. We were considered to be privileged in a sense because every day we were marched out of the compound to be employed as trash workers or to do other menial labor work on other military bases in the vicinity. The experience of being locked-up nevertheless had a big impact on me. All the rules and regulations while serving your sentence were made to remind you that you did not ever want to come back, making sure whatever offense was committed would not be repeated.

My section of prisoners, serving anywhere from two to four weeks, was assigned to a large building totally enclosed by a high metal fence. Inside was one big room with two long lines of metal bunk beds on each side and the main door on one end. Our days started around 4:30 a.m., getting up before dark and spending the next two hours on the daily building clean up, and among other assignments, shaking some nasty and terribly dusty army blankets out before folding them meticulously in a very specific way, which of course was never to the satisfaction of the prison staff. The best part was when we were marched out of the prison around 8:00 a.m. to the envious

Israel Military Service (Tsahal), 1972-1975

looks from the majority of other prisoners. As mentioned before, we were the lucky ones, living in the compound but with our daily trash patrol assignment at the nearby bases. Often while on work assignment, we would get some small contributions of cigarettes or sweets passed quietly to us from regular fellow soldiers, showing their compassion and solidarity with us.

At night, after several role calls and head counts, we were locked inside our dorm building for the night with no access to a bathroom, only a large trash can. The accepted rule was that the bathroom can stayed next to the main door, where newly arrived prisoners were assigned their bunk beds. The more days you were there, the farther you rotated away from the door, moving away from the nuisance and smell of the bathroom container.

A couple days short of completing my sentence, surprisingly one evening on the last night roll call, my name was called up in the list of names due for release. The next morning by 5:00 a.m., I was eagerly packed and waiting to be taken to start the lengthy checkout process. After I recovered my personal belongings and was released, I was so happy and relieved to walk away from that military jail and regain my freedom after eighteen days of extra harsh discipline. One thing I recall from that dreary experience is how we do not really appreciate the small things in life. We take things for granted until we are deprived of them. I remember walking outside into the warm sun. Walking under trees and enjoying the sounds of chirping birds. Walking away from this unpleasant experience and enjoying the first few minutes of total bliss and the sense of liberty. I almost wanted to jump and dance in the warm, comforting sunshine.

I did not have to present myself until the next day to my base, so I decided to pay a visit to two good girlfriends from my Aloney Itshak high school days.

Sarah and Odette were sharing an apartment, living at the time in Bat Yam in southern Tel Aviv. Sarah answered the door and was very happy about my surprise appearance. After hearing about my recent ordeal, Sarah really outdid herself to pamper me, inviting me to spend the night, wining and dining me. She cooked a delicious, comforting meal while I took a long, hot, relaxing bath. We stayed up late talking. I could not ask for a more comforting moment after the deprivation of the last eighteen days and before resuming my soldier duty the next day.

A couple months later, after receiving my orders for the officer course, I presented myself with my file to the new base and officially started the first phase of a three-months-long training and studying process. The first part involved mostly getting back in shape and starting boot camp all over. Not all candidates were assured a spot. After each week of training, the whole platoon took a psychometric test where we had to rate the best ten and the worst ten among our classmates.

After a few weeks of training, I was still feeling a bit isolated and slightly depressed, probably due to a general feeling of loneliness and the lack of a support network. I didn't have a regular girlfriend at the time, and Armand, Prosper, and Jacqueline had gone back to France. I was not very motivated and probably as well was afraid to fail or not be good enough compared to the rest of my platoon. The few letters from Samy in Paris were my only moral support at the time, where he would express his complete support and encouragement, boosting my morale. The only other new immigrant in the platoon of forty or so officer candidates was Zeev Krakovsky from Poland. We talked a lot and commiserated together, assuming that we both were ranked low by our teammates.

Israel Military Service (Tsahal), 1972-1975

One morning I asked for a private interview with our commander, and finally just asked him to let me go since I didn't feel I was inspired or motivated to continue the training. A little surprised by my request, he tried at first to convince me not to quit, that I stood a good chance to make it through. But I kept insisting I just wanted out, to get back to an assignment where I could perform simple tasks and be able to manage my own time. Another small factor, I definitely did not want to add an extra six months of service on top of my mandatory thirty-six months, as each future officer had to commit to serve that extra time.

The commander was not at all pleased with my attitude but after realizing he could not force me to stay, he released me. I just want to add that in hindsight, the decision to quit the officer training course did not take me long to regret. I was so sorry, and for many years wished that I had persisted and stayed to complete the training. I truly believe that if at the time I had around me somebody like a good friend, a brother or sister or a girlfriend to motivate and inspire me, or someone I didn't want to disappoint, I would have found a few more ounces of courage and determination to persevere and get over the temporary low morale that made me take the easy way out. It bothered me so much that in later years, once I became a civilian again, I looked seriously into trying to take the officer course as a reserve soldier, which is a much-complicated undertaking.

Yom Kippur War, 1973

By October of 1973 I had served fourteen months in the IDF. After bailing out of the officer course on my own poor judgment and getting back to my logistics and transportation unit, I was into a daily routine. I would turn twenty on October 14. Nothing prepared me for the big events about to unfold in the early days of that month.

Yom Kippur that year fell on Saturday, October 6. I was at my base located outside Tirat Hacarmel, and like most of the soldiers in my unit, I did not fast that day. After returning to our barracks from having lunch at the base dining hall, I and some fellow soldiers were relaxing in our bunks. We were trying to get radio reception on a small transistor to listen to music, mainly from foreign radio stations since they were no radio or TV broadcasts in Israel during the very holy day of Yom Kippur.

A small argument started between some of the soldiers who apparently had been fasting and objected to being disturbed by the music. As the argument heated up, the music suddenly stopped, and a news report came through mentioning military bombardment taking place somewhere. We immediately switched the dial to the national Israeli station. The station was just starting to broadcast a news report about attacks at the Egyptian and Syrian fronts. Within a few minutes we heard sirens sounding from the adjoining town.

We quickly gathered at our company headquarters to wait for more detailed news or orders. Within a short time, the orders came in and the first few trucks were dispatched to their assignments. Older, more experienced drivers were selected first to be dispatched. I remember all of us getting excited and wanting the opportunity to get out on whatever assignment, just to be in the action, convinced that this was probably going to be a short-lived military operation similar to the last conflict in 1967, the Six-Day War, where Israel quickly won territory from its enemies. After packing my Uzi and a small bag with some personal clothing, I was ordered to join a convoy of four or five trucks assigned to drive to a large, secluded ammunition depot compound located in the north. We would load up and haul tanks and artillery shells closer to the Syrian front, to resupply artillery positions in battle.

Truck convoy, South Sinai, 1973

Yom Kippur War, 1973

On that late afternoon, we drove as fast as we could, with no speed limit this time and an MP, a military policeman, standing at each major junction waving us through as he stopped all traffic for us, giving military trucks priority. As we made our way north, going through different towns and crossing major road junctions, we could see mostly military vehicles zooming by and civilian reserve soldiers on the move trying to get back to their military units. In Israel, after completing his or her compulsory military service, each soldier joins the reserve forces and is called annually to serve three to four weeks in training or service. In times of emergency, when a sudden conflict arises, all reserved soldiers have to stay tuned to the national radio station, and listen for their battalion to announce their special coded phrase, which lets them know that their unit is being called, and that they are to show up at their pre-set meeting place, either to be picked up or to make their way there, by any means available.

My first assignment was to transport a full load of 155 mm artillery shells strapped on large wooden pallets, to be delivered to the outskirts of the Golan Heights to replenish another smaller depot closer to the border. By the time our convoy of four trucks got close to our destination, it was already getting dark. The small roads leading to the Golan were crowded with military vehicle traffic.

That afternoon, several columns of Syrian tanks had overwhelmed the few fortified Israeli military positions along the Syrian-Israeli border. With their massive numbers of tanks and artillery, they were now penetrating deeper into the Golan plateau, rushing toward the main Golan headquarters base of Nafakh. I was very familiar with the area from the last few months of driving and delivering food, ammo, fuel, and troops during the day, but at night with all the commotion going on it was hectic. A thundering artillery bombardment was going on in the background. The IDF forces were trying to equip and organize thousands of reserve soldiers, rigging hundreds of armored vehicles and tanks before rushing them to the front line.

The first few days of the war some tank crews, unable to wait for the trucks to haul them to the front from the big storage warehouses in the north of Israel, started driving on their own to get to the front line. All the roads leading to the Golan Heights were crowded with traffic in both directions. Our small truck convoy, after several hours of delay, was finally able to unload our artillery shells and managed to get back to base for other assignments.

At one point, after all reservist and able-bodied Israeli men were called up to military units, we were assigned an extra driver per each truck, to be able to drive day and night, maximizing performance. Usually pairs were formed by teaming up an experienced reserve driver with a young serviceman. I recall in those first few days joining another convoy delivering Gabriel missiles from Haifa to the Israeli Navy base of Charm el Cheikh on the southern tip of the Sinai Peninsula, along the Red Sea. The Gabriel missile was at the time a very sophisticated Israeli-made sea-to-sea missile mounted on fast-moving Navy ships. We moved lots of ammo, tanks, and artillery shells, which in those critical early days of the war were badly needed since both Arab armies, the Egyptians and Syrians, were inflicting heavy losses on Israel with their surprise assault of massive forces on both fronts.

One day, my driver partner and I didn't quite understand what we were sent to transport as my paperwork mentioned only dry ice, or "hot ice." When we got to this particular compound in the south where large tents were set up, I saw bearded men wearing religious head coverings and stained white aprons. I realized we were to transport several coffins containing bodies or body parts of our own soldiers killed in battle, to be buried temporarily in a specially dedicated cemetery in the Negev while the war was still going on. Later, after the end of the war, these coffins were to be transferred and reburied in the national military cemeteries near the larger cities, where their families could be present.

Charm el Cheikh, South Sinai, 1973

I also recall that a couple days before my birthday I was parked at another base in the south, near Beer Sheva, called Mishmar Hanegev. By then I was a little disillusioned, realizing that the Yom Kippur War, based on news reports of the last few days, was not going too well as our military forces were struggling and fighting hard under the massive onslaught of Egyptian and Syrian attack forces. Both Arab armies had learned from their mistakes and their humiliating defeat in the 1967 War and were now fully trained, much better prepared, and equipped with the latest weapons and military technology thanks to the generosity of their Russian allies.

As was becoming apparent, the new strategy of Egyptian and Syrian armies consisted of trying to handicap as much as possible the military strength of the IDF by first neutralizing the powerful Israeli Air Force with its deep reach and by limiting the maneuverability of Israeli tanks. In 1967, the IDF attack airplanes within the first few hours totally destroyed most of the Egyptian and Syrian Air Forces and airfields. This time they were using a massive umbrella of very sophisticated anti-aircraft missiles, causing many losses of Israeli jets and almost guaranteeing undisturbed clear skies above the attacking Arab forces. The Egyptian and Syrian land forces and infantry were also equipped with hundreds of the latest Russian anti-tank missiles to ambush and surprise the Israeli tanks. The infantry forces were equipped with the latest and very expensive night vision equipment to inflict damage even at night.

The Israeli forces and fortified positions were taken by surprise, and even though way understaffed, were fighting hard. The IDF was calling in all the reserved forces and getting them properly equipped, organized, and in position for strategic moves to defend the country. The most urgent task was to stop the attacking forces while reinforcements were getting dispatched. Eventually, in a second stage they had to prepare a serious counterattack to roll back the gains achieved by both the attacking armies.

The first priority, due to the lack of strategic depth in the north of Israel and the proximity of population centers near the Golan Heights, was to focus on pushing back the Syrian tank advances in northern Israel. This was achieved by a very efficient counterattack of IDF tanks on the Golan plateau after traumatic days of massive invasion by hundreds of Syrian tanks on our line of defenses. The few remaining Israeli tank commanders gave a tremendous show of unparalleled courage and heroism to fight back, blocking the invading wave of Syrian tanks. Among them were Zvika Greengold and Avigdor Kahalani, whose forces fought for four straight days and nights a heroic battle with only a couple dozen tanks. They successfully stopped the onslaught of hundreds of attacking Syrian columns. Both of them survived and were highly decorated, recognized by the whole country for their exceptional display of courage and heroism during those critical first days.

By mid-October, the IDF was gaining back all previously lost ground, and soon enough was in position to start penetrating deep inside Syrian territories. The Israeli generals could now focus on strategic moves in Sinai to push back the hundred Egyptian tanks and the thousands of infantry soldiers that had crossed the Suez Canal into the Sinai.

Sometime during the second week of the war, I was paired with another reserve driver that would be with me for most of the rest of the war. Alex Hazan was in his late twenties and from Casablanca, and although we did not really know each other in Casablanca as he was older than I was, I recognized him. Our families knew each other. We were assigned to a convoy of about fifty or more trucks.

We all had to spend several hours dismantling our side walls and taking down the heavy tarp covers of our truck beds, basically keeping the beds open and flat. We had no idea why or what for. Then we formed a long convoy along one of the roads leading to Sinai. We were on standby and had to wait…and wait…for almost two days we waited on that road. In the end, whatever the plans were, they got called off and we had to put together again our truck beds. Then we were dispatched to a different assignment.

Many years later, I discovered what had happened during those two days. The IDF Chief of Staff, General David Elazar, nicknamed Dado; the Chief of the Southern Front, General Shmuel Gonen, nicknamed Gorodish; General Chaim Bar Lev; and General Ariel Sharon, nicknamed Arik, were debating the exact timing of the IDF's next move. Arik Sharon, then a reserve general and one of the most courageous and daring Israeli commanders on the Egyptian front, was pushing for a swift counterattack, to send forces to cross the Suez Canal and outflank the two attacking Egyptian armies. The Egyptian Second Army had crossed into Sinai in the north and the Third Army was attacking from the south.

General Sharon, who was a popular and well-liked army officer, used to be the Commander in Chief of the Israeli Southern Front until early 1973. He expected to be promoted to the General Chief of Staff of the IDF, but he was bypassed for political reasons. He resigned from the military and helped found the Likud right-wing party, an opposition party at the time in Israel. To help defend the homeland Arik Sharon, like most other officers, was called back into the army for the Yom Kippur War.

While in charge of the Southern Front and Sinai, Arik and the IDF's strategic planning staff had a plan in place, previously rehearsed on the ground. The plan called for armored land forces to be equipped with floating bridges built especially for the purpose of crossing the canal. Special roads leading to the edge of the Suez Canal were built with no curves in order to easily tow the many segments of the bridge. Once the bridge was put together and in place over the canal, the tanks would cross over to the west bank. Arik Sharon had anticipated the exact strategic location where the crossing would take place. The site was called Deversoir, which means "funnel" in French.

Deversoir was one of the narrow spots on the canal not far from where it opens up into the Great Bitter Lake. Arik and his command staff had marked that narrow spot for a potential bridge crossing in the future, and as the war was unraveling, he decided to activate his plan. The strategy was to cross and cut off the supply lines of the Egyptian armies that had crossed over and overwhelmed the under-staffed Bar Lev fortification line on the Suez Canal and were advancing toward the main Israeli headquarters bases in Sinai. Another reason the crossing was ideal in that spot was that it was one of the less protected areas, a weak link between the Egyptian Second Army attacking in the north Sinai from Port Said and Ismailia and the Third Army attacking in the south from Ismailia and the town of Suez.

The bridge was made of huge metal cylinders. The original plan called for those big cylinders to be brought by truck to an area close to the Suez Canal, then the cylinders would be hitched together with a flat place on top. Special tanks would tow the completed bridge along a straight asphalt road the short distance to the canal and float it on the water. The road, named Tirtour, had been previously built with this purpose in mind.

I and my partner, stuck for two days along the road in a long convoy of trucks with bare-metal beds, were waiting for orders to get the bridge parts hauled to the canal. Plans were altered due to intense tank battles and artillery bombardments and fighting taking place on the Tirtour access road. As a backup and emergency last recourse, the tanks had to tow large segments of the bridge through sand dunes.

I went back to the Syrian front to deliver barrels of fuel. When I got close to our front line, I saw the devastation. Charred, blackened remains of Israeli and Syrian tanks were scattered all over the Golan plateau. Some of them looked intact from outside, with just a small hole, but the insides were all burned. Driving along some of the roads, I saw dead bodies of Syrian soldiers lying near their destroyed tanks and armored vehicles. Our own Israeli casualties had been immediately retrieved. This was my first exposure to a battlefield with enemy casualties still on the ground.

Like many young soldiers participating in the war effort, I was looking to get some souvenirs from the battlefield to bring home. After taking a short break, I parked my truck near a small formation of Israeli armored personnel carriers waiting to get unloaded. I decided to venture close to an abandoned Syrian armored vehicle on a small hill, to look for war memorabilia. With my Uzi strapped across my shoulders, I took a quick look inside and noticed no dead bodies but a lot of ammunition boxes. Near the front part of the vehicle was a nice Syrian army hat with a shiny brass badge with Arabic writing on it. I crawled in from the back of the vehicle, over the shells and ammo boxes, and reached for the hat.

Suddenly, a loud metallic sound went off, blasting my ears and scaring the hell out of me. I thought I must have triggered a booby trap . . . or some kind of explosives. I backed out in a hurry, still in one piece and totally frightened but still holding the hat in my hand. Hearing the loud noise, some soldiers nearby came immediately to investigate. We figured out an explanation for the racket. Apparently, the large battery located under the front passenger seat was exposed, and while crawling from the back of the vehicle I must have caused a metal belt of machine gun bullets hanging from the gun turret above to slide and drop onto the battery beneath. The

Yom Kippur War, 1973

metal had made contact with the battery poles and created an electrical short that could have blasted the ammo and me. Thank God nothing exploded, and I got away with just a big scare and a Syrian officer's hat, kept to this day in my home in Austin, Texas.

Soon after, the Syrian front was stabilized and secured, and the war effort turned to focus more on the southern front in Sinai. Many logistics units, including the one I belonged to, were dispatched to service in Sinai. We were sent to be attached to the main headquarters logistics base in Sinai, located about forty miles from the Suez Canal. The base was named Refidim, after the Old Testament battle story in Exodus, and there I spent the rest of my service until 1975.

In Sinai my partner, Alex, and I were first assigned to join a small convoy to deliver large loads of 155 mm artillery shells to several armored M109 self-propelled howitzer batteries scattered among the dunes of northern Sinai. The artillery batteries were posted just off the road appropriately called "the artillery road," which went north-south. They were a few kilometers away from the front line and the main battlefield where our tanks were trying to stop the advances of the Egyptian Second Army tanks. We had to drive on the paved road as close as possible to the firing batteries, then wait our turn for our load to be transferred onto a smaller 6x6 all-wheel drive, off-road truck that would haul the shells the short distance through the sand dunes to the firing batteries.

Each pair of M109 howitzer firing batteries was accompanied by several armored personnel carrier crews parked nearby, to secure the perimeter from potential Egyptian commando units. The Egyptians had been known at the time to be infiltrating, dispatching by helicopters at night commando units to go on foot behind Israeli lines to attack and disturb supply lines. While parked on the side of this narrow pavement waiting for our turn to advance and unload, the artillery batteries were firing every minute or so at a range of about five kilometers west toward the Egyptian forces.

The Bar Lev line of fortification had been the first line of defense on the eastern Israeli side of the Suez Canal. Except for a few outposts, most of the fortifications fell within the first few hours under the massive Egyptian forces that crossed the canal, overwhelming the few Israeli troops posted. In the first hours of the surprise attack, the Egyptian forces used high pressure water hoses to blast the massive sand wall barrier on the Israeli side. Once bridges were put in place, the Egyptian columns of tanks and armored infantry crossed over and advanced toward the second line of defense built by the IDF, the entrenched, fortified positions about ten kilometers east of the Bar Lev line. These positions, after being reinforced with freshly deployed reserve forces, were now fighting back the constant assault by Egyptian infantry and tanks. For the first eight to ten days into the war, the Egyptian forces were held off along that line. While daily armored combat took place, the batteries of armored M109 self-propelled howitzers, like the ones I was parked near, were bombarding non-stop to give our positions some relief.

Alex and I were getting bored standing by the trucks so we decided to walk the short distance among the sand dunes to join the staff standing guard on top of the M113-variant armored personnel carriers, commonly called "Zeldas," securing the perimeter around the howitzer guns. We could at least hang around with them and follow closely through their radios all the communications about the fighting taking place less than four kilometers from us. A lot of the code words I did not understand at first, but after listening for a while and with the help of the Zelda crew, I did better. It was clear from among all the radio exchanges that one of the commanders of a nearby fortified *maoz*, or stronghold, was under constant attack and in a dire situation, asking for some reinforcement. At one time the crew pointed out to us General Arik Sharon heard on the network giving brief instructions and orders in a very composed voice.

We stood there for several hours listening as the combat was raging only a few kilometers from us, the artillery shells blasting off at regular intervals from the batteries we came to supply. The officer in charge of the unit of Zeldas was a reserve soldier like all his crew. He had a heavy bandage on his thigh and his face was unshaven. He looked very tired but was totally focused on the radio exchanges. He apparently had been wounded a few days before when the vehicle he was in was blasted by an anti-tank Sagger missile. These Russian missiles were being widely used by Egyptian special units. The officer was evacuated but quickly returned to the front to assume command of these several armored personnel carriers to guard the positions of the heavy artillery guns.

Occasionally I heard the deafening sound of low-flying IDF jet aircraft passing over our heads and toward the battleground. Near the end of the afternoon, we finally heard reinforcement columns of Israeli tanks coming. The tanks were speeding toward the front line to engage in combat and relieve the pressure on our defending positions. Each commander was sitting exposed on the turret of his tank. We waved to each other. The soldiers we were with waved their arms to make the Armored Corp signal of "full speed ahead" to show the urgency of getting there.

I vividly remember one thought that crossed my mind as I watched the tanks heading forward at full speed. As they passed by so close, I thought about these guys who probably already did their mandatory army service, doing their duty to the country when they were my age. These reserve soldiers only a few days earlier were regular civilians at home living a peaceful, regular life surrounded by their families. They were going to once more risk their lives in battle, while a guy like me, barely twenty years old and single with no wife or kids, still serving my mandatory three-year service, was parked in relative safety.

Wouldn't it have been more logical to have young, single soldiers like me taking more risk first? I guess the answer to that is, it depends how selections are made for matching each individual to his army assignment. Also, the regular enlisted young men represent only a small portion of the IDF. In normal times of no full-scale war, they handle most military duties involving the security of the front lines. During wartime, the full strength and bulk of the IDF forces to fight and protect the country relies at last resort on calling up its reserve units drawn from the Israeli population at large to face the challenges.

Within a few minutes, we heard excitement on the radio communications as the reinforcement tanks engaged the enemy and brought serious relief to the fortified maoz. In that particular area we were in, the Egyptian unit finally disengaged and retreated further west toward the canal, behind their own secured position, with IDF tanks in pursuit. I remember hearing on the radio the request for pursuing IDF vehicles to capture live, if possible, retreating enemy soldiers for intelligence purposes. Then we heard on the radio from one of our armored columns that a few prisoners had been captured and were being brought back.

The next big expedition I recall was toward the last week of October, as the fighting was slowly diminishing and a cease-fire was being negotiated. General Arik Sharon was able to implement his master plan of sending forces to the other side of the canal into Africa, establishing a big Israeli enclave outflanking and surrounding in the south the whole Egyptian Third Army of 15,000 to 20,000 men who were totally cut off from their supply line. This seriously threatened the Egyptian forces, while Israeli columns were advancing every day toward Cairo. The Israeli armored units finally stabilized on a defensive line close to the 101-kilometer marker on the road to Cairo.

My teammate, Alex Hazan, had by now become a close buddy since we had been a driving team for the past few weeks, from the beginning of the war. We were always on the go, eating mostly *manot krav* K-rations and sleeping wherever. We enjoyed conversing, singing, and joking, mostly in French and some in Arabic Moroccan. Being together with Alex was a big plus, and a morale booster for both of us. Alex must have been in his late twenties, living with his parents in the town of Ashdod. His family made Aliyah from Casablanca ten or fifteen years previously. A few weeks before the war, Alex had become engaged to be married.

We joined a convoy of about twenty or more trucks, some of them large fuel tankers, to resupply our fighting forces in Africa on the other side of the canal. The main Egyptian military air base on the other side, recently captured by the IDF, was called Fayid, and that is where we were all heading first before being dispersed to different locations. Leading the convoy were several officers in jeeps. We got underway from Refidim in late afternoon. Our truck was loaded with gasoline—filled five-gallon metal "jerry cans" stacked in several rows. We took the only paved road access, Tsir Akavish, leading to the canal crossing and to the main bridge.

The destruction and the charred remains of armored vehicles scattered along the road and in the dunes attested to the hard-fought battle and bombardment that had taken place. Our long convoy advanced at a slow pace due to the narrow road and the heavy traffic both ways. As it got dark and we were getting closer to the crossing, orders were to drive with headlights off and rely only on our smaller running lights to follow the truck ahead of us. Waiting for our turn to cross the bridge, we had to let several buses coming toward us squeeze by very close as they were passing by. They were packed with Egyptian prisoners of war being transferred to holding facilities in the rear. That was a chilling, sober introduction before we crossed into Africa and the Egyptian mainland on the west side of the Suez Canal.

After waiting a few hours by the side of the road, our convoy was finally cleared to cross the floating bridge. It was rough and bumpy, due probably to heavy use in those first days of constant traffic to resupply our forces on the other side. After crossing, we had to wait for the whole convoy to get reorganized before moving on. It was very dark and hard to see anything, even a couple feet from the road. Occasionally I had to turn on the headlights for a couple seconds just to make sure not to get off the pavement. In the darkness of night, with almost no light, I could not see much beyond the road, but I could smell the change of landscape—more trees and vegetation, palm trees, the shapes of some farm buildings.

As we slowly progressed, the convoy made frequent stops, sometimes waiting for an hour or more. With little visibility, we were anxious and kept our guns close by. The officers in the command car were getting instructions by radio. They would occasionally drive by as we were parked on the roadside, telling us to follow regular procedures in case of an artillery bombardment or an attack on the convoy by ground. The rules were simple enough—if we came under attack, we were to move the trucks away from the road in order to keep the main access road free and open for vital reinforcements and supplies. If the truck ahead of us went left, we were to go right, driving fifty to one-hundred yards away from the road.

After standing still for more than an hour in one spot, it must have been around 1:00 a.m. Somebody came banging on our truck's driver-side door. When I lowered the window, there were some of the other drivers standing there and asking if we wanted to join them for a bathroom break on the side of the road. That sounds funny now, but for the next few days, when it was nighttime this would become routine, to find a couple guys to venture together a few yards from the road to answer nature's call in the dark, keeping safe in the company of others.

After we got moving again, the order came without much explanation that we needed to immediately disperse and scatter the convoy. The truck in front of us took off and veered to the right. I followed suit and veered to the left, trying not to get stuck in the dirt as I drove away from the road until I could see several other armored personnel carrier half-tracks parked for the night. I could hear the sound of their radio communications. Alex and I parked our truck, got off with our Uzis and blankets, and found a spot several yards from the truck to lie down on the ground to try to sleep for a couple hours.

We had barely fallen asleep when the noise of the engines of armored vehicles woke us up. The crews seemed to be in a hurry to move out immediately. The only thing we were able to understand was that they had heard a warning over the APC (Armored Personnel Carrier) radios of a possible shelling in our area. Alex and I quickly rushed back to our truck, not thinking even for a second that there was more danger in getting back in the truck, which had no protective armor whatsoever and was carrying a load of gasoline that could easily be ignited. We were young, exhausted, and slightly panicked.

I got behind the wheel, started the truck, and in the dark, without using our headlights, tried to get back on the road. Another soldier, probably another truck driver that in the confusion could not locate his truck in the dark night, jumped in with us. With the three of us squeezed in the cabin, we managed to get back on the main road. We tried to guess which way we had come from, to try to backtrack our way. Slightly disoriented, I chose a direction and started driving.

I don't know how far we drove, occasionally turning on the headlights to cheat and see where we were headed, until finally we saw a small farm building on the right side of the road, with a few IDF armored half-tracks parked nearby. As I slowed down, I distinctly heard Hebrew being spoken on the radio communications. I decided not to venture further. I pulled off the road and parked near the armored trucks. The three of us decided to stay inside the truck to get some rest and patiently wait for daylight to come in a couple more hours.

Around the time of the 1973 War, a poem written by the famous Israeli journalist, poet, and columnist Didi Menosi appeared in his weekly current events column in the mass circulation newspaper *Yediot Ahronot*. I cut it out to keep as a souvenir. Here is my English-translation of it:

Yom Kippur War, 1973

On the edge of the headlines

On a small narrow road
An ammunition truck
Loaded with artillery or tank shells
Makes its way day or night
To supply and feed
Like a good mother
The war rigs with their dose of iron.

A conventional truck With no extra armor to protect it
Makes its way. Suffice a single bullet or small shrapnel
To turn it into blazing fire.
Its two drivers behind the wheel Looking like the famous
Thriller adventure movie, "Wages of Fear"

Yet the loaded truck keeps moving forward With its team of two drivers
One alert and awake, the other resting and asleep
They rarely get credit or make the headlines
Even though victory without them will be hard to achieve.

And even with morning dawn As the darkness dissipates
And the victory parade to celebrate gets on its way
The ammunition truck will not be present in the parade
As it is already back on other assignments hauling gear,
food, or fuels to keep the troops prepared

As darkness dissipated and the first light of day appeared, we came down to talk with the soldiers on the APCs to help us get our bearings and some directions. I was also discovering our surroundings, finally getting a better idea of the Egyptian landscape west of the Suez Canal. The east side of the canal, which we were familiar with, is a wind-swept desert with large sand dunes. The west bank of the Suez Canal is a completely different landscape, luscious and green due mainly to a sweet water canal running parallel to the Suez canal. This fresh water created a belt of cultivated fields and fruit trees from north to south. Small communities of Egyptian farmers, or *fellahin*, inhabited the land. Most of them were gone now, nowhere to be seen due to the recent fighting and bombardments having taken place. The area was irrigated by several small sweet water canals so the farmers could plant crops and raise livestock.

We drove back, passing several abandoned Egyptian armored vehicles on the side of the road, probably from the recent battle and the IDF push westward a few days ago. We tried to locate our original route coming in during the night. By mid-morning, we finally spotted some of the trucks from our convoy and we regrouped, waiting for the rest of the convoy to be found and herded back to join us.

Most of the drivers gathered in small groups exchanging stories about the adventures of the previous night and how each truck ended up in a different spot, waiting for daylight. Some drivers had already explored the surroundings at daybreak and were proudly displaying an assortment of weapons and ammunitions cases found scattered on the grounds and roads. Apparently, despite the big alarm and scare to all units in the vicinity to seek shelter, no artillery shelling or any major attacks took place during the night in the area we had been in, or at least we were not aware if anything had happened.

Around midday, orders were to continue driving southwest, approaching the recently established new boundary of IDF forces a few kilometers short of the 101-kilometer marker on the road to Cairo. On the way, we saw the destroyed vehicles and tanks of the Egyptian army still scattered among the dunes, and close to the main road were some bodies of dead soldiers.

Yom Kippur War, 1973

After passing a road junction, most of the convoy was ordered to drive off the pavement and park in a wide formation in a large open area surrounded and protected by small sand hills. This would be our staging area and refueling spot for the next few days. Many armored vehicles—mostly half-tracks or M3 personnel carriers, Zeldas, command cars and such from the units securing the new Israeli-Egyptian boundaries nearby would be stopping at our small compound to get refueled. A few tables and benches and some water trailers with a line of water spigots were brought in. For restrooms, we still went in small groups, carrying our guns, to do our business behind one of the sand hills.

The following morning, I happened to notice a few soldiers walking through the area we were in, laden with all kinds of gear, blankets, mattresses, pots and pans. They had discovered that about a couple miles walking distance from our truck park, away from the road and among some big dunes, there was an abandoned Egyptian army compound. After getting more details and directions, together with another soldier we decided to venture out and try to locate the compound. I took some water and my Uzi with several extra clips and started hiking in the general direction of the compound. We were looking mostly for items to improve our camping conditions, as well as some souvenirs from the Egyptian army to show off that we really were in a combat zone and participating in the war effort. I secretly hoped to come across an Egyptian army-issued AK-47 machine gun. Also high on my list was a bayonet or an Egyptian commando knife. I had already found several other guns, like the Russian SKS carbine and RPD machine gun that I didn't really care for.

After walking for a while, we saw the first signs of the abandoned camp, some half-buried outpost bunkers marking the entrance. I was on the alert and kept my Uzi ready just in case we came across any potential danger or surprise. The camp was made up of several small, half-buried barracks camouflaged and protected by small walls of sandbags. Some were living quarters with furniture, beds, desks, chairs, etcetera. It was so strange to find everything in place, plates on the table and pictures on the walls. I still have to this day several IDs and documents found there.

I quickly checked every building. Entering in one of the rooms, I noticed my soldier friend bending to pick up something on the floor. As soon as I realized what he was holding, I knew we were both in danger. He was holding in his hand a triggered, unexploded hand grenade, also known as a dud. It was without a pin or lever. Those should never be disturbed or moved around due to the faulty mechanism. I immediately backed away toward the door while telling him to put it gently back on the floor and run away. Luckily for us both, as he gently put the hand grenade down, nothing happened.

We gathered a few souvenirs, some blankets and a few plates and cups. On the way out, as we were passing a bunker located slightly away from the rest, a barking dog came out from that building toward us. We had been warned that packs of dogs had been seen close to Egyptian dead bodies and to stay clear of any stray dogs roaming around. I immediately cocked my gun, ready to fire away. The dog was moving away from us while still barking, and I thought maybe that somebody was inside the building. As we approached the bunker, a fabric curtain over the small entrance moved with the breeze. That really got my attention, convincing me that somebody might be hiding inside. I switch off the safety on my Uzi, ready to fire a burst through the fabric. Thank God I didn't—when I gently moved the curtain to one side, I saw that the room was full of wooden ammunition cases, of either tank shells or artillery. We could have been blown apart if I had shot through the curtain. At that moment, I realized how some of our irresponsible behavior as young, inexperienced soldiers in search of war souvenirs and trying to slightly improve our camping conditions could easily have cost us our own lives.

I came to understand that this room we had just entered was the ammunition depot for the whole compound. That was why it was the furthest away from the rest of the camp. We also discovered in one corner a litter of puppies, probably only a few days old, inside an empty ammo case. Then I understood why the dog came out from the bunker and was barking. I was so happy not to have shot at the bitch, nor to have released a burst of bullets through the fabric curtain before entering the bunker.

We made it back to camp with our goodies, hoping to improve slightly our camping conditions while we waited to unload our fuel. We stayed parked with our truck for several more days while most of the other trucks were heading back once having distributed their fuel. For some reason our truck didn't seem to be making any progress to get in line to unload. Therefore, Alex and I decided to take an active role in promoting our gasoline distribution in order to unload and be able to get back. We drove our truck to the side of the road and started waving at the passing traffic of military jeeps, armored vehicles, and half-tracks coming from the front line positions and seeking to refuel. Within a few hours we managed to unload all our fuel into the gas tanks of dozens of military vehicles. We gave away most of our "Egyptian camping gear" to new truck teams coming in and headed back to our base on the east side of the canal.

By the end of October, when we were driving back, the cease fire was already in place. Under UN auspices, Israeli and Egyptian top generals met at the kilometer 101 road marker to Cairo and negotiated how to disengage the surrounded Third Army. As we headed back to cross the canal in full daylight and with much less worry or concern, we took our time, taking in the scenery. At the bridge crossing, we even stopped to take pictures of the congested traffic coming and going between Sinai and Africa. After unloading our empty metal jerry cans at the fuel depot in Refidim some seventy kilometers east of the canal, we thought that with all the turmoil and mess of the last few weeks, if we were to disappear for twenty-four hours from Sinai, nobody would notice. Under the strong influence of Alex, not having seen his parents and his future bride for more than a month, we decided to disappear from the radar screen. We drove nonstop, taking turns behind the wheel, all the way to his parents' house in Ashdod, south of Tel Aviv, to spend the night and drive back the next day, hoping nobody would miss us.

We arrived at Alex's house late at night totally exhausted. His parents were so surprised and delighted, and relieved at the same time to see us. After refreshing, extra-long, hot showers, we had a delicious hot meal served by Alex's mom, his whole family sitting around us wanted to hear about our recent adventures. His father, a religious man like my father, was praying and blessing us, telling us that it was really a biblical miracle that strengthened the IDF soldiers during the war, to recover from the trauma of the first days and turn the tide against both armies attacking us.

Early the next day Alex went to see his fiancée for a couple hours. He dropped me off at Rishon Letzion to pay a surprise short visit to my father's sister, my aunt

Tata Sol. She was so happy to see me and with tears of joy in her eyes kept blessing me in Arabic and praying for my well-being. Tata Sol, my sweet and gentle aunt, was herself a mother of five boys. Four of them — Albert, Jacquie, Armand, and Samy — had been called up as reservists and were serving in different locations. I remember thinking to myself how with her own sons to worry about, she was nevertheless so happy and relieved to see me, forcing me to eat and eat her delicious food spread in front of me.

After this refreshing, quick break from military routine, we made the long drive back to the main Sinai rear headquarters base at Refidim. Fortunately, nobody seemed to have noticed our brief absence.

On the bridge over the Suez Canal, right after the Yom Kippur War of 1973, wearing an Egyptian officer's cap.

On a Centurion tank on the edge of the Suez Canal after the Yom Kippur War, 1973

On the banks of the Suez Canal, me standing in front center. Sitting behind me is my driving mate, Reservist Alex Hazan, 1973

Road to the Suez Canal

Within a couple weeks after the cessation of combat, some restructuring and regrouping started taking place. The first priority was to give some of the called-up reservists short leaves to visit their families. Leaves of forty-eight hours were arranged first for the older reservists. Much later came the turns for younger, mostly regular soldiers — single people like me.

For my leave, I decided to go to my kibbutz, Givat Oz. As luck would have it, I had previously arranged through letters and long-distance phone calls to meet a nice French girl I had met a few months earlier while visiting the kibbutz. Françoise was a few years older than me and was spending a few months living and working as a volunteer at the kibbutz. I was very attracted to her but, unfortunately, at the time she was already dating a local Israeli kibbutznik and all my efforts were fruitless.

After a few months, Françoise went back to Paris. We kept in touch by letters, and I must have given her my brother Samy's phone number in Paris. As the war broke up, she called Samy asking about my well-being. Françoise was employed in Paris by an airline company which allowed her to benefit from advantageous passes for international flights. Once we reconnected by phone, she insisted on coming back to meet me at the kibbutz on my first official leave after the war. I felt very flattered and thankful. I had something to look forward to, after the intensity, fear, isolation, and rough conditions of the last six to eight weeks.

My reunion with Françoise was a real blessing and a big dose of pleasurable relaxation, rejuvenating me and giving a serious boost to my morale. The kibbutz members were so welcoming, and before I left to go back, they spoiled me with all kinds of goodies, from cigarettes and cookies to underwear, socks, and toiletry items. The kibbutz had suffered several casualties from the war, as I was to find out later. Several of its young members serving or called up during the war had lost their lives in combat.

Back in Sinai after the ceasefire took effect, my unit had several new logistics missions and new assignments. A big priority was the layout and construction of a new road parallel to the existing Tsir Akavish. A large presence of Israeli infantry and armor were positioned all the way to the Egyptian port city of Suez in the south and Ismailia in the north. IDF forces now numbered many thousands and were well established on the west side of the canal. Tsir Akavish, or "Scorpion Road," was the only paved road to the bridge over the canal and was now a heavily congested bottleneck. My logistics battalion, together with military engineering units, was assigned to help build a second road to help resupply the forces.

All available drivers, including me, were assigned without much preparation to drive brand new Mercedes dump trucks to carry sand and dirt. The IDF was able to import in emergency several hundred of these trucks. We were sent all the way to the port of Haifa in the north of Israel to take delivery directly from the ship bringing them in from Germany, then drive in a convoy all the way down to Sinai. Due to the urgency of the task ahead, these new civilian trucks were still in their original, factory-bright, civilian colors and were to remain so for months due to the lack of time to repaint them. These trucks were easily spotted and stood out among all the conventional military vehicles circulating in and around the Suez Canal.

We were to build as fast as possible an alternate access road in order to relieve the traffic pressure on the Scorpion Road. It would be in a location farther south, away from the artillery guns of the bridgehead positions established by the Egyptian Second Army on the east side of the canal. To build a new road across the ever-expanding sand dunes to reach the canal and the bridges, first the bulldozers went to work to make a path. Next was to haul large quantities of caliche gravel as road base, to lay a thirty- to forty-foot-wide roadbed before laying on any kind of pavement.

Our job driving the new Mercedes trucks was hauling the caliche road base from nearby improvised quarries to dump on the new road path. To speed the process, the fleet of trucks and drivers were divided into two large work units. A tent compound was established at each end of the new road, so one group worked on the road from the shores of the Suez Canal going east and the other from the opposite side going west.

Learning to handle a heavily loaded dump truck on a paved road was a new experience but getting off the asphalt road and venturing onto a soft, gravel, unpaved portion was another challenge. The complicated part was making a U-turn in a limited, unstable space and backing up the heavily loaded truck to the edge of the dirt roadbed, then using the hydraulics to raise the truck bed at a proper angle to dump the contents without flipping the whole truck over. Unfortunately, in the first few days with the rush against time and lack of experience, accidents occurred. Many trucks flipped over, many slid off the main road. There were several head-on collisions.

There was a lot of pressure to speed up the process at any cost.

Several large tents were set up to establish the two camps, one on each end of the new road. Conditions were very basic as far as amenities. This was in the wintertime, the end of 1973 and the beginning of 1974. The days were very hot and dusty, and the nights were cold and windy. Some of us chose to sleep inside our truck cabins where it was dry and slighter warmer than in the large, breezy tents that frequently had muddy floors due to winter rains.

It was during this period that my friend Eric Binia made a surprise visit at the camp. I had met Eric while living in Haifa in early 1972, before moving to Jerusalem. Eric and his family — his parents and brother, Daniel — immigrated to Israel from Egypt. His family was one of the well-established Jewish families from the big Egyptian port city of Alexandria. His father owned a tie factory and was doing quite well until after the 1967 Six-Day War when the Nasser government dispossessed them from all their assets and property, just for being Jewish. The Egyptian government accused the father of being a Zionist collaborator, and like most other Egyptian Jews, he was put in jail for several years. Eric, his brother, and their mom managed to escape and took shelter in France.

Mr. Binia, the father, who I met later in their home in Haifa, was a very interesting, well-travelled, and charming man. While languishing several years in Egyptian jail, he was persecuted, tortured, and punished — one of the repercussions from the Egyptian army's humiliating defeat by Israel on the battlefield in the 1967 War. He was released after a few years and was able to reunite with his wife and sons and move the family to Haifa.

Eric and I became good friends, and I was often invited to his home in Haifa, where we conversed in

French. The Binia parents were always happy to see me, very warm and welcoming. I always enjoyed seeing them, chatting and spending time at their home.

Eric, who enlisted about the same time as me, volunteered to serve in a combat unit with the paratrooper battalion belonging to forces under General Arik Sharon. His regiment was among several that fought their way across the canal and was the first infantry unit to cross the Suez Canal and establish a bridgehead in Africa, on the west bank of the canal. I must have run into his paratrooper unit somewhere in Sinai and left a message with my location for him to look me up.

One late afternoon, Eric came by our camp on the shores of the Bitter Lakes of the canal, south of Deversoir. We were so happy to see each other and spent time catching up on recent events, mostly what he had endured with his unit. Therefore, during that cold and windy winter night, we stayed up late talking. The cabin of my Mercedes truck was much more comfortable than in my regular army truck, with one of us on the floor on a small foam mattress and the other on the bench seat.

I was mostly listening to Eric describe what he went through and the casualties inflicted on his unit during the second week in October, with the intense fighting and the heavy bombardment they were subjected to while crossing the Suez Canal on small, inflatable rafts. The paratroopers had always been the spearhead combat units of the IDF, and during the Yom Kippur War they fought some of the bloodiest battles. One of those battles became known as the Battle of the Chinese Farm.

The Chinese Farm, a small, agricultural enclave, was called Chinese because of Asian writing found on the equipment, although the equipment turned out to be Japanese made. The farm was close to the canal, and well-equipped Egyptian forces strategically entrenched fight, the paratroopers cleared the way for the IDF to advance to the shores of the canal. The paratrooper units, most of them reserve units, fought valiantly and suffered a lot of casualties. Moshe Dayan, who was the defense minister during the war, expressed the grief of the country as he recalled the Battle of the Chinese Farm in his memoirs: "I am no novice at war or battle scenes, but I have never seen such a sight. Here was a vast field of slaughter stretching as far as the eye could see."

We stayed up most of the night as Eric related to me his experiences and the series of events leading to the first combat unit crossing the canal on floating rafts. His paratrooper unit secured a bridgehead position on the other side before reinforcements were finally able to join in and secure the area as the first floating bridge was brought in to allow columns of tanks and armored vehicles under the command of Major General Avraham "Bren" Adan to roll over to the other side.

Another interesting encounter I had during that time was going to visit my cousin Armand Bitton, one of the sons of Tata Sol. Somehow, I learned he was posted with his reserve unit in Africa, on the outskirts of the old Egyptian main air force base of Fayid. One day I was sent across the canal with my truck to bring several loads of sand and gravel to help build a military observation post close to the new ceasefire line between Egypt and Israel. After completing my assignment, on the way back to camp I decided to look up Armand. I ventured around several military camps asking for his unit until I was directed to a small group of tents. I walked in one of the tents and there was my cousin with a group of soldiers seated around a table playing cards. We kissed and hugged each other and were so happy to meet. We visited for a while, then he wanted to take a spin in my truck.

He insisted on giving me some extra stuff, like blankets and K-rations.

A few months later as we were making serious progress on the completion of the new road, while having dinner at the big mess tent, somebody came looking for me. I was told to put on a clean uniform and get ready to drive a truck to the main headquarters some seventy kilometers away to report to the base commander. I figured this could only be bad news, meaning I had to be in some kind of trouble. This was in general the usual procedure when you had to present yourself and answer for some out-of-line behavior.

Driving alone in the night toward the base, I wondered what rules or orders I might have broken. Once inside the military base, I went straight to report myself to the main headquarters. In the office of our company commander, Major Barukh, I was ready to answer for and accept the consequences of whatever transgression I was guilty of. After a proper military salute, I stood waiting at attention across from Major Barukh, who was seated at his desk reading from a file. He asked me a simple question: "Why don't you write letters to your family?"

I was not sure I had heard him properly. I kindly asked him to repeat the question. Standing there a bit nervous, and tired after a long workday, I was taken by surprise by the question. As it turned out, Major Barukh had in front of him a letter from France sent to the official address of my army base, to his attention as my commanding officer. Each soldier's mailing address is composed of his name, rank, and soldier ID number followed by the four- or five-digit number for the military base he is posted at.

Apparently, my brother Samy, without my knowledge, had taken the initiative with the help of our brother-in-law Sylvain Marciano, who was fluent in Hebrew, to draft a letter to the commanding officer of my base. In the letter, they shared with him their worries about me, asking about my whereabouts after the war, my well-being, and why my family in Europe and Morocco were getting little news from me. Brother Sam mentioned in the letter to my commander, based probably on info I had previously shared with him, that I should be able to obtain a special thirty-day leave. A leave I was entitled to as a single soldier with no immediate family living in Israel, in order to travel abroad and visit my family. Samy added that an airline ticket had been paid for and issued for me, waiting only for proper authorization to release me to travel.

I was relieved immediately to learn first that I was not in any trouble, and almost flattered by the sudden attention. I regained my self-confidence and confirmed to my commander that I had indeed applied for the special leave a few months back but without any answer so far. Major Barukh was probably surprised that my French family was reaching out directly to him at the highest level, asking for his assistance as my supreme military commander. Major Barukh used his desk phone to get the officer in charge to immediately show up at his office. Once the officer showed up, he was given special orders, to make sure that within one week's time I got the proper clearances to depart to France for my special leave.

Then Major Barukh noticed in my personal file that I had been sent to the officer training course. He suggested that after I returned from my leave in France, I should come back to see him, and that he would like, due to my background, to send me to a special five-week course to be trained as a noncommissioned officer, or NCO.

Today, looking back, I have to admit that the letter from Paris, France, written in early 1974 by Samy and Sylvain and addressed to my army commander, brought my records to the attention of my officers and changed the status of my remaining fourteen months of service in Sinai. After my return from Paris and another interview with Major Barukh, I was dispatched to the NCO training course and came back as a corporal and junior NCO.

Visit to France, 1974

While living in Israel, I had always been in contact with my brother Samy in France, exchanging numerous letters. Since I couldn't send mail directly from Israel to an Arab country, in this case Morocco, all correspondence to my parents in Casablanca had to transit through France to Sam's attention. I always kept him informed of my whereabouts and my life. My letters to him every few months were like a personal diary, where I summarized and expressed my feelings about experiences I was going through while finishing high school and then serving in the IDF. After the Yom Kippur War, Sam, who was in touch with our parents in a more direct way by phone and letters, convinced our father in Casablanca to splurge and participate with him in purchasing an airline ticket to fly me from Israel to Paris. Sam offered to coordinate my visit and host me, so that I could spend my special leave having R&R in Paris.

I remember packing my personal belongings from inside the tent on the shores of the Suez Canal and some of the drivers in my unit asking me was this for real that within a few days I would be on my way to Paris. And if so, did I ever intend to come back to this dreary, forsaken place. When I acted surprised, that I had never considered the idea of not coming back, their response was that I must be completely mad . . . or very naïve. I should add that most of these guys serving as drivers I would have under my command in a few months as their

NCO, and they were mostly not very educated, from very modest backgrounds in Israel.

A few days later, with all the proper authorizations and paperwork stamped and approved allowing me to depart the country, I picked up my prepaid, round trip flight ticket and flew to France for the first time since my coming to Israel five years earlier. Sam was at the Paris airport to welcome me. He and Genevieve, his sweet French wife whom I had already met earlier in Israel during the summer of 1969, welcomed me to their new apartment located in the 14th arrondissement at 35 Boulevard St. Jacques. This was my first visit to Paris, and they both made sure to show me all the major tourist sites across town. They went all out to make sure I had a great time during my stay.

Paris, 1974, visiting Samy after the war

Visit to France, 1974

Paris, Cathedral Notre Dame, 1974

    One weekend I joined Sam and Genevieve on a road trip in their VW Beetle for a family visit to Genevieve's retired parents living in the small town of Tulle in the Corrèze region of central France. I very much enjoyed discovering the scenic back roads, small picturesque villages, and magnificent countryside. Genevieve's father, Mr. Colin, had been an officer in the French army during World War II. After a short combat period against the invading German army, he ended up for the remainder of the war in a POW camp for army officers.

While in Paris, I was also able to see my brother Prosper. At the time, he was trying to find a job after making his decision to leave Israel and move to Paris. He was living in a very small studio and struggling, barely getting by.

Patricia, whom I had been staying in touch with by letters, insisted on seeing me and invited me to have dinner at her parents' home. She even arranged for her fiancé, Gerard, to drive me there. It was a bit awkward for both of us. Gerard and I had not met previously, but we knew about each other from stories Patricia had told. After the events of the last year, though, I was absolutely at ease with Patricia and was just looking to have a good time and take advantage of every opportunity while away from the military. At Patricia's parents' home, I had a true hero's welcome. I was seated between Patricia and her sister, Micheline, and enjoyed a delicious French dinner served by their mother. Most of the conversation focused on Israel and the recent war, making it a little awkward for Patricia's fiancé who must have felt left out while the spotlight was mostly focused on me. After dinner, Gerard kindly drove me back to Samy's place in his nice sports car.

Another night, Samy and I joined my friend Françoise and a small group of her colleagues from work for a restaurant outing, which was a great experience and an opportunity to socialize and meet interesting young mainstream French people. Toward the end of the night, Françoise asked me to accompany her home, which I had been hoping for the whole evening but wasn't sure if she was seeing somebody from the group we were with. All went well, and once more I had a great time—a great reunion and more badly needed R&R.

Visit to France, 1974

My trip to France, thanks to Samy's initiative and hospitality, really made a big difference and boosted my spirits. I was treated so well and honored by family and cousins insisting on inviting me to nice dinners in their homes. When the time came to go back, it was difficult to say my good-byes, but I had to focus on the road ahead and be ready to complete my remaining time in the army.

Bir Tmadeh

Soon after returning to my base in Sinai, the road project was completed. After a brief meeting in my commander's office at the base headquarters, I was dispatched as promised to a five-week training course in Tzrifin, near Rishon Letzion, to become an NCO, or *mashak*. Once I completed this successfully, I was assigned to a recently established transportation outpost.

The new transportation logistics unit consisted of about sixty military trucks, three officers, four NCOs, four corporals, and about eighty soldiers, mostly drivers and a few mechanics. The small compound was created on the site of an old abandoned Egyptian airfield called Bir Tmadeh. The two large runways of the airfield were

Wreck of an Egyptian plane on an Egyptian airfield, 1973

attacked by Israeli jets in the early hours of the 1967 War, leaving the runway tarmac intact but destroying great numbers of Egyptian military aircraft based there. Many rusted military airplane carcasses were still lying there, seven years later, scattered all around the runways.

The new base was established at the end of a small road leading to the first runway, adjoining two large, existing metal warehouses. A large square area had tents that were the living quarters of most of the drivers. Portable buildings were set up for the dining hall, kitchen, offices, and officers' quarters. Four old Egyptian train cars were brought in next to the tents to be used for a warehouse, a storage building, a cafeteria, and a clubhouse. On one end of the camp, we had our two large diesel generators working alternately 24/7 to supply power to the compound. Water was brought in on a regular basis by tankers to refill our water tanks sitting on metal towers. Two small, portable shacks were used for common showers. For bathrooms, several latrines were dug on the outskirts of camp. Our trucks were

Bir Tmadeh, Sinai, 1975, fleet of trucks in the background

parked on the tarmac next to two metal buildings used for their mechanical repairs and maintenance. With our large fleet of trucks, we also had our own above-ground diesel fuel cistern for refueling our fleet.

At first my job, together with two other NCOs, was to assist in pairing up, assigning, and dispatching the fifty or sixty drivers and their trucks to carry out the daily transportation needs of military units in our vicinity. Every morning we got a list from our headquarters, fifty kilometers away, that had the transportation needs for that day. We were to have each truck in good mechanical shape and properly equipped before assigning an able driver to it. The truck would then be dispatched on time to carry out the assignment, either just for that day or sometimes for several days to remain on-site with another military unit until completing the task. Within a few months, I was promoted to sergeant and took over a new assignment within our small base. I was in charge of logistics, maintenance, and discipline within the whole compound.

Somewhere around that time, my brother Armand came back to Israel and within a short time was hired as a bus driver for a company called United Tours. Most of their buses were large, luxurious coach buses mostly reserved for tourist visitors to Israel. Our main base headquarters in Sinai, in charge of all transportation needs in the region, had on permanent standby a small fleet of civilian chartered coach buses. Their civilian drivers were always on base ready to be dispatched to transport troops in comfort, either within Sinai or all the way to central Israel. Those buses were under special monthly contracts to the IDF from the main bus companies in Israel, like Egged and United Tours. Civilian bus drivers willing to work temporarily on a military base in faraway Sinai were motivated to do so by the extra premiums and bonuses paid to them while full room and board was included on the base.

Armand, knowing that I was serving in Sinai, jumped at the opportunity and took one of these assignments, finding himself at our main base headquarters with his big red bus for a few months. I would occasionally run into him around the headquarters, or after work he would drive his bus all the way to our isolated compound to visit me.

During one weekend leave, while Armand and I were staying with our grandmother Meme Hninah, Armand asked me if I had any information about our old apartment in Jerusalem that we had shared. He needed to find a place to stay on his own now that he was back in Israel. After I joined the military, Prosper was the last one living in it. Before he left Israel for a new start in France, he found some students to sublease the apartment for a very low amount paid upfront in cash, without a formal lease. With no keys or any information on the past or present tenants, Armand and I decided to take a trip to Jerusalem to find out for ourselves about the apartment and possibly try to claim it back. While Prosper had a fifty percent ownership, Armand had the other fifty percent ownership and was hoping to reclaim the apartment and move in.

We got to Jerusalem on Saturday in the early evening. After ringing the doorbell of the apartment for a while with no answer, we decided to wait to see if anyone would show up. After a couple hours, we tried a neighbor on the same floor. She recognized Armand, and under the excuse that he forgot his key inside, he asked the neighbor if he could use her window to try to enter our apartment window. Fortunately, after safely crossing from one window to another while suspended dangerously in the air three stories high, Armand found an open window and within minutes he was able to open the door from inside and let me in.

It was strange for both of us to find ourselves back inside the apartment after almost one and a half years. Very little furniture was there, mostly some mattresses on the floor, a few sleeping bags, and an old rug in the living room. We decided to spend the night, sleeping on the mattresses and waiting for the next day, Sunday, to decide how to proceed. Around 7:00 a.m. we heard a key in the door and a young man came in completely surprised to see us. Armand and I quickly got up and reassured the guy that we were not burglars but the real owners of the flat coming back to claim our property. He did not have any qualms, just wanted to retrieve some of his clothes. He gave us the keys and left.

Apparently, after a few months of the students living in the apartment, several students ended up with copies of the key and the apartment was used sporadically by whoever had keys. Our first task was to change the locks and initiate a major clean up of the whole three-room, one-bath apartment. For several months after that, we—Armand mostly—started investing our small savings in refurbishing the place. On my special leaves, I helped put a fresh coat of paint on the walls and repaired the bathroom. We had to get the utilities reconnected. Most importantly, we had to pay all the outstanding utility bills and city taxes. I was able to locate and buy some used beds, mattresses, and blankets and very basic furnishings for the apartment.

Rahel

In Sinai I was getting comfortable in my new role as a sergeant NCO, forming a good working partnership with the staff and commanding officers of our small logistics unit. One of my duties was to frequently shuttle to our headquarters fifty kilometers away for supplies, repairs, and our logistics needs. During one of these visits, I was in the office of Major Barukh, waiting to see him for some special requests, when a female soldier conversed with me in Hebrew and noticed my slight French accent. She was his assistant or secretary, and she asked me some personal questions. I didn't expect to get attention from her and was flattered, a bit confused but agreeably surprised.

Our headquarters at Refidim base was made up of about three hundred soldiers, with a staff of about fifteen to twenty officers and six or seven women soldiers, mostly in office clerk positions. Except for the commissioned officers and the office staff, where most of the women soldiers were assigned for desk work, very little social interaction took place between male and female soldiers. The women had their own barracks which was off limits to regular male soldiers. They ate their meals at the special officers' tables in the dining hall. As much as I was flattered by this woman's attention and inquiries about my background, I did not dare speculate about any potential positive outcome. She mentioned my connection to the "Frenchie civilian bus driver," referring to Armand, my brother. He was one of the few civilians posted with the small group of bus drivers on base and was probably trying to flirt with her whenever she rode in his bus.

Rahel was a petite, charming, and cheerful brunette with long hair and pretty brown eyes. She was very outgoing, friendly, and engaging. She was born in Israel from Moroccan parents who were living in the same small town, Tirat Hacarmel, near Haifa, as my grandmother Meme Hninah—in the same neighborhood, several blocks away.

On one of my weekend leaves, Armand and I with his big bus visited Meme Hninah for Shabbat. We decided that since we had the luxury of wheels—a whole huge coach—we would drop by Rahel's parents' home to see if we could interest her in joining us to go to a disco with some of our friends. Hearing us honking the bus horn, Rahel came to the window and was delighted to see us. She agreed to join us if we could pick her up later. As mentioned before, I had kept in touch with a whole group of Moroccan Jewish girls studying at Haifa University, and the plan was to pick everyone up in Armand's bus and go out on the town, in the Carmel district of Haifa where most of the trendy bars and nightclubs were located.

My belief then was that the military uniform made us blend in among the thousands of other uniformed soldiers, so it was hard to stand out. Once I changed from my drab uniform into my fashionable, dressy civilian clothes, I had my individual style and personality back, and I regained my self-confidence. Once we picked everybody up on the bus, we had a small group of ten to fifteen mostly university students speaking French and Spanish, laughing and joking on a Friday night. We had a private limousine bus driving us to an outing on the town.

Later that evening, while having drinks and dancing in the nightclub, it appeared that I was making serious progress with Rahel. The next day we decided to meet again and go out to the movies. However, once we got ready to make our way to the theatre, a last-minute plan was improvised. Since we both had to get back to base early the next day, we decided to go back to Tirat Hacarmel, change into our uniforms, get our guns and small backpacks, and catch a ride to our recently reclaimed apartment in Jerusalem to spend the night there—an exciting and welcome turn of events. The next day we took the long bus drive to Sinai and parted as Rahel went to the main headquarters base and I took another ride to get to my small compound at Bir Tmadeh.

I was not sure if Rahel, once back in a military setting with all the rules and constraints, wanted to maintain the new relationship between us. Rahel was an attractive girl, one of only a few women on base, so most likely she would opt to date one of the officers with whom female soldiers mostly interacted with while performing their daily tasks. To claim me, a mere sergeant, as her boyfriend and to make our relationship known around base would attract attention and maybe even cause resentment against both of us. I left it up to her, and to my pleasant surprise, she opted for our relationship, making my life much improved as I found comfort, affection, and emotional support with her.

At a review a few months later, my commanding officer asked me if I would like to be transferred from our Sinai Peninsula base to mainland Israel. As a soldier without parents in Israel and having served in war and peacetime for more than six months "on the line," meaning on military controlled territories like the Golan, West Bank and Sinai, I was entitled to be posted closer to home. I declined the option. I also did not mind staying in on extra weekends, covering for my two officers by staying in full command of our small base while they went home. Rahel would join me many times during those weekends.

The commute from Sinai base to mainland Israel was mostly done by long bus rides of six to seven hours on narrow roads. Shortly after the 1973 War, with thousands of reservists that had been called in, the IDF chartered large civilian airplanes manned by military staff, as well as assigned old Air Force cargo planes to shuttle all the soldiers going on weekly leaves from the main Sinai airport to Lod Airport near Tel Aviv. The Logistics Corps that my unit belonged to was in charge of staffing the terminals at both ends and issuing passes for airplane seats, which put me at a slight advantage. One of my good buddies from my driving days was assigned at the terminal and would always get me priority seating, as if I were on special official duty.

To get home and back from Sinai, we flew in all types of aircraft after the war, from the very old military planes like the Boeing C-97 Stratofreighter and the Douglas C-47 to the more recent Lockheed C-130. Later on, a small fleet of used civilian Boeings were assigned full time to assure the connections. Since many times I was flying directly from Sinai to much smaller airports, like to Haifa or Jerusalem, I was on small chartered civilian airplanes as well, like the nine-seater Piper Navajo reserved mainly for officers only. My buddy Ilan Langhaus always made sure I got a seat under "Official Army Business." The rides on these small airplanes were not only fast, but also very exciting and enjoyable, particularly when having the advantage of being assigned to the co-pilot seat in front.

Sometime toward the end of 1974, I benefited from my second thirty-day leave that I was entitled to as a "lonely soldier." This time, I decided to find a job and earn some needed wages. I was hired as a driver for a civilian contractor supplying civilian car services for shuttling high-level officers around to the different bases in Sinai. I had met Ynon, the contractor, as he came to our base often while driving officers around. Ynon owned several Volkswagen minibus passenger vehicles. He offered to hire me for the thirty days to drive one of his minibuses since I already had all the necessary security clearances and was familiar with all the bases in Sinai.

The pay was very good, and since I did not have to worry about room and board, I was able to save most of what I earned. Having my own girlfriend on-site was perfect, as I could stop by to visit her. For a full month, I got to drive around army bases in Sinai in civilian clothes with my civilian Volkswagen minibus, getting most of the soldiers and officers a bit confused about my status. I was a soldier stationed in Sinai and working in the same spot on his long leave instead of being home or abroad.

One night after dropping off my last officer for the day, I stopped by to pick up Rahel and go for a spin. Next to an adjoining large base, I pulled off the road to get away from the main traffic and drove for a short distance on a small dirt road, then turned off the lights. We parked there surrounded by total darkness. As we were chatting and enjoying each other's company, suddenly we heard a loud engine roaring, coming in our direction. I quickly realized it was an armored tank moving fast toward our general direction where I was parked with all lights off. We were in danger of being run over and smashed by a unsuspecting military tank moving at full speed.

I immediately started the vehicle, turned on the headlights, and got out of there as fast as I could. This scary experience taught me never to venture off-road at night with headlights off in the vicinity of a military armored tank base, which most large compounds in Sinai were. The tanks might be involved in night training or simply moving around without lights and not expecting to encounter a small civilian vehicle in their path or among the low dunes with its lights turned off.

Rahel and I enjoyed our weekend leaves going straight to the apartment in Jerusalem. She helped me locate some furnishings as well as decorating our small flat, adding her special woman's touch. I spent most of what I had earned working those thirty days on improving the place. It really started to feel like a warm, welcoming place to come to when on leave from the army.

Yom Haatzmaut, Independence Day, 1975

I was feeling lucky and happy as I was getting more responsibilities at my job, had a girlfriend serving in the same unit, and had a nice apartment to go to in Jerusalem. Armand, on the other hand, was trying very hard to find a stable, fulfilling way to live, and spent his time shuttling between Israel, Canada, and France. He would spend several months at a time in each of these countries, trying to establish a life for himself. In Israel, since he had the experience and the necessary licenses, he always could find work as a bus driver and earn enough money to help him take off on his next try in Paris or Montreal, and later, all the way back to Casablanca, Morocco.

In early April of 1975, I was invited to appear in front of my new base commander. This time I gladly went with no hesitation. Once in his office and at ease, I was told that I had been selected to represent the whole Logistics Corps of the IDF at a special ceremony at the residence of Israel's president, to celebrate the twenty-seven years of Israel's independence. Each year, in honor of Independence Day, the president of the country holds a special ceremony to honor the IDF troops and welcomes in his official formal residence the representatives of all the corps or major units of the defense forces. Each major branch of the military chooses a soldier with an exemplary service and performance record to be sent to represent them and be awarded a special certificate of Excellent Merit Service. I was asked if I would do the honors, and I gladly accepted.

The ceremony was to take place in Jerusalem on April 16. I had a second meeting in my commander's office to make sure I was prepared and ready for this national event. A couple days before the event, I went to Jerusalem and joined a group of other soldiers that were selected from the various branches of the IDF. We were briefed, coached, and taken to rehearse our moves and marches.

All I remember is that we marched into the beautifully landscaped courtyard of the official residence of the president of Israel and then stood in special formation with our starched and nicely pressed new uniforms and our shiny boots. Then we marched into the big reception hall of Beit Hanassi, the president's residence. Facing us was the fourth president of the country, Ephraim Katzir. Next to him was the minister of defense, Shimon Peres, who much later became the prime minister and later the president of Israel, and then General Motta Gur, the general chief of staff. Most of Israel's top generals were present in the room.

After short speeches by the general chief of staff and the president thanking us for service to our country, we were called each by name to come forward and get a personal handshake from the president as well as a photo op and a certificate signed by the president. We were all invited for drinks and snacks in the garden afterwards. I remember being interviewed in French later by the national Israeli radio service, Kol Israel. The station broadcasts news in several languages — English, French, Spanish, and many more, including one in the Moroccan, Jewish Arabic dialect. My few comments were broadcast later that day. I know that because the parents of my friend Eric told me they heard me on the French news broadcast of that day.

After being seen on the Israeli national TV channel by my father in 1971, as a young child in Casablanca in that old documentary on Moroccan Jews, this time I was heard on the national radio station as a young soldier. This was a nice way to slowly enter my last few months in the military and get ready to be discharged in mid-August of that year, after finally completing my three years of mandatory service.

Sergeant Robert shaking hands with then-president Ephraim Katzir (Israel's fourth president); Shimon Peres, acting defense minister; and Motta Gur, military chief of staff, second from left. Excellent Merit Service at the President's Ceremony, Israel Independence Day, 1975.

At Bir Tmadeh, last picture taken in uniform, May 1975

Simon

Around July of 1975, my younger brother Simon was coming to Israel on an organized trip with a group of Jewish kids from his high school in Casablanca. Not having seen him for six years since I left home in 1969, I was not sure I was going to recognize him. I asked him to mail me a picture of himself, and to this day I still have the photo, with him standing with some friends and a small arrow marked "that is me" pointing to him. We met at a hotel in Tel Aviv where he was staying with his group. I very much enjoyed seeing him, reconnecting with the new eighteen-year-old Simon who was twelve when I left home. We spent a couple hours catching up on family news.

Simon was probably the last of the six Benayoun boys still living at home with our parents, together with our youngest sister, Nanou, both staying on track to complete their studies in high school. A few years after Prosper and I left for Israel, Evelyne, and later Michel, opted to leave home as well, without graduating from high school, and ventured to France and later to New York.

Simon, whose Hebrew name is Shimon, was born in November of 1956. He was named after our father's brother who was murdered in the city of Rabat by Moroccan militants fighting for independence from France. Simon was the Benayoun boy who stayed home the longest, accommodating our parents and giving our father much satisfaction by staying the conventional course, playing by the rules, respecting religious demands and expectations, and finding the right compromises that most of us refused to play by.

Our father developed a unique bond with Simon and drew a lot of *nahat*, or satisfaction, from finally having one son that didn't rebel or aggressively oppose him like most of the other siblings did. Simon was able to find the right middle ground and managed to have a very loving, constructive relationship with our father. Our father drew a lot of pride from his one son who not only remained close to home so long but also chose to pursue his studies while following Jewish religious traditions, attending synagogue services wherever he was living at the time, in France or Morocco. This was very soothing to our father.

Simon not only shared some physical resemblance to our father but also inherited a similar nature of temperament and character. On the other hand, after seven sons and daughters chose to oppose him and opt to take the first chance to leave home, my father must have realized the trend and probably was willing to compromise more as he was getting older. In any case, that does not take away the merit of Simon who was able to provide support and give satisfaction to our hardworking father who unbeknownst to all his children scattered in different corners of the world was to pass away suddenly. Simon also played a big role in returning home for a few months after our father passed away in order to help our mother manage logistics and assets before moving to Montreal.

Simon was able to achieve his own goals while balancing what was expected of him and at the same time following his own agenda. He was a great athlete, dedicated to his passion, the game of soccer, which we call football. His soccer team played in a Moroccan minor league. Simon also had great social skills, developing and maintaining meaningful, long-term friendships that last to this day.

A few years ago, I learned that after I left Casablanca for Israel, Simon had difficulties in high school and failed two years in a row to pass to the next grade. Apparently, however, he was able to finally surmount these difficulties and graduate with honors. He was accepted into a French university in Paris, and after four years of college in Paris and Toulouse, he received a business degree as a Certified Public Accountant in France.

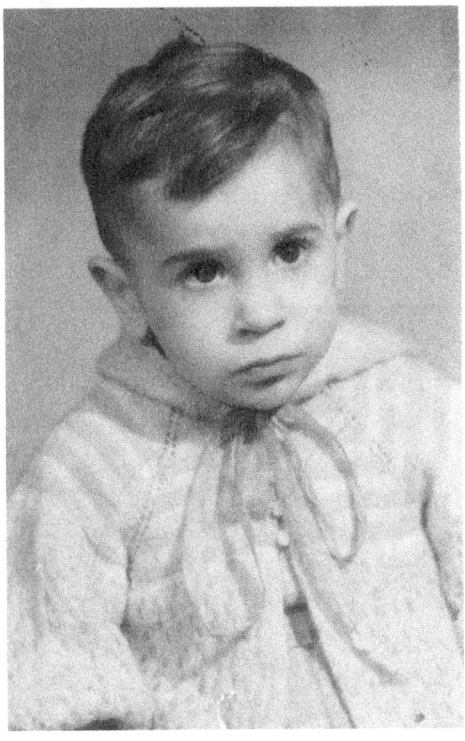

Simon, 1958

Looking For Home

Simon, Casablanca, 1975

Simon, Paris 1993

Civilian Life and Neot Hakikar

Knowing that I was going to be discharged from the army, I was considering my options and my next steps in entering back into civilian life. I had a modestly furnished apartment at a subsidized rent, which was a big asset, but not much savings to anticipate my next move. I did ask my father for a small contribution to help me until I could get a job. With the modest amount received from him, I was able to purchase a used fridge — badly needed in my kitchen in the Jerusalem apartment. In the army, before being discharged it is traditionally accepted that we have the last thirty days off, to be able to make arrangements and start the reentry process into civilian life. During the month of July 1975, I was mostly living in Jerusalem. Around that time my younger sister Evelyne, after having lived in Paris a few years, was spending time living and working as a volunteer on a kibbutz in the north of Israel, close to the Lebanese border.

She came to visit me and spent one weekend in Jerusalem accompanied by her new boyfriend, Charlie Beriro. He would later become her husband and the father of her only child, my nephew Nathan. We had a great time together while we visited all the great historical tourist sites around Bethlehem and Jerusalem. Charlie, a tall, handsome, friendly guy, was also from Morocco, loved travelling and volunteering at Kibbutz Bar Am for a few months every year.

I flew one last time back to Sinai to say goodbye to all my friends. A nice get-together was organized in my honor. A group gift from all the staff in my unit was offered to me and after exchanging parting wishes and promises to stay in touch, I flew back from Sinai to Jerusalem.

My first step was to register for fall courses at Jerusalem University. In the meantime, I needed a job. Within a few days, I was hired by a local surveillance company to be an armed guard at the entrance gate of a big shoe factory in Jerusalem. The Hamegaper factory was famously known in Israel for producing most of the boots for the IDF. Armed with a handgun at my waist, my job was to staff the entrance gate controlling the incoming and outgoing traffic during regular working hours, and on the night shift to patrol the whole compound.

My romance with Rahel was slowly wrapping up as we both were heading in different directions. She still had another year in the military, and I really didn't know how I was going to sustain myself, being independent and earning a living while waiting for the possibility of starting school. I was also very adamant about not wanting to commit to a serious relationship while entering a new civilian life, not knowing if I was going to even continue living in Israel. Like my two brothers and sister, I might decide to possibly relocate to France.

I started taking some college requirement classes and realized very soon that taking notes in Hebrew at the college level was not going to be an easy task. I seriously considered the travel industry and went for an interview at the Israel national airline company, El Al, for a flight attendant job. I was invited back to take a lengthy test, and after waiting a couple weeks, was told to apply again in the spring.

After a few months of looking at the newspaper for job openings, one ad got my attention. A touring company for tourists, based in Jerusalem, was looking for young Israeli guys who, after army service, had good knowledge of foreign languages such as English, French, or German and were already licensed to drive big trucks. The company was named after a moshav, a co-op village south of the Dead Sea—Neot Hakikar. This is a name mentioned in the Old Testament. Their office was located by the main avenues close to the famous King David Hotel.

At the interview place, a bunch of guys were waiting to be called in. When my turn came, my interviewer, Avi Amir, one of the partners in the agency, asked me questions about my background, my army service, and my knowledge of languages. During the interview, the main owner, Rudy Golan, who was sitting at a nearby desk, jumped into the conversation asking me questions in French to test my knowledge of that language. Avi wanted to know which country I came from. I answered Morocco, and that I had immigrated to Israel by myself. I remember mentioning that my plans were to try to stick it out on my own for another year or so before deciding if I really intended to remain in Israel.

Avi looked at me with a smile on this face, then he told me that in all the years that he was involved in the company, they had never hired a guide with a Moroccan background. I knew about some of the prejudices in Israel against Moroccan Jews, but I was taken by surprise and slightly embarrassed hearing this unnecessary statement. I disliked his attitude and decided on the spot as far as I was concerned to get up and end the interview. As I got ready to leave, Avi realized I was offended. He asked me to please stay, and he told me, "Listen, you see all those guys waiting out there? They all want this job badly, but they don't interest me. If you really want this job, it's yours. You can start next Sunday at 6 a.m." I was surprised, but gladly accepted. The problem was, I did not have a clue as to what kind of work I was agreeing to. All I knew was that it involved driving groups of tourists and touring around a certain area of the Sinai desert peninsula.

Sunday morning at 6 a.m., with a small backpack on my back, I presented myself at the agency office. I was then driven to East Jerusalem, on the Arab side of town, where located among several private Arab homes was a warehouse and a large yard where the touring vehicles were kept. I was introduced to Yossi, who was going to be the official guide and in charge of the upcoming trip. We first had to load the vehicle with all the gear and food needed for the trip.

The vehicle, an REO M34 2½ ton, was an old American-made surplus military truck that was commonly used by US and NATO armed forces. This 6X6 all-wheel-drive vehicle was sturdy and tough, an ideal all-terrain truck for venturing off-road. The team in Neot Hakikar was able to locate these military surplus trucks in Europe and import them to Israel where they were adapted so each could accommodate up to twenty passengers seated comfortably for off-road expeditions. They had a metal frame with canvas roof and five rows of four seats each. Water storage tanks were added and a metal cargo box was welded onto the back to carry gear, food, and luggage. The cabin in front was completely open and had room for the driver and two passengers.

Once we loaded up all the gear, like sleeping bags, ice chests, tools, food and water for five days, we drove off to meet our group of travelers waiting to be picked up outside the agency main office.

I was a little surprised at first to see that such a rough truck, open on all sides and with just a canvas roof to protect from the elements, was going to attract and carry tourists visiting Israel. In my humble knowledge at the time, I was under the impression that foreign tourists were always transported in luxurious, air-conditioned coach buses, staying overnight in comfortable hotel rooms. I was not yet understanding the whole concept but enjoying the experience so far.

Once the whole group was seated on board with all their luggage properly stored and tied up in the back, we started our long drive to Eilat in the south. Yossi asked me to drive. As we descended from the hills of Jerusalem into the Judean Desert toward Jericho, he told me that this five-day camping trip to Sinai would be a try-out for me to test my skills in general and evaluate if I would be a good match for this type of work.

We stopped for a short break near the oasis of Ein Gedi on the shores of the Dead Sea to serve a light breakfast to the group before continuing our drive for a few more hours toward Eilat on the shores of the Red Sea. As mentioned before, I had been several times to Eilat, first with my brother Samy and then a couple of times on my own in high school and in the military. After passing through the town of Eilat, a few kilometers south we reached the old Israel-Egypt boundary and finally crossed officially into the Sinai Peninsula, our main destination and the focus of our camping expedition.

Yossi, a big, blond-haired *sabra* from Eastern European parents, was a native Israeli born in Rishon Letzion and was a veteran from a famous IDF recon combat unit. He addressed the group, explaining in good English how our itinerary for the next five days would take us deep into Sinai, mostly off-road through the valleys, mountains, and canyons of the Sinai desert. Most importantly, he mentioned some essential rules about our drinking and cooking water, trying to conserve and minimize waste while making sure to stay hydrated, and rules about bathrooms, trash, snacks, etcetera.

The rest of the afternoon, we drove along the main road built by Israel along the Red Sea shoreline of the Gulf of Aqaba. We stopped for lunch in a scenic, pristine, isolated cove away from the road. Masks and snorkels were distributed for those interested in discovering the marine wildlife and colorful coral reefs a few feet from the shore and just below the surface of the water.

The Sinai Peninsula, covering some 37,200 square miles, is a large, triangular wedge between the Gulf of Aqaba in the east and the Gulf of Suez in the west. It connects the continents of Africa and Asia from east to west and the Mediterranean and the Red Sea from north to south. It is divided into three regions.

In the north is the sandy, coastal Mediterranean plateau with low hills and deep and not always passable sand dunes — some are seventy-five to one hundred feet high. There are brackish wells and oases. Several battles were fought here between Egypt and Israel, and this is where I was posted during my military service. This was the area I was familiar with during my last two years in uniform.

The center of the peninsula is a formidable, mostly limestone plateau known as the El-Tih Desert. The southern Sinai is composed of igneous rocks, with deep wadis and high pinnacles. The wadis are like canyons and drain water toward the Gulf of Suez or toward the Gulf of Aqaba. This area of high mountains includes Mount Katrina, or Catherine, of elevation 8,668 feet (2,642 meters); Umm Shumar, 8,482 feet (2,585 meters); Al-Thabt, 7,997 feet (2,437 meters); and Mount Sinai, 7,497 feet (2,285 meters). The mountains are in the center and separated from the Gulf of Suez to the west by a narrow coastal plain, but on the eastern side they rise sharply from the Gulf of Aqaba.

After the Israeli takeover of the Sinai in the 1967 War, a paved road was built from Eilat all the way to Charm el Cheikh at the southern tip of the peninsula. The first half of the road followed the shoreline coast until the oasis of Nuweiba. All along the road were magnificent and spectacular views of the many bays and coves on the Gulf of Aqaba. As I drove our REO truck along the coastal road, making my way further south into the southern Sinai region, I was discovering at the same time with our group the amazing wild, scenic beauty of this remote landscape.

As the sun was starting to set, we made our way to our first night camp, near the oasis of Dahab. We camped under the palm trees in a small cove, right by the water. Under the instructions of Yossi, there was a whole routine of how to set up camp—park the truck a certain way to use its special side lights so we could see, set up the kitchen, get our group situated and supplied with sleeping bags. After a coffee, tea, and cookies break, dinner preparation got underway with the help of the four first-row passengers, the designated volunteers for that first night's kitchen duty.

After dinner seated around a crackling campfire, we had a short get-acquainted session where each participant introduced himself. The group was made up of travelers from many different countries but mostly from the US and Europe. By the time I got to my sleeping bag, I was totally exhausted but felt very happy after such a long day of discovery.

The next day, after visiting and discovering several other spots along the Red Sea shores and isolated coves, the time came to abandon the paved asphalt where our REO was doing an okay job and switch to all-terrain mode. The real expedition was just getting started. We slightly deflated the air pressure in the six big tires and lowered the glass windshield. We wrapped our Bedouin *keffiyeh* on our heads to protect from blowing sand and dust, then engaged in low gear and drove deeper into the mountains using the large, dry riverbeds, or wadis. This is when I realized the capabilities and the amazing performance of the REO truck. Loaded with twenty-two passengers plus gear and food, it drove smoothly on such rough terrain.

As we got further west and away from the road, the whole landscape started to change. We drove through canyons, gorges, and valleys connected through narrow mountain passes while gradually gaining some altitude. Yossi was at the wheel first, then we switched as he wanted me to experiment with handling the big truck on the rough terrain. Maybe it was on the third day, the truck slowly climbed a winding, narrow trail to get to a pass that would descend into the next wadi. We finally made it to the top of the mountain and drove a few minutes on the plateau. I remember vividly that suddenly this huge, incredible view opened up in front of us and drew an enthusiastic reaction. Everybody reached for their cameras.

In that moment, I realized that this is what I wanted to be involved in. This is what I would love to master and work in, this concept of organized Sinai desert tours using an unconventional all-terrain vehicle to lead participants willing to explore nature, escaping city life and navigating in remote, pristine wilderness. I decided that even without pay this lifestyle suited me perfectly. It was an escape for me as a young man fresh from my army years, looking for a direction to begin making a life for myself. From that moment on and through the continuation of the tour, I was eager and totally invested in wanting to learn and master all the technical details and, most importantly, impress Yossi so he would give a positive review of my performance and my potential to one day become a guide.

The scenery continued to constantly change as we entered the mountains and valleys surrounding Mount Sinai and the Saint Catherine Monastery. I discovered my Arabic language skills were an added benefit with the native Bedouin tribes living with their herds of camels and black goats in Sinai. By the end of the tour, as we made our way back to Jerusalem, Yossi let me know that he thought I did a good job. He was definitely going to give a positive recommendation.

Back in Jerusalem, I was officially hired. While waiting a few months before being sent to a training course to study to become a licensed guide, I was to continue to go on weekly trips as an assistant guide, or what we called a "second" to the main guide, or *movil*, the trip leader. As excited as I was to have been selected, I realized after a couple trips that as a "second," the job required quite a few skills. Guiding was certainly one of them, but most important was the ability to drive and navigate off-road terrain and to be able to maintain the vehicle and to repair most mechanical breakdowns while far away from civilization, deep in the isolated wadis and mountainous regions of the desert.

The REO was an incredibly tough, resilient vehicle that was built to perform in a variety of rough terrain, from sand dunes to rocky mountain paths, but with the strong demands, and the year-round busy touring agenda, they frequently needed mechanical attention. The lead guide had to be prepared and well equipped with an array of mechanical tools and a list of spare parts for repairs on-site. He had to take care of and ensure the safety of the tourists, being able to give first aid in case of emergency, to properly cook for and feed them, and to make sure they stayed hydrated in the hot desert summer months. We carried a machine gun in each vehicle as required by the military but did not have any way of communicating once we got off the main coastal roads. Each trip leader had to make sure not only to properly pack enough food for all meals, but to keep constant watch on water usage by the group so as not to run out.

Later I learned that one of my biggest assets for the Neot Hakikar desert tours was my French language. Club Med was one of their major contracted clients and had a very profitable partnership with the agency. I was to work closely with Club Med and guide the specially chartered groups during each summer. Neot Hakikar was under contract by the French Club Med to offer a weekly six-day Sinai expedition during the three summer months, and a weekly three-day tour the rest of the year. I became the main French guide for the agency, mostly handling all French groups signed up to tour Sinai with Neot Hakikar.

After a few months working with a variety of groups from Israel's kibbutzim and schools and for organized groups from Europe, learning how to prepare and pack for the trips and to repair minor mechanical breakdowns, I was sent along with several other new guides to start our official Sinai guiding course. The study and training course lasted several months and focused on the different geographical regions and habitats present in Sinai—the geology, archaeology, the flora and fauna, and the history of the desert with its current native Bedouin tribes. The Bedouin population numbered about 10,000 people and was divided into several tribes, each occupying their own delineated territory for grazing their camels and flocks of black goats. Our studies involved many field trips to different corners of the Sinai, led by our professors and with the touring vehicles and special logistics supplied by our company. During the course, I realized for the first time my true passion for nature that had been within me all along, and it was finally able to be recognized, expressed, shared, and widened.

My first few trips as a leader, I made sure to select as an assistant a new "second" that had better mechanical skills than me. That is how I discovered Hillel, a recently hired future guide who was a shy, soft-spoken, sweet person who could repair and deal with any mechanical situation or breakdown. The guiding team of Neot Hakikar, mostly native Israeli guys in those years, became a really tight, friendly group. We were working constantly and usually as paired teams on the road, guiding, camping, living outdoors, and working with weekly groups. Most of us shared a love of nature and enjoyed the escape offered by the Sinai desert with its wild, scenic beauty, its fascinating variety of landscapes, its rugged canyons, its refreshing oases hidden in narrow gorges, and its large remoteness. We loved the illusion of being in control of this large desert as we made our way through the many wadis, discovering hidden, sheltered coves among the sandstone bluffs to set up night camps in. Coves that we nicknamed based on the name of the guide who was first to discover it.

Most of the guides, like me, came to the Sinai to get away after their army service, the majority having served as officers in the special forces and combat units. Several came from units like the famous Sayeret Matkal and the Shayetet 13 reconnaissance units or were Rangers from the paratrooper battalion. There was Timy from Argentinian parents, who was an ex-officer and an incredible, gentle, generous big guy; Joel, a kibbutznik from Yemenite parents; Moti, from Polish parents, who became my roommate in Jerusalem and a very close friend for many years; Tsvika, from German parents, who guided the German groups; Bruce from the northeast of the US; Udi who guided the Germans as well; and Ephy, Mikha, Aran, Shay, Moshe, Aaron, Zeevik, and Gadi.

*Ras Mohammad National Park,
Southern Sinai on the Red Sea, 1976*

Neot Hakikar, the company, was originally created by a group of young farmers and their families living on a newly created settlement, or moshav, by the same name that was established south of the Dead Sea. This small farming community was in the middle of an arid, unfriendly, and desolate area. When not working on their farms, for their leisure they went exploring under the guidance of a creative young sabra man by the name of Amiram Avrutsky and his wife Devorah.

In the typical pioneering Israeli spirit and with the love of discovering the natural assets of their surroundings, they used some old jeeps and other four-wheel-drive vehicles to explore the canyons and valleys around their remote location. They ventured into the Negev and Arava desert areas, exploring during the day, camping out at night, roaming all the way to the new port city of Eilat at the southern tip of Israel, long before the existing paved road was built.

They soon realized that they could commercialize the concept, mostly to attract young Israelis eager to be in the outdoors to explore while camping out in the remote, hidden valleys and canyons around the Dead Sea and the Negev desert. The creative and venturesome young team of settlers from the Neot Hakikar Moshav, with Amiram as their main motivator and visionary, acquired and retrofitted several jeeps and old military surplus vehicles from the army. With these "command cars" they were soon able to put together and market a few itineraries for exploring and camping out.

The tourism industry in Israel was just picking up steam, and Club Med, one of the biggest companies running resort villages all around the Mediterranean, was looking to offer their French visitors to Israel a new concept and a more out-of-the-ordinary way to experience touring the land. They signed a contract with Neot Hakikar to offer desert tours to their clients. Soon the desert tour company got busy and expanded, eventually moving out from the farming settlement but keeping the original name. They relocated to Beer Sheva first, then Eilat, and then Jerusalem.

After the 1967 War, Israel took over the whole Sinai Peninsula. The rugged southern portion of Sinai has long miles of shoreline along the Red Sea, a high mountain region in the center of the peninsula, and numerous oases inhabited by the local Bedouins. Neot Hakikar had a staff of young guides, most of them ex-military officers freshly discharged from IDF combat units and able to read topographic maps. They were willing to venture out and explore mostly for fun the new possible itineraries deep into the Sinai, adding to their original trips. Soon the Sinai desert tours became the focus of the company. After importing several REO trucks acquired from NATO surplus military stock in Europe, they retrofitted them locally to accommodate up to twenty passengers plus two guides.

The REO in action, Sinai, 1976

The REO in action on a mountain pass

I enjoyed every moment of my work, meeting and guiding interesting participants from different backgrounds, my interactions with French groups from Club Med and others. Everything was going extremely well. My language skills in English and Arabic were seriously improving. I very much enjoyed my constant interactions with the local Bedouin, being able to finally put to good use my Arabic knowledge from my childhood growing up in Morocco.

The following is a poem I kept, written originally in French and sent to me by a participant of one of my guiding trips in Sinai, circa 1976.

> *"After we get back to our country*
> *We will dream of Sinai.*
> *Every picture of this beautiful desert*
> *Will also include Robert.*
>
> *We ventured into the desert after the leisurely life of Eilat Club Med.*
> *We took our places on this fancy truck with natural air flow,*
> *With ejectable seats, movable ladder, and*
> *Self-service bar with drinks at room temperature.*
>
> *In order not to shock our civilized souls,*
> *You drove us first on the asphalt road*
> *And slowly you took the time to make us*
> *Discover, appreciate, and love this desert that is your passion.*
>
> *Noontime you put together a garden party*
> *With a multi-colored menu.*
> *Every day in a special, magical setting chosen by you,*
> *You provided us with the daily manna needed for a desert traveler.*

In the afternoon we reclined in our special bouncy chairs,
Digesting and dozing off while the magnificent, magical, diverse scenery
Kept flowing in front of our eyes,
This landscape that you so cherish.

Around sunset, you chose for us a "one thousand stars" location
That we surprisingly discovered to be quite comfortable for the night,
With your special gourmet dinner around the fire.

Together around the campfire, we listened to your biblical tales,
Bedouin legends, and stories peppered with your special sense of humor.
You enriched us and contributed to our dreams of the desert night . . .
A little too short.

With my group, hiking on Mount Sinai after watching the sunrise from the summit, 1976

Day after day, as Moses guided the Hebrew tribes,
You led us through this unique journey
Through the Sinai desert.
You made us enjoy the whole experience."

The three managing partners running Neot Hakikar then were Rudy Golan, Avi Amir, and Menahem Dreiblatt. Rudy was born in Istanbul, Turkey, from German parents. He spoke fluently about six languages and was the main finance director, PR guy, and marketing manager for international sales for the desert tours. Rudy, an interesting individual, was very cultured and well-travelled, always enjoying the moment, the good life, and never missing an opportunity for gourmet meals, drinking, and smoking. He was a womanizer par excellence. I later became very close to him. He was almost as a father figure to me. Avi Amir was in charge of logistics and operations. He originally started working in the company as a young guide and eventually made it as a partner. Menahem, the third partner, was in charge of all mechanical aspects of the fleet of trucks.

When not on a trip, we had several company-paid apartments in Eilat for the guides' use. While working and spending most of my time in Sinai, I was not very often at my apartment in Jerusalem, maybe one weekend every two or three weeks. I was kept very busy either leading a tour or preparing to go on one. Most of my French groups from Club Med were picked up and returned from the big resort hotel in Eilat. During the summer months, we had a French group every week for a six-day, five-night tour, and very often I was guiding two trucks, sometimes three. At the end of every tour I was always invited for dinner with my group at the resort, where I loved the festive ambiance and famous Club Med mood of singing and dancing celebration.

At the end of the season, the tradition was that our company offered a special tour in Sinai for some of the staff at the Club Med resort, before they moved on to their next assignment in the worldwide network. It was at the end of one of these trips, when we drove all the way back to Jerusalem, that a big surprise waited for me. After parking the REO near our office and saying goodbye to my group, as I walked with my French girlfriend into the office, one of the girls working there told me that my brother had been waiting for me inside. When I asked which brother, I remember her answer was "the Orthodox rabbi . . . ."

I was convinced this was some kind of joke until I entered the room and a bearded man in a black hat and a long black coat came walking toward me with a big smile and open arms. As he called my name, I realized it was my brother Prosper. He had become a very pious and religious Hasid, studying in a French yeshiva. After hugging and greeting each other, he let me know that he needed to have his apartment back and that I was welcome to live with him on the condition that I would abandon my secular lifestyle and accept all the religious customs. He was staying temporarily at a local yeshiva in the Old City of Jerusalem and I had a few days to make my plans.

We parted, and I was totally in shock from the encounter and his manners, his language, his disrespect for me. My brother Prosper, whom I hadn't seen since we last met in Paris three years previously, had completely changed, transforming himself into a very religious man. As much as I was distraught and upset, I also felt sorry for him as he had also mentioned that he could use any financial contribution from me.

Prosper was legally half owner of the apartment with Armand, but in his rush to leave the country several years ago he had completely abandoned the flat. It took Armand and me a lot of work and money not only to claim it back but to pay all the accumulated debts and renovate, repaint, and furnish it and keep it well maintained. The next day, I went to visit Prosper, looking for him at the yeshiva in the old Jewish quarter within the walls of the Old City. I found him napping in his room.

Prosper tried to explain to me and justify his demands and duty to claim his apartment. He also requested once more any financial contribution I could spare as well as help getting for him some clothing, which I happily did. However, after a few days I realized the situation was more complex for me to share the same apartment with him, and it was not going to be feasible. Prosper had so many religious requirements and could not tolerate or accept me as a secular person with my own lifestyle. I had to move out as soon as possible.

I had worked so hard to get where I was on my own and was stable, happy, and fulfilled in my professional occupation. I very much enjoyed my new life and work as a Sinai desert guide. This was such an unexpected turn of events, and I was destabilized by it. I couldn't really get back to work without having first resolved the issue of finding my own new, comfortable apartment to move to. When it was time to go back south, I told Rudy, my boss, that I had to postpone getting back to work until I could make arrangements to find a new place to live. Rudy kindly offered for me to move in with his family for a while until I could get my own place.

Rudy and his wife, Yofit, and their two kids lived in a beautiful, spacious bungalow villa in the country outside Rishon Letzion, on a ten-acre orange grove. They kept a couple of horses nearby. Rudy commuted daily to the office in Jerusalem. I moved my things to their home and was able to get back to my work in Sinai. After a few weeks, Rudy offered to help me with whatever rent I could find, and through another Sinai guide's mother I was able to find an amazing three-bedroom apartment in her building in a great neighborhood on Pinsker Street, centrally located and only two blocks from the office. It was very close to the prime minister's official residence and the famous Jerusalem Theatre. The rent was more than I could afford, but Rudy and the office agreed to subsidize part of it until I could make arrangements or find roommates to split the rent.

Since I was spending most of my time on tours in the south of the country, I did not see much of Prosper. I was to learn later that after living for a few weeks in the apartment, he leased it to a young couple for an upfront amount of money and returned to France to make his way back to Casablanca from there.

Prosper (1952–2007)

My brother Prosper was born in February 1952, some twenty months before me. Growing up we were very close. Prosper was a sweet, gentle, and very affectionate child, and I looked up to him. Armand, who was two years older than Prosper, was most of the time his play partner and Prosper looked up to him. As a teenager in high school, Prosper was a good student. He was talented in writing French essays and always obtained some of the best grades in his class. He was very popular among his small group of friends and was a great dancer during the get-togethers of the local neighborhood.

At the beginning of the school year of 1968, we both decided to convince our parents to let us continue our schooling in Israel. After a few weeks of confrontation and arguments, Prosper was persuaded to go back to school and wait until the summer of 1969, after the school year was over, which in hindsight was a wiser decision and a much better attitude than the one I adopted at the time. When we finally left together in the summer of 1969, we became very close, spending the first few weeks of our journey and our time in Israel within the same group of boys and girls.

After several weeks, we finally separated as we were sent to different study programs at separate locations. Prosper's study program was to keep following the French curriculum, while I had to transit to a whole new Hebrew-Israeli curriculum starting from tenth grade on. While in Israel, we stayed in touch, visiting each other often as well as spending occasional weekends together visiting our grandmother or our aunts. Prosper's suicide attempt in 1971 did not seem to have endangered his life, although he must have been going through a very difficult phase. He had to be confined for a few days in a mental institution. Prosper seemed to have recovered well and successfully resumed his studies with his group of friends and classmates. He went on to academic studies first at Tel Aviv University and later transferred to Jerusalem.

A few months before I enlisted in the military, Armand, Prosper, and I were able to move in together and share the apartment in Jerusalem, spending quality time together. That was a fun period. We had some great moments and experiences, enjoying being reunited. We explored the great city of Jerusalem and often cooked and celebrated together for Shabbats and other fun events.

In late 1972, Prosper decided to leave Israel to study in Paris. He tried very hard to make a living there without the proper visas to live and work legally in France. He struggled financially while attempting to pursue his studies at a French university. Our parents in Morocco tried to help financially, but after a couple years of facing harsh conditions and constant economic struggle, Prosper turned toward religion.

When I came to Paris on my thirty-day leave from the military in early 1974 after the war, I was able to spend time with Prosper. Shortly after that, I heard that he had rediscovered Judaism and wanted to reconnect. It seemed to be soothing to him and so he embraced the faith and decided to join a yeshiva, a Jewish center for studies. After spending several months at the yeshiva totally immersing himself in studies and the practice of Orthodox Judaism, he completely renounced his previous secular ways, grew a beard, and changed his style of

Prosper (1952-2007)

clothing, dietary rules, and daily worship. A couple years later, he was dressed all in black as a conventional Hasidic Lubavitch rabbi, then he came to surprise me and to claim back the apartment in Jerusalem.

Prosper later decided that his best option was to make it back to Casablanca and join the local Lubavitch branch there. He became active in the local organization, helping them raise funds for their many community outreach programs. As traditionally done within the Orthodox Hasidim, a marriage was arranged. Prosper got married to a local religious girl, Michelle, and together they had six children, all born in Casablanca. Their three sons are Mendy, David, and Dov-Beer, and their three daughters are Haya, Hannah, and Sterna.

My siblings and I kept in touch by letters and occasional phone calls, helping Prosper through the years with some financial contributions. He was a familiar face around the Jewish community in Casablanca. He was known to be very generous, helping and comforting older and needy members of the community. Prosper died in 2007 in Casablanca from diabetes complications. He was fifty-five years old. I am in touch with my nephews and nieces, three of them living in France, the other three in Israel.

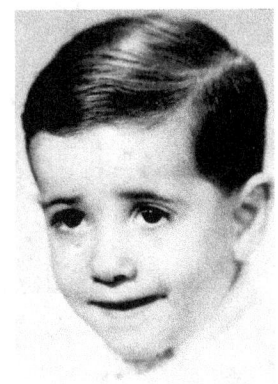

Prosper, 1952

Looking For Home

Prosper, Israel, 1969

Prosper, Casablanca, 1991

Visit to Morocco, 1977

I was very happy in my new apartment. Located in a great neighborhood, the apartment was half furnished and belonged to an Israeli professor teaching in a California university. The apartment had a spacious balcony with a great view. After a few months, my friend Moti moved into one of the other bedrooms and became my roommate. Moti Kaufer was born in Rishon Letzion to Polish parents who immigrated to Israel in the early 1930s. Moti was working for Neot Hakikar before my arrival, and he joined me and a few other new guides as we participated in the same guide training course. Moti and I got along very well and spend a lot of time together either guiding or leading trips. I was invited several times to his parents' home, and we stayed in touch long after the Sinai years.

During the winter, which was the slow season, I usually would take a longer break and visit my family and friends in France. While in Paris, I decided to explore the possibility of a surprise visit to Casablanca to visit my parents. After checking with the Moroccan embassy in Paris and hiding the fact that I had been living in Israel, I was able to get an extension on my expired Moroccan passport and got on a plane headed for Casablanca. This must have been around 1977, close to eight years after I had left as a fifteen-year-old boy.

Landing in Casablanca felt strange and awkward. I had strong, mixed emotions. Passing through customs and walking out of the new airport, it seemed many things had evolved and changed within me in the eight years I was away. I had a feeling of having become very Israeli in my identity, having served in the military and experienced the military conflict of the Yom Kippur War. It felt strange being back in an Arab land even though it felt so familiar.

Wanting my visit to be a total surprise, after landing in Casablanca I took a cab from the airport to 22 Rue Berthelot and rang the doorbell. My younger sister Nanou answered the door, and for a few seconds she was not sure who I was. She was eight years old when I left, and she was now about sixteen. My parents were so surprised and happy to see me.

On Shabbat I accompanied my father for Friday night services at his synagogue on Rue Colbert, where he was now the main *shaliyah tsibour*, leading his congregation in daily prayer services and officiating as the main rabbi. This was the same synagogue that was to be renamed "Or David," the light of David, in his memory after he passed away suddenly a couple years later in December 1980. My father was very proud introducing me to his congregants as his Israeli son. Some of them later told me that my father, during the intense weeks of fighting during the Yom Kippur War, would approach the Aron Hakodesh, where the Torah scrolls are stored, at the end of each prayer service and with particular fervor recite a special prayer for the safety of all Israel's soldiers, me included, during those difficult times. Many years later I was to relive a similar scenario as a father myself, praying for the safety of our two boys when my own sons were soldiers in the IDF, particularly when Daniel was on dangerous missions with his special forces unit or David crossed into Lebanon during the Israel-Hezbollah War in the summer of 2006.

In all the years I had been living in Israel, I seldom attended synagogue, so being back in Casablanca and honoring my father by joining prayer services with him was a treat. Friday services traditionally begin with the chanting of the poetic, sensuous Shir Hashirim, the Song of Songs, a beautiful love poem attributed to King Solomon. I was very familiar with the text and the melody chanting it from attending regular prayer services while growing up, but never really understood the meaning of the words in Hebrew. Now, after living in Israel and speaking modern Hebrew fluently, I was shocked to discover that I suddenly understood the text. What we were chanting was erotic and descriptive, a beautiful love poem with so many sexual references.

I had a great time during my visit reconnecting with a few of my old school friends still living in town. I was able to go with my parents to Rabbi Yehya Lekhdar and pray once more at Synagogue Ettedgui. I saw my friend Daniel Mechaly who so kindly hid me in his family's storage room in their building during the conflict with my parents to try to force them to let me move to Israel. I went with Daniel and a small group of local friends on a side trip to discover for the second time the city of Marrakech. Also, I introduced Daniel to Nicole, a friend I had met at the University of Haifa campus. Nicole had decided to return home to her parents in Casablanca. A few years later, Daniel and Nicole were to get married and move to New York.

Sinai

The Sinai desert in the 1970s was very isolated and difficult to access due to lack of established roads leading to its interior. The main asphalted road went along the shoreline on both sides of the peninsula, and if navigating the rough terrain off-road, hopefully you had a high clearance, four-wheel-drive vehicle. The remoteness, the difficulty, and the isolation made it a unique destination to seek solace and enjoy scenic wilderness. We, the guides of Neot Hakikar, were passionately fascinated and attracted to its natural beauty. We were constantly exploring, trekking through its canyons and climbing its mountain tops, wanting to reach and discover its most isolated corners. Among our team of guides, the ultimate challenge was to find a new wadi, a new shortcut to a mountain pass, a hidden canyon or secret valley, or a new vista.

The logo of the company with a fennec, or desert fox

Looking For Home

We spent a lot of time with our local Bedouin friends, quizzing them about the topography and distances and about the history of their tribes. With our all-terrain, six-wheeled vehicles, we felt like landlords of the desert, in total control, roaming the vast expanse of land, constantly on the move. Equipped with plenty of fresh water and a food supply to last a few days, we roamed from the Sinai High Mountain Region in the center to the sand dunes, sandstone bluffs, and canyons to the east and west, and to the magnificent, isolated coves and fine sand beaches along the shoreline of the turquoise waters of the Red Sea.

I loved every minute of my work and took great pleasure sharing my passion and fascination with Sinai with the variety of groups coming from faraway places to experience it. Having a captive group audience which most of time included single, attractive female travelers who were attracted to the guides did enhance the whole experience. I was in my mid-twenties working long hours outdoors, driving, guiding, cooking, and leading long hikes, and I was enjoying some occasional romances as well.

Neot Hakikar Sinai Tours, 1975

It usually took about a day or two for participants to get a feel for the concepts of our desert camping safari tours. Many times a special bond would be created between me and a particular group, mostly the French Club Med groups. On the last night of camping, wanting to enhance their experience, I would arrange with a local Bedouin friend to purchase from him a live lamb and have it slaughtered on the spot, to be processed, cooked, and served for our last dinner. At the end of the day, after having chosen the right spot for our camp, we would unpack the gear, unload everything, getting the kitchen organized, and choosing a good spot for the nightly group campfire. Often some Bedouin friends camping out nearby would show up and sit with us around our campfire. We would chat and exchange stories with them.

Sometimes, to break the routine and to really enhance the group experience, I would decide with my teammate to make a change to our itinerary by driving extra miles to reach on the last night a hard-to-get-to magic spot along the coast. Ras Abu Galum is an incredible, deep blue lagoon located in a cove surrounded on all sides by steep cliffs. The access was either by sea or along the coast coming from the north. On most trips, I would be coming from the west, through the interior and heading east to the coast before heading back north to Eilat to conclude the tour. Coming from the west, one difficult access to the lagoon was a shortcut driving down a long, narrow, winding, rocky riverbed for a few hours. The dry riverbed, a wadi, required some hard driving and extra effort navigating through it, but at the end of the narrow canyon, after one last twisted curve, it suddenly opened up almost like a river finally reaching its destination as the canyon walls finally opened up to a beautiful beach on the edge of the deep blue sea.

Looking For Home

Sinai Tours 1975

If timed properly to arrive in the evening hours, the group of tourists would be completely taken by surprise. They never expected that after such a long, bumpy ride they would suddenly emerge from the deep, dusty, rocky canyon to the expanse of deep blue sea, with red granite mountains in the background on the other side of the gulf waters. The setting sun reflecting on the mountains enhanced their deep red-purple color, possibly one explanation for how the Red Sea got its name. Once close to the water, after driving the last few yards approaching the cove, I would stop the truck, killing the engine, then jump out and start running toward the water, followed shortly by most of the group. Within minutes, all were swimming, on some occasions totally naked, in the deep blue, clear water, being refreshed after several days roaming in the dry desert.

Several canyons in the Sinai had spring water running through them for a short distance in their most narrow segment. One of the most scenic natural features in Sinai are the oases formed from underground rivers or aquifers such as an artesian aquifer, where water can reach the surface naturally by pressure or through man-made wells. Sometimes as the wadi between the canyon walls narrows, underlying rock can trap water in pockets or on underground fault ridges or volcanic dikes. The underground water can collect and rise to the surface to create pools and swimming holes. I am thinking of the Ein Umm Ahmed oasis and Ein Fortaga that we often visited on our tours and refreshed ourselves in the flowing fresh water on a regular basis in South Sinai.

My brother Sam was one day walking along the banks of the Seine River in Paris browsing the many used booksellers' stands along the river and found a rare, out-of-print book about Sinai, published in 1951 in Egypt. It was a full study and complete survey of the Sinai desert, written in French by a couple based in Egypt. This French couple built a home in one of the valleys on the western part of Sinai and while living on-site began an extensive, detailed study of all the natural aspects of the peninsula, including terrain, topography, flora, fauna, and also the Bedouin tribes, as well as drawing detailed maps and pictures. Sam and his wife offered me the book with a nice dedication written on one of the pages, dated February 1977.

An interesting anecdote regarding that book about Sinai. At least once a year Neot Hakikar, as a special treat to its staff of guides, used to put together a special outing in the desert just for the guides to relax and bond, spending a few days together touring and exploring some hidden or out of the way areas. These guides-only trips often involved trekking to a mountaintop or riding camels into remote areas, accompanied by their Bedouin owners. During one of these outings where we were using several camels to haul our camping equipment, I was relaxing one evening lying on my sleeping bag and reading my French Sinai book. When I noticed that seated nearby was one of the older Bedouin men, I laid down my book and we started conversing. I quizzed him about certain details of the area where we had just set up camp, and after a while he asked me about my book. After I explained some about the author and the contents, to my total surprise he recalled as a young boy knowing the author and his wife, describing to me in detail his general appearance as a tall man. He knew his name, the fact that he was French, and the exact location of the house they built and lived in for a few years while conducting their study and survey of the Sinai Peninsula.

Military Reserve Duty (Miluim)

While living and working in Jerusalem, I, like most Israelis, continued doing my military duty, which involved serving between thirty and forty days each calendar year in military service, commonly called *miluim*, or reserve duty. I had to present myself for an interview to decide what type of unit I was going to be assigned to. The first time, to my great surprise the officer interviewing me was an old friend of mine, Zeev Krakovsky. We were so happy to reconnect after losing track of each other. Right away we decided to go to lunch and catch up on our lives.

Zeev was the only other immigrant with me during the few weeks I was in the officer-training course. He tried to influence me not to give up, telling me that even if we were not the top candidates, with only a basic knowledge of Hebrew compared to the native boys, that we should make them kick us out and not bail out on our own. He followed his own advice and stayed on to finally graduate and become a lieutenant. Zeev, still in uniform, was serving the extra year required when becoming an officer.

Since most of my guide buddies at Neot Hakikar were from prestigious combat units, I felt I needed to do better. I asked Lieutenant Zeev to assign my file for duty in combat units as much as possible. After a few months, my first miluim service order came by mail. I was assigned to an infantry unit guarding the border south of the Golan Heights, at the corner of the three countries—Israel, Jordan, and Syria. I would patrol at night in an armored vehicle, a BTR-152, a segment of the border between Jordan and Israel.

The border was relatively quiet. It was controlled and guarded during the day by several bunker observation outposts on high ground, scattered along the border every couple of miles. Every night before going out on patrol, we lined up to check our gear and weapons ammunitions as well as to hear special instructions to follow before opening fire on suspicious activities along the border. A squad of infantry combat soldiers in an armored personnel carrier equipped with a powerful spotlight would drive the whole night back and forth along a segment of about five or six miles. We would inspect the metal fence with concertina barbed wire on top, but most important, we examined the sand path along it.

The IDF back then had created along most of its borders a series of obstacles. A tall metal fence ran the whole length of the border. Just inside the fence was a fine dirt and sand path the width of a vehicle, and next to it was a regular paved, narrow road. The idea was that before sunset every day, a special armored vehicle would drive on the dirt and sand path along the metal fence, dragging a large rake to comb and smooth the path. As soon as it got dark, the first shift of the night patrol on the BTR was to start driving on the paved road while pointing the spotlight along the parallel sand path and the high metal fence, and checking meticulously for any footprints or markings on the sand, making sure nobody tried to breach and cross the border coming from the Jordan side of the border.

I was in charge of driving the six-wheeled armored BTR. Next to me, sitting on top and handling the big spotlight, was an Israeli-Arab Bedouin scout, a full-time, career IDF soldier from the Bedouin Scout company. His job was to decipher any suspicious print or marking left on the freshly combed sand path as well as look for any possible breach of the metal fence. The first shift was for the first half of the night, and the second shift for the second part until daybreak. After sunrise, the orders were to have four soldiers from the squad on foot, with full combat gear, walking in front of the vehicle in a special formation behind the scout. They actually had to walk the whole distance of our assigned segment before declaring that segment officially open for the day.

One night, after volunteering for it, I was assigned to a different night activity. Without too much explanation, I was asked to get behind the wheel of an armored M3 half-track with a heavy mortar unit set up in the bed behind the driving compartment. I joined a whole convoy of several armored vehicles, and after dark we drove a few miles toward the Jordan River and parked on a hilltop, on the side of a small road. Our orders were to remain there most of the night, waiting for more instructions.

After a while, most of the soldiers in the convoy became bored, so they gathered around one of the vehicles which had a radio and listened to activities going on nearby. Within a few hours, I realized that I was part of a backup force on standby while a special forces unit was conducting a secret exploratory mission on the other side of the Jordan River, on Jordanian territory. They were to check, measure, and make a quick survey of the surroundings, like the riverbanks and other important strategic features. Apparently, this was an annual thing to secretly send a special task unit to locate and mark specific potential crossing points along the Jordan River, just in case war broke out between Jordan and Israel and it was necessary to send tanks and troops across the other side.

    The Israeli ranger unit was supposed to operate in total radio silence unless coming across trouble, and apparently during that night they did break their radio silence rules. A couple of special forces soldiers, operating in total darkness, strayed from the small group and found themselves in the middle of a minefield on the Jordanian side. It was either not properly marked or just overlooked on their maps. Luckily, nothing was triggered, but they had to freeze and stay put in their tracks, waiting for help to reach them. A special unit was on their way bringing special mats to line up on the ground all the way to the soldiers in order to extract them one at a time without anybody getting hurt. We followed the whole operation on the radio exchanges for several hours through the night until all was completed successfully and the unit made it back home to our side, undetected. The convoy I was part of was just normal procedure for backup fire power in case things went completely wrong. That would have been highly unusual since the border with Jordan during the mid-70s was considered very calm and stable, with farmers on both sides tending their fields during daytime.

    For my second miluim service a year later, I was sent to Mount Hermon to serve as a military ambulance driver, among other things. Mount Hermon was commonly nicknamed "the eyes and ears of Israel" on Syria and Lebanon. This important Israeli military outpost, sitting on the highest mountain in the whole region at 9,232 feet above sea level, was taken over in a surprise attack by Syrian commando forces the first day of the Yom Kippur War. Later during the war, it was claimed back by Israeli combat units from the Golani Brigade after a long, bloody battle. On the summit, due to its strategic importance, it is heavily fortified with bunkers used to observe and guard as well as serve as living quarters tunneled inside the rock. Halfway to the summit, there is another military base which is slightly bigger to accommodate and service all logistics for the large bunkers at the summit. I was to spend time at this location, driving mostly the military ambulance and a special large military truck with double axles and ten wheels to supply the summit outpost.

    I had to spend many nights at the summit, deep inside the heavily fortified bunker tunnels used as sleeping quarters for the soldiers. I remember that while on the summit base, certain areas of the compound were off limits and required special access codes. The reason was all the secret electronics devices constantly monitoring the Syrian capital Damascus which was only forty kilometers away, as the crow flies on the plain down below.

Turkey

At different times my brothers Samy, Armand, and Simon came to visit me in Israel. Moreover, I was able to arrange for them to go on a tour and enjoy for free a Sinai desert trip and a probably memorable camping experience. Armand, having lived in Israel and being more familiar with getting around the country, surprised me one day by coming all the way to Eilat and looking for me at our local truck compound in town. I was just finishing one of my tours and was on the last stretch, driving back along the coastline from Sinai. Our last stop was a secluded beach for a final swim and lunch before heading back to civilization.

    I noticed a jeep coming toward us, and as the vehicle got closer, I recognized one of the guides from Eilat. Seated next to him was Armand. I was very surprised and happy. Armand must have convinced whomever he spoke to in the office that he really needed to see me and surprise me, and that he did.

Since the tour was pretty much finished, the other guide switched places with me. I got in the jeep and drove back with Armand, catching up on the last three years since we saw each other. Armand decided to spend time in Eilat with me and was eager to join me on one of my desert tours. He went on several tours where I was guiding, meeting new friends enjoying the whole experience of discovering a total new style of travel and camping out in the desert. Samy and Simon got a chance as well to tag along with me on several trips and had their own fun experiences discovering the Sinai desert.

The Jerusalem apartment on Pinsker Street that I was sharing with my friend Moti and another guy, Dany Shemesh, was becoming a comfortable and enjoyable home to come back to every couple of weeks for a short break, like for a long weekend. The apartment was nicely decorated, and I enjoyed having friends over, often spending time in the kitchen cooking all kinds of meals for them. During my time off, when not in Sinai, I really loved living in Jerusalem and taking long walks through the different neighborhoods. Pinsker Street was conveniently located close to downtown Jerusalem, the German Colony, Mishkenot Sha'ananim, Yemin Moshe, Rehavia, and, of course, the Arab Old City and its famous historical sites where most of my hikes always ended up leading me, one way or another. Jerusalem will always remain for me one of the most unique sites in the world. I loved and cherished living there. The city fascinated me not only with its history, but its spirituality and its own unique architecture.

During the winter months, when the tourist season was not as busy, I would try to take a few weeks off and travel to Europe, spending time roaming around France visiting family and friends. While in France in 1977, I watched live on French TV as the Egyptian president, Anouar el Assad, made his now famous historic visit to Israel, starting the process leading later to the Camp David Accords between Israel and Egypt. The peace treaty that would result in the Sinai desert being gradually returned to Egyptian control.

With that peace treaty being negotiated, Rudy, Avi, and Menahem, the three main partners in Neot Hakikar, had to be considering all their options in light of unraveling political developments and the possibility they would lose their main source of revenue if Sinai was returned to Egypt. Rudy, being the main person in charge of marketing, finances, and PR, was considering expanding or developing alternative tours. Originally from Istanbul, Turkey, Rudy moved to Israel in the late 1950s and developed an extensive network of connections within the tourism industry.

One idea Rudy had was to expand to neighboring Mediterranean countries like Greece and Turkey. Neot Hakikar Desert Tours was doing an annual desert trip for a church group from Switzerland, and their leader and his organization were in charge of a Christian ecumenical program. They were considering taking a large group to tour Turkey. Within a few months, with Rudy traveling back and forth between Tel Aviv and Istanbul, he was able to offer them a twenty-one-day bus tour of Turkey. And since the group was Swiss and French-speaking, I was delegated to be in charge and accompany the group as a tour manager onsite. Therefore, in the summer of 1978, I was to spend three months in Turkey being in charge of the tours in that country.

Rudy and I left for Turkey and spent several days in Istanbul getting ready for the arrival of our first group. The idea was to use a custom-designed Christian itinerary called "In the Footsteps of St. Paul" to explore the country. Later we were able to market our own version of a tour exploring the best tourist sites in Turkey. While we were getting ready, I was able to reconnect with some of my Turkish friends from Aloney Itshak high school who had returned to live in Istanbul.

Rudy and I on the appointed day were ready at the Istanbul international airport to welcome our first group with trays of *lokum*, the Turkish gel candy. We had a luxurious bus with a Turkish local driver and a young, bilingual French-English, licensed tour guide. Our first group would go on an extended, almost three-week tour of the country. After spending a few days visiting the main sites in Istanbul, we were on the road. My job was to make sure all the logistics during our two-week drive across Turkey went smoothly, handling the technical details like hotel and restaurant reservations. This was a big change from the Sinai desert trips, but I enjoyed discovering Turkey with all its major archaeological sites, museums, and rich history, before it became such a popular tourist destination in the last three decades. Our itinerary took us south along the Aegean coast, connecting with the Turquoise Coast on the Mediterranean Sea, heading east and then north and inland into the Anatolian Plateau, then completing the loop by coming back to Istanbul.

After Turkey, the plan was to develop another itinerary in neighboring Greece and market it in Israel and Europe. Back in Jerusalem I was put in charge of exploring and scouting a circuit through mainland Greece. Meanwhile, the Camp David Peace Accords between Egypt and Israel were signed, agreeing for the Sinai Peninsula to be handed back over to the control of Egypt. After the last three years guiding in Sinai, I was getting slightly worn out from being on the road constantly, leading consecutive trips. I started looking at my options and considering several possible moves.

One idea I had was going back to school to get a national guiding license for the whole country as well as a special driving permit so I could get my own private limousine to cater to small groups and individuals for personal, private tours. I applied and got accepted to start my studies in the early part of 1979.

Rudy, upon hearing of my plans to move on, put a lot of pressure on me to remain in Neot Hakikar. We had developed a very warm and special relationship. He started making me enticing offers to join the office staff based in Jerusalem, creating for me a new position. He offered for me to be in charge of logistics for Greece and Turkey group trips as well as to continue marketing the Sinai desert trips to several French touring agencies interested in starting their trips from Egypt. I would still have to guide or train new guides for ten days a month down in Sinai, but the rest of the time I would have my own desk to work from in the Jerusalem main office. After giving it serious consideration, I decided to postpone my training course and accept his offer for the new position. At the end of fall of 1978, as I was training a new guide in the Sinai, I was to meet my wife-to-be, Deborah.

Deborah

I was in Eilat getting my truck rigged and ready before heading out to the meeting place to pick up my group coming down that morning by bus from Jerusalem. In the warehouse, while packing the REO, I met Ephy, the younger brother of my good friend Timi (RIP), one of the most experienced, knowledgeable Sinai guides. I would be leading and training Ephy on this trip, letting him practice his English to address the group on one of his first guiding assignments. Moshe, another new guide who had been working in the shop for several days, was dying for a change of scenery and begged me to let him join us to escape the boring work in the shop. Since the trip was not completely full, on my own initiative I let him get his small backpack and jump in with us for the trip.

Once my group was on board, we started our five-day, four-night typical itinerary. The seventeen or eighteen men and women participants were from different countries and backgrounds. As we headed south, due to the weather and the early winter season I decided that after lunch on the first day we would leave the shoreline and the main paved road along the Red Sea coast and head inland toward the dunes and sandstone bluffs of the oasis of Ein Hudrah.

For our campsite the first night, I selected a wide, sandy canyon surrounded by amazing sculpted sandstone bluffs. As the sun was setting, its last rays reflected a variety of pink and golden-yellow colors on the sandstone rocks, I was enjoying what was always one of my best moments of the trip. As I was unloading the trailer, humming to myself a Jacques Brel French song, one of the ladies walking nearby and overhearing my singing, surprised me by addressing me in French. She asked me in perfectly good French if I spoke French. She had assumed we guides were native Israelis. I had assumed, having heard her previously conversing in Spanish, that she was either from Argentina or Latin American. This was my first introduction to Deborah, who came all the way from the state of Texas, which sounded like an exotic place and brought memories of the popular Western movie culture. I thought how unusual it was for an

Deborah on Mount Sinai during our first encounter, 1978

American to be fluent in two foreign languages, French and Spanish.

Later that night, small cooking tasks were assigned in the camp kitchen with four volunteers, Deborah being one of them. She decided to argue with me about how to cut the tomatoes for the fresh salad. I wanted them in small cubes, the typical Israeli way, but she wanted them in larger slices, the American way. And something else about the cooking of the schnitzel . . . . It seemed like we would be a challenge to each other from right off the bat.

The next morning at first daylight, Ephy was standing next to my sleeping bag letting me know he had had a rough night. He was feeling ill and losing his voice due to what seemed to be a throat infection. Ephy would require getting evacuated as he couldn't really continue on the trip. Once everyone was packed and on board, I cranked up the engine and noticed right away a problem with the motor. The water pump was making a hissing noise, alerting me that its ball bearings and belt were on the verge of breaking. I was confronted with two major issues to solve—one mechanical in nature, to have the motor repaired right away before getting any deeper into the desert, and a second, slightly less urgent, to find a way to evacuate the official guide trainee, Ephy, and take over the group guiding myself.

I came up with a plan of how to achieve both. I decided to take my chances and drive another half hour with the hissing pump to a small Bedouin store I knew was located close to a crossroads. Once there I would try to get a message to Eilat headquarters, to either send me another vehicle or a new water pump and to transfer Ephy and have Moshe step up as my assistant for the continuation of the trip.

Once we made it to the Bedouin camp with the motor still working, I luckily ran into one of our company jeeps driven by Avi, who happened to be on his way to Eilat. Everything got sorted out, and while the mechanical engine part was on its way to me, I decided that instead of having the whole group stuck waiting for the vehicle to be repaired, I would come up with an extra fun activity for them. I asked my local Bedouin friend Jumaa to round up and bring to us a dozen camels, saddled up to take my whole group on a three-hour ride to visit a beautiful green oasis nearby, to include a hike through a scenic white sandstone canyon. A few hours

Deborah on camelback in Sinai, 1978

Deborah

Deborah and I spent more time together, having some interesting conversations, mostly in French, late at night around the campfire, under the magnificent desert night sky peppered by thousands of shining stars. She was visiting Israel with a good friend of hers, Suzanna, originally from Mexico. Suzanna had stayed behind in Jerusalem. Deborah and Suzanna were both living in Houston, Texas, and were on an extensive trip traveling around and visiting several countries. They had started in Eastern Europe, stopping to visit for a few days the major cities and tourist sites. After Istanbul, Turkey, they made it to Israel and planned to continue on to Egypt, Italy, and France, finishing their itinerary in Paris and from there returning home to Houston.

On Thursday morning, the last day of the trip as we were heading back to Eilat, Deborah and I made plans to stay in touch and get together in Jerusalem during the upcoming weekend. I was supposed to wrap up the tour and bring the group to the town of Eilat on the edge of Sinai, where a bus would be waiting to drive them the rest of the way to Jerusalem.

My plans were to fly the next day to Jerusalem and spend the weekend with Deborah showing her around the city. When I got back to the guides' apartment in Eilat, I had a message to call the office and report. Once on the phone with Rudy I understood that plans had changed, and a lot of pressure was put on me trying to convince me to stay in Eilat over the weekend in order to lead another group to Sinai the following Monday. I strongly objected, explaining to Rudy that I had just met a special girl whom I liked very much. I even told him I thought I had met my future wife. Rudy convinced me to stay, begging me to help him out by taking this VIP French-speaking group because he really did not have any other French guide available.

Upset and disappointed by the change of plans, I decided the next morning to call the phone number in Jerusalem Deborah had given me. Suzanna and Deborah were staying at a small bed and breakfast. While explaining the change of plans, that I had to remain in Eilat to get ready for my next group, I suggested for Deb to get on a bus the next day and come back south to spend the weekend with me in Eilat. My suggestion sounded great, except that she couldn't abandon Suzanna alone in Jerusalem. Would I consider extending the invitation to include her as well?

While waiting for the girls to get to Eilat, I decided to make a good impression by cleaning up and sorting out our guides' apartment. Our tour company put at our disposal several apartments for the team of guides to use while in town either before or after trips. I passed the word around the local office that we were not to be disturbed. I got the apartment cleaned and got the place ready. I decided to cook some food and get some wine, looking forward to the visit.

The weekend went very well. I enjoyed very much spending time with my new girlfriend. The next day, Saturday, I even came up with a brilliant idea—to introduce Suzanna to my friend Moti, who was just getting back in town from Sinai. Saturday night we went out together, the two couples. All was going super well, and it looked like Moti and Suzanna were hitting it off rather well. That night, we made plans for the next day.

Since Suzanna hadn't yet been on one of our desert tours, she was invited and gladly accepted to join Moti on his next group departure scheduled to start Sunday midday. Deborah was also invited to tag along. She couldn't really join me and my upcoming tour since my group was traveling together and were all acquainted with each other. The idea was that Moti would have the two girls with him since his group was made up of individual participants coming from Jerusalem. They would leave on Sunday and I would leave on Monday with my French group flying in together. I would try to catch up to Moti in order to meet at night by setting our group campsites near each other.

Our plan worked perfectly. Suzanna discovered the Sinai desert Neot Hakikar Safari-style with her friend Deb by her side, and at the same time she fell in love with my friend and roommate Moti. I have a funny memory of that trip, while I was trying to catch up with Moti's group and not miss our point of rendezvous.

On the second day of my trip, I was approaching the Saint Catherine Monastery located at the foot of Mount Sinai for the traditional visit after the climb to the mountain. A small group of young Bedouin boys was always hanging around welcoming us as we pulled next to the monastery. These boys knew all the guides and always looked forward to our weekly visits as we would always joke with them in Arabic and often give them small treats. This time one of them had a message for me from Moti letting me know where to meet up with him later for camping and making sure to add with a big smile on his face that my American girlfriend would be there as well. So even the Bedouin knew that Deborah was someone special to me.

After that second Sinai trip and return to Jerusalem, the four of us — Moti, Suzanna, Deb and I — spent time living together in my apartment on Pinsker Street. During our first Sinai trip, when I asked Deborah about her occupation, she had responded that she was an accordionist, which I thought was a joke of some kind. As it turned out, she had been playing that instrument since she was seven years old and played professionally. Additionally she had also founded a language school and technical translation business called Professional Language Services which she had sold before leaving on her world trip. While living together in Jerusalem, she was able to rent an accordion, and a couple of times brought it out at different parties and social gatherings with our small group of friends in Jerusalem. To everyone's enjoyment and admiration, she played some great music.

Deborah and accordion, Houston, 1977

While in Jerusalem, Deborah had to suddenly leave to travel home to the US due to a family emergency. Deb's father back in Texas was terminally ill, and she needed to be by his side. During that time, I also had to travel to Greece to explore and check out a new fifteen-day itinerary that we were planning to market and offer in the upcoming summer of 1979. Moti decided to join me and requested as a special favor that I extend an invitation to Suzanna. Even though this was strictly a working trip, I agreed, and soon we were all four or five of us packed in one vehicle crisscrossing the whole country of mainland Greece from the south to north, putting together a detailed future itinerary.

Once we all got back to Jerusalem, we two couples developed a kind of routine sharing the apartment on Pinsker Street. One morning, Moti and I were sitting on the balcony sipping our morning coffee while admiring our beautiful view from the apartment, with Deborah and Suzanna seated on our laps. Very famous for his sarcastic, funny, particular Israeli humor, Moti started a short conversation in Hebrew so the girls could not understand us.

"Life is good, man...what else can a man wish for, but maybe a nice, good-looking girlfriend sitting on his lap right now..."

I responded laughing, as that is exactly what we had at this moment.

Moti asked, "So Buddy, are you happy?"

"Yes, I am."

"Are you falling in love? Getting attached?"

"I think so...how about you?"

"Yes, I am too." After a moment of silence, he said, "I have never been here before. So what are we supposed to do next?"

We both burst out laughing and decided to switch from Hebrew to English and let the girls participate in the conversation, trying to figure out what could be the best way to move forward, to continue our simultaneous romances.

Within a few days, after considering all our options we came up with what we thought might be the best scenario for all. Since the girls were in the middle of a big trip and already had airplanes tickets, it was decided they would continue on to the previously scheduled two more countries of their original itinerary, Italy and France. Once in Paris at the end of their trip, the four of us would consult by phone and come up with a solution. We would either join them there, or they would come back for good to Jerusalem. In essence, we were just postponing major decisions while Moti and I looked into our options with local jobs. Before the girls left to continue their trip, I wanted to tour Israel with Deborah and show her the main tourist sites, so just the two of us rented a car and went on a road trip for several days driving all over the country.

Sometime around the end of 1978, at the same period of my romance with Deborah in Jerusalem, both my parents were visiting Israel from Morocco and came to visit me in Jerusalem. My father had four of his sisters living in Israel and he enjoyed very much spending time visiting them. He took great pleasure being around them, particularly Sol and Fiby. His sisters always showed him great love, respect, and admiration, my father being the only surviving boy after losing his two other brothers.

My father as a religious man had always entertained the dream of one day making the big move from Morocco to the Holy Land, coming to settle and retire in a small cottage similar to that of his younger sister Fiby, surrounded with a small yard planted with different fruit trees. I remember when he was in Israel and I was visiting him at my aunt Tata Fiby's small cottage in Migdal Haemek. I would find him usually outside in the front yard seated with family members around him under the shade of a lemon tree, often mentioning how he would love one day to retire and live nearby.

My parents came to spend the day visiting me in Jerusalem, and I showed them my apartment and took them around to visit the city. I took my father to visit Yad Vashem, the Holocaust history museum. I could see on his face how difficult it was for him to have maybe for the first time discovered through the exhibitions the grueling details and the extent of the methodical massacres suffered by the European Jewry.

During that year in 1978, when my father was on his way back to Morocco from Israel, while stopping in France for a few days he had to be hospitalized with his first minor heart attack. He was fifty-eight years old. He was released after about a two-week stay in the hospital and was prescribed blood thinner medication and probably some follow up treatments that I am not sure he stuck to. Jacqueline, my sister living in Paris, was very helpful during his hospitalization, constantly by his bedside making sure he was well taken care off, especially with his kosher diet requirement.

Once Deborah and Suzanna left, I was back working at the office in Jerusalem getting ready for a busy summer putting together and leading new tours and circuits in Greece. Neot Hakikar in the last few years was also involved in a real estate project, building and running a small motel located at the Sinai airport, a short distance from Mount Sinai and the Saint Catherine Monastery. I was asked at one time to move there for several weeks, to replace temporarily the local manager and run the motel, which was an interesting experience spending time living in Sinai.

Sometime later, Deborah and Suzanna, having reached their final destination and staying in Paris, had to make some decisions. Deborah decided she wanted to stay longer in France and to study music in the fall. In the meantime, she had found a job during the summer playing the accordion in a local French band in the south of France. Suzanna went back to Houston while Deborah moved to live in the town of Nice in southern France.

Early in the summer of 1979, Deborah flew to meet me in Athens, Greece, where I had just arrived and where I would be based to run the Greek tours. Our reunion was very emotional, and we were both very happy to be together after the numerous letters and phone calls of the last couple months. After our reunion, Deborah had to get back to Nice for a few days to fulfill some gigs she had committed to play with her touring French band. She promised to come back and catch up with our tour somewhere along the way.

After a few days in Athens, we welcomed our first small group and the first Neot Hakikar fourteen-day Greek road trip got under way. I had Aaron and Carolina helping me. On the third night of the trip we were camping out on the outskirts of the historical ruins of Delphi. Deborah surprised everyone by showing up at the campground by taxi directly from the Athens airport, dragging behind a suitcase and her famous accordion. Her presence and the sound of the accordion contributed tremendously to a fun ambiance and very pleasant experience at the campground.

During the Greek trip, while camping and discovering mainland Greece with our small group, Deb and I came to realize that we wanted to be together and make plans for our future. I knew I wanted to marry her. I proposed to her one night while we were camping in a small village in the northwest corner of Greece, not far from the border of Greece, Albania, and at the time Yugoslavia, now North Macedonia. We had our tents set up in the backyard of the local village church with the approval of the bearded Greek Orthodox priest. That night I had organized to have dinner with the whole group in a typical Greek restaurant overlooking a beautiful lake nearby in the mountains.

The two of us were making our way back at night through the alleys of the small village. I got down on my knee to propose and almost got run over by a herd of sheep following their shepherd to cross the little main square of the village, right across from the church. We decided to get married and decide later where to live together.

After completing the trip and getting to our final hotel in Athens, Rudy welcomed us in the lobby, wanting to make sure all went well. He wanted us to be ready for the next group coming a few days later. A couple hours later, from my hotel room I phoned Rudy in his room and told him the latest news—that I had decided to get married. I also had to let him know that I was resigning and would not be able to continue working for the company in either Greece or Israel. I made sure to explain to him as well that I had taken detailed notes about the whole itinerary and trained my two assistants, Aaron and Carolina. I assured him that both were up the task to take over and run the next group.

Thessaloniki, Eastern Greece, 1979

Rudy got upset and was very disappointed. He hung up on me. After a couple hours, the phone rang in my room. It was Rudy calling back with a totally different attitude, first to apologize, and second, since I had made up my mind and there wasn't much he could do to dissuade me, to invite both of us to go out and celebrate our engagement. Rudy had previously met Deborah on different occasions, like at parties and get-togethers in Jerusalem. He called around town and reserved a dinner table at a local steakhouse, appropriately called Texas. During dinner, many toasts were raised, and Rudy offered us his best wishes for a happy life together wherever we might end up.

Athens, Greece, 1979

Deb and I had made the decision to get married, but we were not sure at all where we would settle—in which country, or how we would make a life together. The main thing was to stay together. One idea I considered was the possibility of applying to study at a hotel management school in Europe, either in France or Switzerland. But first things first, we had to let our families know.

Deb wanted to introduce me to her family back in Texas, and for that, I needed to look at getting a tourist visa with my Israeli passport to get into the US. Therefore, the next day we went to the US embassy in Athens to look into our options. I explained my case to the young American staffer behind the desk about wanting to join my fiancée to travel to Texas to meet her family. As much as he sympathized with our love story of having first met in the Sinai Desert in Israel and deciding to get married while on a Greek tour, the agent went on to explain that since I was an Israeli citizen, I had to make that request in Israel at the local consulate in Tel Aviv. The US embassy in Athens was only supposed to process Greek nationals.

The agent was curious about my background, asking me about my military service in Israel and the 1973 Yom Kippur War. When I responded that I was enlisted at the time and actively involved, he mentioned that at that same time he was serving in the US military, posted somewhere on a major US airbase in Germany, and was busy for several days loading up airplanes full of gear and ammunitions to resupply the Israeli military in the prolonged days of the war that lasted more than three weeks. I thanked him and assured him that, indeed, all the US aid, clothing, equipment, and military gear was highly appreciated and put to good use by the troops. Toward the end of the interview, seduced by our love story and wanting to show his support for us, he took it upon himself to stamp my passport and give me a three-month visa to visit the US, without the hassle of going through the embassy process in Israel.

A few days later, Deb and I flew together from Athens to Nice, where we spent a few days in Deborah's rented apartment meeting her friends. Deborah had been living in Nice and playing the accordion with a small band. The plan was to go to Paris together to introduce Deb to my older brother Sam. After that, she would continue on to Texas to start planning our wedding, while I would fly back to Jerusalem and make my own plans to join her in Texas about a month later.

When we got to Paris, the situation with Sam was not ideal. He had just been notified that Genevieve, his wife, had filed for divorce. Nevertheless, Sam made his best efforts to welcome both of us. He was delighted to meet Deborah and was totally charmed by her. He took us around Paris and one day organized a scenic outing to visit Normandy and the picturesque town of Honfleur.

Honfleur, Normandy, France, 1979

Back in Jerusalem, I finalized my plans, arranging with my roommate at Pinsker Street to be gone for possibly a couple months. I also had several phone calls and letter exchanges with my parents in Casablanca, letting them know about my engagement and plans to get married in the US. My parents were very disappointed and concerned by the fact that Deborah was not born Jewish. They disapproved of my plans, but I was committed to Deborah and knew that we would build a good life together. And we certainly have created a wonderful family life with two exceptional sons, our lovely daughter-in-law, Sivan, and our sweet grandchildren. When asked about the secret to the success of our 40 plus year marriage, I like to paraphrase George Burns by saying the key to a great marriage is to marry Deborah.

A Texas Wedding, 1979

After about a month in Jerusalem, I flew from Tel Aviv to the small town of San Angelo, Texas, with two large suitcases. I spent two nights on the way—one night in Amsterdam and the second in Dallas. Until then, I had never been to the US and really didn't have much interest in visiting there. But because of the world-famous American movie industry, I had always been fascinated by the Western cowboy culture and the somewhat exotic history of the West and Texas.

When I landed at the Dallas airport, it was late at night. I had a hotel voucher reserved and paid for in Israel to spend a night at a Holiday Inn somewhere in town while waiting to catch the next day's flight in a small plane to the town of San Angelo in West Texas. When I got on the shuttle bus, the driver asked me which Holiday Inn I wanted, mentioning the existence of five or six in the Dallas area. No address details were mentioned on my voucher. The shuttle driver tried to help me find a few Holiday Inn locations around the airport, finally dropping me off at one.

The front desk did not have any record of my reservation. Exhausted as I was after such a long flight, I just wanted to book a room. Unfortunately, that particular hotel was fully booked and could not accommodate me. By then it must have been around two in the morning. The front desk clerk was a very nice person, and realizing I was a foreigner and stranded in the middle of the night, he tried to be helpful and find a solution. After waiting for a while in the hotel lobby, I asked the clerk to get me a cab. I decided the best thing to do was to get back in a cab with my luggage and drive around to the many hotels around the airport until I could find a room somewhere. Around 3:00 a.m., very exhausted, I was finally able to book myself a room in a luxurious five-star hotel, just to get a few hours of sleep and clean up before catching my connecting flight to San Angelo.

The next day, Deborah was happy to see me. Her parents, who had always lived and worked in the Houston area, had decided after reaching retirement age to enjoy living next to their older daughter, Holly, and her husband, Jim Bob, in Eldorado. Holly and Jim, who was a physician, had decided to get away from life in the big city of Houston and find a small rural community to raise a family and where Jim could practice medicine. Eldorado, Texas, forty-five miles south of San Angelo, ended up being their choice. It was a tiny town of fewer than 2,000 people, in the middle of nowhere.

Jim was able to have a small hospital built, then a nursing home, and now there is a larger hospital and even a wellness center. He practiced medicine there for many years. Fay and Winnie Helen, Deb's parents, moved from Houston to Eldorado to be near Holly and Jim and for Fay to get personal medical care at the small hospital. I never had the chance to meet Deb's father, Fay Joseph Hilliard, but I have heard that he was a very good man. He passed away early on in 1979 after battling cancer for the last four years of his life.

Deborah wanted me to meet her mother, Winnie Helen, and her sister, Holly. Winnie Helen was very courteous and polite meeting me for the first time, but she, like my own parents, made sure to let me know politely but with a firm stand that she did not approve of our union. She was deeply concerned that with our

A Texas Wedding, 1979

different cultural backgrounds, religions, and mentalities, we stood very little chance to make a viable couple trying to make a living in Texas. She was a very admirable woman who lived her life with great integrity, and over the years we came to have a mutually respectful and affectionate relationship.

Deborah and I were married in Houston on September 16, 1979, in a civil ceremony by a local judge friend of the family. We had a patio ceremony at a beautiful Mexican restaurant, la Hacienda de Los Morales. Deborah's family and friends were there, and on my side my brother Sam flew in from Paris and my twenty-year-old younger brother Michel flew in from upstate New York, where he was living as a student.

Houston, Texas, September 16, 1979

Hilliard - Ben-Nun Patio Ceremony

Miss Deborah-Doris Lisette Hilliard of Houston will become the bride of Robert Ben-Nun of Casablanca, Morocco (a resident of Israel for the past ten years) in the patio of La Hacienda de Los Morales on Sunday, September 16, 1979. The double ring ceremony will be performed by Judge Lee Duggan, Jr., at five o'clock in the evening. A dinner dance for one hundred and fifty wedding guests will follow the ceremony, with music provided by the Bernie Hatch Orchestra and Roberto Compean.

The bride is the daughter of Mrs. Winnie Helen Hilliard, a native Houstonian who currently resides in Eldorado, Texas. Mrs. Hilliard will wear a gown of medium green with a flowing chiffon overlay of pale green with a darker green fern print for her daughter's wedding. She will wear a white orchid corsage.

The groom is the son of Mr. and Mrs. David Benayoun of Casablanca, Morocco.

For her wedding, the bride has chosen an all-lace gown with bouffant skirt flowing into a cathedral length train. The sheer fitted bodice features a high neckline and ruffled yoke which forms the suggestion of a sleeve. She will wear a Spanish comb in her hair with bridal illusion flowing to waist length and will carry a fan embellished with a bouquet of white gardenias, pink roses and ivy.

The groom and his attendants will wear traditional black tuxedos, white ruffled shirts and black bow ties. The groom's shirt will feature a wing collar.

Serving as her sister's matron of honor is Mrs. Helen Bramer of Eldorado, Texas, who will wear a pink chiffon print with lavendar flowers. Maid of honor is Suzanne Lezana of Mexico and Houston, moving to Israel. Bridesmaids are both nieces of the bride — Amy Hilliard of Houston and Elizabeth Brame of Eldorado. The attendants will wear floor length pink gowns with lavendar sashes. All of the bride's attendants will carry pink silk flowers made by Mimi Hilliard, sister-in-law of the bride, and will wear matching flowers in their hair. The groom's attendants will have matching pale pink silk boutonieres. The groom will wear a white rose.

Best man is the groom's brother, Sam Benayoun of Paris, France. Groomsmen are Michael Benayoun, brother of the groom, of New York, New York; Chris Hilliard and Bud Hilliard, brothers of the bride, of Houston; and Dr. J. B. Brame, brother-in-law of the bride, of Eldorado, Texas.

Pre-nuptial parties included a formal catered dinner for about thirty people in honor of the bride and groom on Friday, September 14, at the home of the bride's aunt and uncle, Dr. and Mrs. L. M. Vaughan; and an informal rehearsal dinner at the home of the bride's brother and his wife, Mr. and Mrs. Chris Hilliard, on Saturday, September 15th.

The bride and her family are all native Houstonians. She is a graduate of St. Mary's College, Notre Dame, Indiana; and the founder and a stockholder in Professional Language Services, Inc. Most recently, she has been affiliated with an orchestra playing on the Riviera in Nice, France, as an accordian player.

The groom resides in Jerusalem, Israel, and has been working with a tour agency, conducting tours through the Sinai Desert, Greece and Turkey.

A Texas Wedding, 1979

At our wedding. Sam on the left, Michel on the right, 9/16/1979

We debated for a while where we were going to settle. My vision of starting a new life in Texas, one of the largest states in the US, with so much open land and large pastures, was more of trying to find a place in a small town in the countryside, a rural setting. I was dreaming of a small ranch. During my first few days in Eldorado, I visited some of the ranches owned by family friends of Holly and Jim and was very attracted by the concept. Of course, I also knew I didn't have the slightest notion how to even start to get involved. The best advice given to me back then was from an older lady friend of the family, Mrs. Coop. She had been ranching all her life, with large land holdings of many thousands of acres that had been in her family for a couple generations. She recommended first going back to school and studying the field I was interested in and getting a degree before venturing into ranching. That was a most common sense piece of advice.

While trying to decide where to start our new life, we took a road trip across Texas in an old 1970 Cadillac Deville, the old Hilliard family car kindly sold to us by Deborah's mother. We visited several small towns across Texas, like Kerrville, Fredericksburg, Llano, and Blanco. We checked out San Antonio and finally decided to settle in Austin, a town of about 300,000 people back then in 1979. All the family, friends, and acquaintances in Texas were mostly in agreement in highly recommending Austin to us.

After spending a few days at a hotel near 290 and IH35, we found a small two-story, two-bedroom unit in a duplex located in Northwest Hills and signed a one-year lease. Deborah was able to get her furniture from storage in Houston delivered to Austin. A few days later, on my birthday in October, the doorbell rang at the duplex. My brother Michel, with a big smile on his face and with his suitcase and his *darbuka* drum, his favorite percussion instrument, was standing there wishing me a happy birthday. A surprise visit it was, after three days on the bus from New York to Texas. Apparently, Deborah had stayed in touch with him after he went back to New York after the wedding in September and convinced him to move to Texas, as a total surprise to me. She asked him to give up New York and move in with us to share our little two-bedroom apartment. I was very happy to see him.

Evelyne, Michel & Nanou

Evelyne was the sibling next in line after me. I always remember her as having a strong character. She was born on August 16, 1955 so she was 13 when I left. I didn't have much contact with her until around several years later when she came to Israel to volunteer on a kibbutz and ended up marrying her boyfriend. She had various adventures including working as a fille au pair with a family in New York and ended up moving to Montreal with her husband and young son, Nathan. She was instrumental in helping my younger sister and mother immigrate to Canada following the death of our father. She worked for many years as a social services youth counselor for the Quebec government and I admire that she went back to school at a relatively late stage in life to get her master's degree.

Michel the youngest of the six Benayoun boys, was born in August of 1959. His Hebrew name is Meyer-Shalom. He is 6 years younger than me. When I left Casablanca to move to Israel in 1969 he was about 10 years old, and after my departure for Israel, we lost touch and would not see each other again until a few year later in the late 1970's. While growing up in Casablanca, Michel, being the younger boy of the family, was the center of attention and very much loved. He was showered with much affection and love, not only by our parents but by us all his older siblings.

Michel always loved to play the Darbuka drums and would occasionally join in and play music with a local Moroccan band at different night clubs in town. When he was 16 years old, he quit school, decided to leave home and move to Paris to try his luck on his own at different sales jobs. After a few years in Paris Michel decided to move to upstate NY and attended school for a while at a community college also doing menial jobs such driving cabs and working selling clothes at a local flea market. When I invited him to come to Texas to attend my wedding, we reconnected, talked a lot about different options and possibilities of maybe creating a business together.

After the wedding, Michel moved to Texas and "Bonjour Boutique", an exclusive women's high fashion clothing store, was inaugurated towards the end of 1979. My friend from High school Albert Arditi was living at the time in NY and was himself a very successful owner of a dress factory in the garment district in Manhattan. Deb and I travelled frequently to NY, and with the coaching and advice from Albert, were able to establish lines of credit from different designers in the Manhattan Garment district and to fine tune our own selection of unique styles. The three of us Michel, Deborah and myself, worked very hard to make the business a success. Michel was an excellent salesman helping customers to find the right blouse, cocktail dress, dressy suit or designer jeans while charming the ladies with not only his French accent but his very unique and sharp taste in ladies fashion wear. In 1982, we sold the "Bonjour Boutique" store before moving away to Canada. Michel developed his own wholesale and retail shoe business in Austin before finally deciding to move back to live in Paris.

And finally we arrive to Nanou, the baby of the family. She was born on November 18, 1960. When I left she was 8 years old. She was very cute and being the baby of the family, she was spoiled with attention and love. Our father had not been a particularly demonstrative man, but with Nanou he was able to show his love and affection for her as the last of his children to leave home. She was very close to both our parents and she immigrated to Canada with our mother after our father died, living together with her until she got married. She has two wonderful children and still lives in Montreal having a successful career in the travel industry.

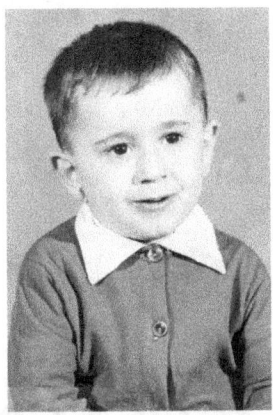

Michel, 1960

Michel, Estepona, 2006

Evelyne 1972 Morocco

Evelyne 2019 New York

Nanou 1970 Casablanca

Nanou France 2004

Visit to France, 1980

Before we met, Deborah had already been exploring Judaism. After our wedding, Deborah and I attended Judaism classes together at the Hillel center on the University of Texas campus, for her to get ready for her official conversion to the Jewish faith. The classes lasted for several months and were beneficial to me as well, allowing me to rediscover my strong connection to the faith. I felt that I had never truly understood or explored many of my religion's practices, always taking them for granted.

In 1980 we flew to France to spend a few days in Paris and to introduce Deborah to my family. My father was passing through Paris on his way to Israel. I was happy for my dad to finally meet my new wife. We spent time hanging out in Paris, taking long walks and discussing life in general as well as options regarding my parents' possible move from Casablanca to Paris. Our cousin Jack Benayoun organized a nice dinner at his home in the 16th arrondissement, inviting my father and my brothers Sam, Armand, and Simon. My sister Jacqueline and her husband, Sylvain, joined us as well. It was a very nice occasion for all of us to celebrate a family reunion.

Unbeknownst to all of us gathered for that dinner, this would be one of the last opportunities to be with our father. He passed away later that same year in Casablanca from a sudden heart attack, in December 1980. Strangely enough, earlier that same year, in the spring of 1980, for the celebration of Pessah, many of my siblings decided to go back home and celebrate the holiday with my parents. Sam, Armand, Simon, Nanou, and Evelyne and her one-year-old son, Nathan, attended. Again, unbeknownst to all present at this Pessah holiday family celebration, this would be the last one with him officiating.

The great Seder of Pessah reunited everyone at our famous old dining room table. Sam had the great idea that night, and I am deeply grateful for his initiative, to record on an audio tape cassette the whole Seder, with all the blessings, prayers, and singing. It was intended to be mailed to me and Michel in the US. That audiotape, two to three hours long, which I converted much later to an MP3 track, is a beautiful legacy. It is a very emotional memory of my father's last Pessah, surrounded by his sons, daughters, and a baby grandchild.

My Father, 1920–1980

In Austin, in December 1980, I received a phone call from Sam announcing to me the terrible news of the sudden loss of our father. Our father had succumbed to a massive heart attack while at work. He was only sixty years old. I flew the next day to New York to try to find a way to straighten out my passport situation and catch a flight to Casablanca. Michel could not join me because he had been living in the US without a visa. If he left the country, he would not be able to re-enter legally. We had just hired an immigration lawyer in Austin to try to get him a work visa.

In New York, I went straight to the Moroccan consulate. Once seated in the consul's office, I explained to him my situation. I had my old Moroccan passport with my original Benayoun name from when I was fifteen. It had expired long ago. I was holding a current Israeli passport and a US green card as a permanent resident in the US under the name Ben-Nun. I needed urgently to attend my father's funeral in Casablanca. Morocco, being an Arab country, would not allow me to enter the country with an Israeli passport. The consul was very understanding and respectful of my wish to pay my last respects to my father. He arranged right away not only to issue me letters and documents allowing me to enter Morocco, but also booked me on a direct flight from New York to Casablanca that same night with the Moroccan national airline.

In Casablanca, I had a confusing few minutes passing through passport control at the airport, but once I showed my recently issued letters from New York and explained the reason for my trip, I was waived through with no problems. All my brothers and sisters, except for Michel, were present together one last time at our home at la Rue Berthelot as we mourned through the traditional seven-day period. We were in shock and inconsolable, trying to digest and cope with the sudden, terrible loss of our beloved, dedicated, hard-working father who was taken from us too soon. A large crowd of family and friends came every day to attend daily prayer services at the house. Many of our father's Arab workers came to pay their respects, among them the ever-faithful Ali, accompanied by Bouazza, Hmed, and Omar.

At the end of the shiva, I and my siblings made the decision to have my father's remains transferred to Israel to be reburied next to his mother. Since he was already buried in the local Jewish cemetery, the regulations required us to wait twelve months before we could proceed. Since most of us, his children, were already living outside Morocco, and knowing my father's strong religious connection and attachment to Israel, always wishing he could have moved there to retire, we decided it would be the right decision.

Strangely enough, when I saw my father last in Paris a few months earlier, I dared to ask him if he had any type of last will or written letter. He responded by telling me that our religion provided for all these types of life situations. I was confused and could not understand how or what he was referring to since he was living in an Arab Muslim country under the jurisdiction of Moroccan law. Since apparently no written will existed, after the traditional seven days of mourning some of my brothers and I went to meet with the official Chief Rabbi of the Jewish community of Casablanca. The Chief Rabbi, who is officially appointed and paid as a Moroccan government employee, knew my father very well, being from the same small town of Settat. Rabbi Shimon Levy explained to us the common way that wills seem to function in the community. It all depended on the Hebrew wording in the Jewish marriage document, better known as the *ketubah*.

The rabbi asked me if I could read and understand Hebrew. He told me to locate the ketubah to check for one of two key words in it—*Toshavim*, belonging to the community of natives, or *Megorashim*, belonging to the newcomers from Spain as a result of the Inquisition. Apparently, within the Jewish community of Morocco, when a couple gets married, the ketubah is drafted to stipulate all the traditional details about the couple, depending on their backgrounds or family histories. The ketubah reflects by its text and wording one of the two regimes. Each one implies a distinct set of laws pertaining to, among other things, the will for the deceased husband. My parents' ketubah was drafted under the Megorashim regime, and once more my father was right when during our Paris visit he mentioned that everything was taken care of within our religion and our Jewish law.

Shortly after the loss of my father, we decided as a family to have my mother, widowed at the age of fifty-eight, together with my youngest sister, Nanou, to apply to emigrate and move to Montreal, Canada, where our sister Evelyne had recently rejoined her husband, Charlie Beriro. To honor my father's legacy and as a tribute to his memory, the members of his synagogue decided to rename the temple in his honor and call it Or David, meaning the "light of David."

Twelve months after my father was buried in Casablanca, we transferred his body to be reburied in

Israel. His body was exhumed and taken first to Paris, where all necessary paperwork and special permits were obtained, before continuing on to Israel. I flew directly from Austin to Israel to wait for the body. A small crowd of family and friends took part in the reburial ceremony on the same day the body landed in Israel. My father's four sisters living at the time—my aunts—and their numerous children and other relatives were present at the Cemetery of Rishon Letzion, where my father was laid to rest not far from the grave of his mother, my grandmother Meme Mryem.

My Father, 1923-1980

Several synagogue plaques renaming the temple in memory of my father

Austin, Texas

In 1981 Deborah and I purchased our first home, a two-story house on Appalachian Drive in Northwest Hills, with a beautiful view of the hill country around Austin. Our house had plenty of space, so Deb and I decided to get a dog. After considering different breeds, we opted for a Labrador retriever and soon found a local breeder to sell us a puppy. We named her Sandy.

Deborah completed her Jewish study classes and did her conversion. We had a small ceremony to celebrate our Jewish wedding. My mother flew in for the occasion. The wedding took place in Austin at the University of Texas Hillel synagogue with Rabbi Neal Borowitz officiating. After that, Deborah decided to get in touch with Rabbi Sheinberg, an Orthodox rabbi leading Congregation Rodfei Shalom in nearby San Antonio. She started taking Jewish classes under him as well in order to get an Orthodox conversion. So that same year, we got married for the third time in an Orthodox synagogue in San Antonio with Rabbi Sheinberg officiating, just to make sure our future children would be recognized as Jews if we ever decided to move back to Israel. That same year Deborah got pregnant, and the following year we were blessed with the birth of our first son.

David was born by C-section in January of 1982. My mother and Nanou came to be with us and help prepare for the big event and the official naming and circumcision. David was a healthy baby with broad shoulders, weighing more than nine pounds at birth. I remember the doctor congratulating me while finishing the delivery, saying, "You got a real football player over here."

While Deborah recovered from her operation, my mother and sister Nanou helped us prepare for the circumcision that was to take place in our house after the traditional eight days. We were able to locate a Jewish physician in Houston who was also a ritual mohel and he agreed to fly in for the day to perform the *brit milah*, the ritual Jewish way with the special blessings and naming ceremony. My friends Albert and Nathalie Arditi flew in from New York to be with us for the happy occasion.

My mother and Nanou did a wonderful job cooking and baking plenty of food. We opened our home to many friends and acquaintances from the community. The circumcision ritual is a very intense and emotional moment, and I made sure to have a strong drink before, in order to face this ancient Jewish ritual and the way of our ancestors. Our first-born son was named after my father, David, who passed away in 1980, and his middle name of Joseph is after Deborah's father who passed away in 1979.

When David was a few months old, my mother-in-law, Winnie Helen, who was the owner of an old motorhome, graciously agreed to let us use it. Deborah and I drove our car to Eldorado with baby David to get the motorhome and take off for a few weeks on a road trip, driving the motorhome to explore the Grand Canyon and the West Coast.

During our first years in Austin, a city of about 350,000 during the early 1980s, we became friends with local French expats, with the help of our new European clothing boutique. We became close friends with one particular French couple, Bernard and Monique Darques from Paris. Bernard was working for IBM France and was posted in Austin for three years at the local IBM offices. They had two young teenagers.

Bernard enjoyed sports and the outdoors, and we got along very well. The two of us decided to take a rafting trip to Colorado. This was before David was born. We signed up to go down the Colorado River in Utah with a local outfitter and raft for five nights and six days in Cataract Canyon. This was my first rafting trip, experiencing for the first time the fun and intense white-water action as we floated down the powerful rapids within the canyon. Camping and rafting on the river reminded me so much of my Sinai days. It was basically the same concept except the REO truck was replaced by seven-man rafts carrying all the needed gear and food for the group. The guides were so similar in a certain way, always busy either operating the oars, guiding, cooking, setting up camps, etcetera.

A few weeks later, Deb and I decided to go on a long trip to Mexico and Guatemala together with Bernard, Monique, and their two kids, Florence and Loic. We flew to Acapulco and rented a car to explore the area. Deborah, having spent three years living in Mexico City after her college years, teaching English for a Berlitz language school, was very happy to get back into the country. She spoke fluent Spanish. While in Mexico, the portion of our trip continuing to Guatemala was cancelled due to political unrest in the country. Instead, we decided to fly to Cancun and spend a few days at a beach resort. Cancun in the early 1980s was the newest beach resort being developed in Mexico.

The Darques moved back to France at the end of their three-year period, but the following summer of 1982, after David was born, they made plans to come back to Texas for three weeks. Our two families decided to rent a house in Lakeway on Lake Travis and enjoy the summer boating on the lake. That same summer, with David less than six months old, we found out that Deborah unexpectedly was pregnant again. We would have another baby in the spring of 1983.

Living in Austin as a young couple raising a family, I was trying to envision a future of creating a Jewish home and conveying somehow my language, culture, and background to our children. I was also trying to adapt to the local culture and mentality and was making my best effort to assimilate and fit in, just like I had to completely adapt myself to a new culture when transplanting myself from Morocco to Israel. I had to learn a new language and assimilate to my new Israeli identity, even going to the extent of taking a new biblical Hebrew last name, like so many new immigrants did after coming to settle in the historical Jewish homeland.

In Israel, a country mostly built by Jews coming to settle from the four corners of the world, it was widely accepted and even encouraged by the local government agency to change old diaspora last names to Hebrew or biblical versions. As a matter of fact, most Israeli diplomats or statesmen had to do this. Ben-Gurion's previous last name was Grun, Moshe Dayan's was Kitaigorodsky, Benjamin Netanyahu's father's name was Mileikowsky. While living in Israel and convinced that I would permanently make my life there, I decided early on to formally change my last name and adopt the Ben-Nun last name which very closely resembles Benayoun. Ben-Nun is a typical Hebrew name from the Old Testament, after Joshua Ben-Nun, a famous military leader in Jewish history and a well-accepted, recognized Israeli adopted last name for a reborn generation.

In Austin, we were in touch with Deborah's family and would occasionally make the drive out to West Texas to visit Deb's mom and her sister Holly and her family. We often saw her two brothers, Bud and Chris and his wife Mimi who lived in Houston. Bud was a sweet, gentle, and very funny person, always ready to joke around and have fun. He loved his sister and was very warm and welcoming to me. Bud, as well as my brother Michel, gave me a surprise visit on my first birthday in the US. When I answered a knock on the door, Bud was standing there. He had flown in with his small private airplane to surprise us and spend the day with us.

My wife and her siblings—her two brothers, Bud and Chris, and one sister, Holly—each inherited from their mother's family some acreage in Lee County. Their land, commonly called "The Farm," used to belong to Deborah's maternal grandfather, Roy Beaman, and was passed on to his two daughters, Winnie Helen and her sister, Doris. Winnie Helen in turn gifted the land in four portions to her four children. Bud ended up with slightly fewer acres but with the existing old farmhouse on his portion.

Bud, like many native Texans, loved the outdoors and was particularly attached to their land in Lee County, located about ten miles northeast of the small town of Giddings. Since Giddings was only about an hour's drive from Austin, we often drove in to join Bud to spend the weekend at the farm. Bud noticed that I also loved the outdoors and took it upon himself to initiate me into fishing, offering me a full set of fishing tackle and taking me to the different ponds and small lakes on the family land and also to the numerous, well-stocked bass ponds in the vicinity. My only previous fishing experiences were during my childhood with my father in the port of Casablanca. I was skeptical of trying to fish in such small ponds versus coastal waterways, also mainly using spoons and artificial lures. Sure enough, under the guidance of Bud I started hooking some huge, magnificent, shiny largemouth bass, anywhere from two to six pounds.

When deer season came around starting in early November and lasting for two months, Bud insisted on me joining him in hunting on the family land in Lee County. At first, I would not hear of it, but he insisted I just join him in taking long walks in the woods, with only him carrying a hunting rifle. I realized how hunting, fishing, and the outdoors in general was such a big part of the Texan culture. The following year on my birthday, we ended up going together to the local gun store in Austin and Bud convinced me to finally purchase my first deer rifle. He chose one for me, picking the brand of rifle and the scope for it. Bud and his brother, Chris, like many proud, native Texans owned each a few dozen rifles and shotguns, some of them collectibles.

Around 1981, Bud and Chris wanting to get further away from the flat Houston region and the humid weather decided to buy some ranching land in the Texas hill country, just outside the scenic town of Kerrville, an ideal region known for its scenic hills and canyons, as well as for great deer hunting. The ranch they decided on was a four-hundred-acre parcel with a stream, some valleys, and canyons, as well as a hilltop with an incredible 360-degree view of the surrounding hills. It had a modest, basic, cinder block cabin very close to a live running creek and a second smaller old bungalow, in need of repairs, about five hundred yards away, adjoining a large, old, red barn. I was very happy with their choice and one weekend volunteered to help them move some furniture into the main ranch house.

Montreal, Canada

In those early years in Austin, when I was in my late twenties, I had difficulties imagining raising our kids in Texas, without a strong connection to my background, be it Jewish, French, Moroccan, or Israeli. As I helped my mother move from Casablanca and settle her and my sister Nanou in Montreal, joining my other sister Evelyne and her two-year-old son, Nathan, Deborah and I started giving serious consideration to one day moving there, too. Montreal had a substantial Moroccan Jewish community that was already well established, with vibrant cultural and religious activities.

Montreal, in Quebec, Canada, could be a good compromise for us — a big, cosmopolitan city with a rich French cultural background and good Jewish bilingual French and English schools. I also had numerous friends and family members already living there who were well established. I liked the proximity to my mother and my two sisters. While visiting Montreal during 1982, we made an offer on a vacant house in one of the most prestigious Jewish neighborhoods — Hampstead. During that time, the province of Quebec was in the middle of an economic recession and real estate values were at their lowest in years. Our offer was accepted, and we became the proud owners of 52 Glenmore Road at an incredible price. Our plans were to initiate some badly needed remodeling while getting our paperwork started in Texas to apply to the Canadian consulate for visas to move to

Canada and become permanent residents the following year, 1983.

In February 1983, Deborah was rushed to the hospital in Austin to give birth prematurely—four weeks ahead of time—to our second son, Daniel. Luckily, all went well, and after a few days in special care, Daniel came home with Deborah. The circumcision and naming ceremony took place in our home in Austin. The same mohel doctor made the trip again from Houston to perform the ceremony. My brother Michel was designated as the godfather, holding baby Daniel Benjamin on his lap while the circumcision was performed.

A few months later, with the remodeling completed in our recently acquired house in Montreal and our visas on order, we sold our home in Austin. We sold our store and our vehicles and bid goodbye to our friends. With David about eighteen months old and his brother Daniel about six months old, we left Austin to start a new life in Canada.

In Montreal we encountered a series of unexpected complications. First, David became sick and had to be hospitalized for several days to treat a complicated and potentially very dangerous eye infection. Luckily, he responded well to strong IV antibiotics. After that, I suffered an ankle fracture and had to wear a cast for several weeks. The worst news was the sudden death by what we think was a heart attack of Deborah's older brother Bud while on a commercial flight to Japan for a business meeting. Bud was only forty-two years old and had no previous heart problems. The family was devastated, trying to cope with the sudden loss at such a young age of the always smiling dear Bud.

The winter season of 1983 to 1984 was one of the harshest to hit Montreal, with record snowfall over the city that made us realize how rigorous the six to eight months of winter there would be to put up with. Until then, I had never experienced long, cold winters. The winters combined with some peculiar double-tax laws of the federal Canadian government made it difficult for us to remain living full time in Montreal as permanent residents. We would have to comply and pay substantial extra taxes to the Canadian government in order to stay. Deborah and I decided to reverse course, while still within the legal allowed time frame, and move back to Texas. During the Thanksgiving holiday of 1983 we traveled to Texas to be with her family at their new ranch in Kerrville and we started a search for a new home in Austin.

We didn't know it then, but Austin was to become our home for many years, providing a dynamic community in which to raise our sons who have both grown up to accomplish amazing things, becoming admirable men and making us very proud of them. Using Austin as a home base, Deborah and I have continued our incredible adventure together, spending time with friends and family and traveling all over the world. All made even more special by Deborah's delicious cuisine and talents for making life magical while creating a wonderful, loving life together.

The Kerrville and Giddings Ranch

By January of 1984, we had moved back to Austin into our newly bought house at 4208 Woodway Drive. It was a big relief to get out from under the cold and snow in Canada and get back to the mild winters of Texas. Soon after moving, I became involved in real estate investments and became very active in buying and selling large tracts of land in the northeast part of town, between Austin and Round Rock, which was a very active and booming area.

As Austin was growing and expanding, most of the surrounding ranches and farmland on the outskirts of the city limits were being bought up. The longtime landowners, most of them still living on site farming and ranching on their lands, were approached to sell their property. Real estate brokers, land investors, and speculators were all trying hard to get signed commitments and solid real estate contracts from the landowners. With the continued expansion and new construction, particularly in the northern part of Austin, these old ranches and farmlands were only a year or two away from being annexed by the city and developed into residential and commercial lots. I seemed to be either very lucky or very skilled in doing my homework to find very profitable tracts of land. The timing was perfect back in the mid-1980s.

After Deb's brother Bud passed away suddenly, my other brother-in-law, Chris, being the designated executor for Bud's estate and his partner in the Kerrville ranch, needed for estate purposes to either sell the ranch or find another partner to buy Bud's fifty percent ownership. Deborah and I decided to buy Bud's share and we became partners with Chris on the four hundred acres of the ranch outside Kerrville.

The little two-bedroom, one-bath cottage was very basic. I had hoped to convince Chris, who was a custom home builder in Houston, to build us a nicer, new ranch house. Chris convinced us to start making some minor remodeling changes to the existing cottage. We added a covered patio to the front, extended the back patio, and put in new kitchen cabinets. Chris very cleverly turned an old shed into a great bunkhouse for the kids. A new well for water was drilled, and most importantly, a dam was built on Fall Creek nearby to create a nice reservoir, with the creek water constantly running over the spillway in the center of the dam. We added a large wooden deck along the edge of the pond so we could swim and fish just one hundred feet from the house.

After a few months, we found a local couple living and working on an adjoining ranch who would move into the rundown second cottage on the property. Wesley and Polly were able to make all necessary repairs and restore and update the cottage into living conditions. In exchange for living on the property for free, they took care of all the maintenance and repairs on the ranch. We also had a big wooden barn which was restored, freshly painted, and brought back to good use.

When we first met Wesley, he was already in his late sixties, having lived all his life in the hill country around Kerrville as a cowboy. I suspect Wesley never learned to read or write. He was a great shot with firearms, skilled as a hunter and angler, living off the land by trapping, shooting, and fishing. He spoke with a heavy Texan drawl, sometimes hard for me to understand. Wesley liked to trap wild hogs on the property and sell them to neighboring ranchers for organized hunts with special dogs. He knew how to train hunting dogs to detect and pursue only the scent of hogs and not be distracted by other game.

Polly was Wesley's second wife, after he was widowed. She was almost like his daughter — she was twenty or thirty years younger. She was an excellent horse rider and kept a mare on the ranch. She was very attached to this beautiful, gentle quarter horse mare, very well trained to work cattle as a cutting horse. Polly took great pride in participating with her horse in many rodeos and tournaments in the region. A few years later, Chris and I decided to buy Polly's horse as well as buy another horse to keep at the ranch under the care of Wesley and Polly. On my visits to the ranch from Austin, I would ask Wesley to saddle both horses and often we would ride together around the property.

Robert with David and Daniel, Kerrville Ranch, 1987

Looking For Home

Daniel, Kerrville Ranch, 1988

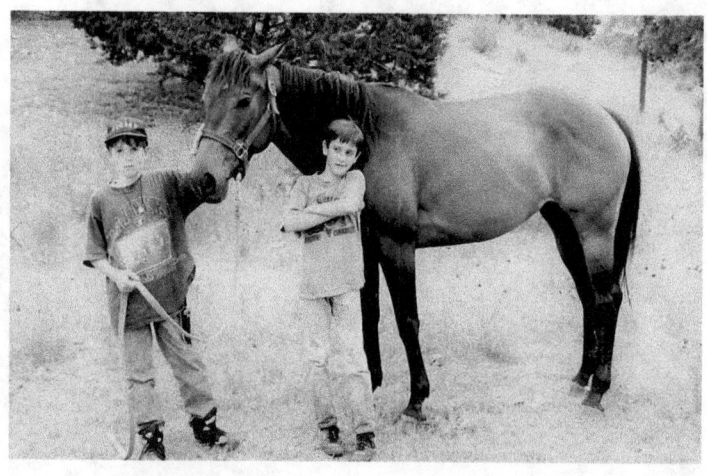

David and Daniel, Kerrville Ranch, 1986

The Kerrville and Giddings Ranch

*Robert with David and Daniel in front of the
Kerrville Ranch cabin, 1986*

With the many dirt trails among the small valleys and around the hilltop, I also decided to get a small all-terrain vehicle. We already had a couple of ATV four-wheelers, but I really wanted a four-wheel vehicle like in my old days in the Sinai Desert. One day, driving on IH35 on my way to visit my Israeli friend Moti and his wife who were living and working in the Dallas area, I spotted an old US military surplus jeep for sale on the side of the road. It was an old M-151 jeep, the same model used in the Israeli army back in the mid-1970s when I was serving in the IDF. It had been improved, and I got a good price on it and was able to have it delivered to Austin a few days later. I kept it as a surprise, so David and Daniel were delighted and very excited to discover it parked on our driveway one afternoon when they came home after school.

The jeep was definitely a substantial play toy and a major addition to the ranch. The whole family would climb on board, including our dog, Sparky, and go adventuring on the rough, rocky trails leading to the many hidden corners, canyons, and springs on the property. Later, as the boys grew up, the jeep became their first driving experience. They experimented with getting behind the wheel and driving with a stick shift, taking short spins in the open field by the house.

The ranch outside Kerrville became a major interest for our family, particularly for me and the boys as we started spending weekends there hiking and exploring the heavily wooded acres. I taught David and Daniel how to catch fish from the creek, as well as get familiar with handling and firing small caliber guns, like the .22 rifle and a small caliber shotgun. It was important to me to teach them first and foremost gun safety while practicing target shooting. I took great pleasure in sharing my love of the outdoors while bonding strongly with our boys, giving them as much exposure to nature as I could by taking them on long hikes.

The four-hundred-acre land tract was divided in two by an access road—a single-lane dirt easement passing through our property and giving access to the other three ranches up the valley behind us. On one side of the road was an eighty-acre valley with a large, flat, open field, with the stream meandering along the edge of it. The small cottage was located in the middle of the open pasture field, in proximity of the creek. On the other side of the road, the land slowly rose to the crest of a wooded hill.

A narrow dirt track led to the hilltop plateau, meandering along the hilltop and making a full loop through the bulk of the remaining 320 acres. From the dirt road on the hill, I was able to gradually clear away some of the thick cedar brush and undergrowth and open several short hiking trails leading to small valleys and canyons on both sides of the trail. As I learned my way around, I discovered several natural springs and other features like small caves and wet-weather streams.

The looping track led to the highest point on the property, with a spectacular 360-degree view of the surrounding hills, a majestic place to watch the sun set. Often we would bring along folding chairs and drinks in a small ice chest and enjoy the great view at the end of the day. From the hilltop, the dirt track dropped down into a scenic valley with a seasonal wet creek running through the center of it.

In the mid-1990s, Chris and I decided to build a massive earth dam across the valley and thereby create a big pond holding water coming down from the creek, the springs and runoffs. The edge of this pond became the perfect overnight camping spot for David and Daniel while growing up. The boys would load up their camping gear on the ATVs and head out from the cottage toward the pond to set up their tent by the water. They would build a campfire for cooking. Deb and I would drive the jeep over to check on them at night before going to bed. David and Daniel became very attached to the land and looked forward to spending weekends and other school breaks at the ranch. They often invited some of their school friends to join them for a weekend in the country.

At the ranch we started a tradition of once a year, usually in the spring or fall, inviting a small group of our close friends to join us for a camping weekend. Since the small cottage was not big enough to accommodate all our guests, most of the families were asked to bring tents to set up around the cabin. The Warenoffs, Schneiders, Bidermans, Simons, Eisenmans, Marzes, and Wishnews became regulars each year, joining us in a cook-out gathering of camping, swimming in the pond, fishing, and following me on hikes to the hilltop and around the ranch.

In 1993 for my fortieth birthday, Deborah managed to put together a memorable and amazing surprise birthday celebration to mark the occasion. It started as the usual close group of friends coming to the ranch for our annual camp-out, but later many of our larger group of Austin friends showed up for a surprise elaborate, seated gourmet dinner on Saturday night, specially catered by our friend Pascal and served under the stars. Most of our visiting friends had made plans to stay in nearby hotels in town.

The Kerrville ranch, being located in the heart of the Texas hill country, was abundant with wild game, mostly whitetail deer and wild hogs. Around that same period, I initiated a new, typical Texan tradition of a guys-only weekend gathering at the ranch, held once or twice a year and also known as the "boys' hunting weekend." Except maybe for my friend Mark Simon who was the only native-born Austinite Texan, none of my other Jewish friends were really hunters, but most of them loved the idea of getting away to spend time in the countryside, learning about firearms, fishing, hiking, cooking, playing cards and enjoying the outdoors.

Kerrville guys-only hunting weekend.
From left: Mark, Irwin, Bruce, Enrique, Robert, Rob

The Kerrville and Giddings Ranch

Kerrville Ranch, 1991

David, Daniel, and their cousin Lionel on the jeep

Other fond memories at the Kerrville ranch were of spending Thanksgivings with Deborah's family. Chris, Mimi and their two children as well as Bud, his kids and his wife were always there and often Deborah's Mom, sister Holly and her husband Jim and their children would join in. It was a treat to see how Americans celebrated Thanksgiving.

After several years Chris let us know that he was going to need to sell the Kerrville ranch, so reluctantly we had to let it go. We were all sad to sell that piece of paradise. I started thinking about the unimproved land that Deborah had inherited from her grandfather outside of Giddings and came up with a plan to build a house there which was finished in 1998.

In the beginning this new ranch did not have the charm of our Kerrville ranch however slowly over the years I worked hard to improve it. I have cleared pastures, opened up paths thru the woods, cleaned out underbrush, created a fire pit area, dug a new well and done many other projects to enhance the property. One of the most spectacular projects I have done is to create a pond with our very own "Bellagio" fountain which we love to watch from the house.

As at our previous ranch, we have enjoyed having campout weekends with friends and Thanksgivings with the family there. An added dimension of this ranch is that there is a lot of family history in this area including an old cemetery with ancestor's graves over a hundred years old. Also Deb's family all have ranches nearby, so often a niece or nephew or Deb's brother, Chris, will stop by to visit.

The Kerrville and Giddings Ranch

Robert and Deborah 2008 Giddings Ranch

Constantina

During the spring of 1985, wanting to share our new recreated life in Austin since coming back from Canada, Deb and I extended an invitation to my brothers and sisters from France and Montreal to join us for a family reunion in Austin and to celebrate Pessah together. They all came to be our guests and spend about ten days. Present were Jacqueline and her husband, Sylvain, Armand and Simon came from Paris. Evelyne and her son, Nathan, and my mother came from Montreal; Nanou joined us with her fiancé at the time. Also present my younger brother Michel at the time still living and working in Austin.

We had a memorable Pessah celebration, with everybody taking part in helping Deborah cook and prepare an incredible feast. The theme song that stayed engraved in our heads from that joyous family gathering was a recently released song by Enrico Macias which was very popular in France at the time. We kept playing that song, "Constantina," at every opportunity and dancing to the beat of it.

We celebrated the first two nights of Pessah in our home, where Deborah and my mother and sisters outdid themselves cooking fabulous traditional gourmet meals for this unique family gathering. Then we packed our group into two large vehicles plus a cargo trailer for luggage and food and headed out to South Padre Island on the Texas coast to spend a full week at the beach. I had arranged to rent two large beachfront apartments on the water. Luckily, during our stay at the coast the fishing was exceptional, and my brothers and I, using my fishing tackle, spent long hours on the rock jetty catching enough nice-sized fish to fill up one large ice chest. My mother, happily surrounded by her seven children, surpassed herself in making delicious tagines.

During that family visit we also took a drive to Lake Conroe near Houston, where my brother-in-law Chris generously offered to let us use his beautiful waterfront lake house as well as his ski boat. That Benayoun memorable family gathering in April 1985 became known as "the Pessah Constantina." Looking back thirty years later, that was one of the most joyous, fun get-togethers to be remembered among the brothers and sisters.

A few months later, my sister Nanou got married and moved out of my mother's apartment in Montreal. My mother found herself living on her own, with the long Canadian winter settling in and limiting her activities outside. During the winter of 1985 our mother had a bad fall, slipping on an icy walkway on her street in Montreal breaking her wrist. A decision was made to ask her to move south to Texas. She gladly accepted, and I made all the arrangements to move her and her furniture to Austin.

My mother was able to move into a nice three-bedroom apartment, part of a duplex rental property that we had previously purchased with her in mind. The duplex on Mesa Drive was only a five-minute drive from our home on Woodway. With my mother now living full time in Austin, we spent a lot of time together, celebrating Shabbat and Jewish holidays. We saw Mamie Suzanne on a regular basis, almost every day. She often helped us babysitting David and Daniel. We were able to vacation together as well and took several family trips to destinations locally as well as out of the country, like to Mexico and the Caribbean.

Pessah, 2019, Austin, Texas.
From left: Robert, Adam, Daniel, Deborah, Sivan, Lia, David

Jews in Canoes

Sometime in 1990, Deborah and I and our two boys went on a family road trip to West Texas. We picked up my mother-in-law, Winnie Helen, and decided to spend a few days in the Big Bend National Park region. We took some hikes around the beautiful Chisos Mountains and signed up for a one-day rafting trip down the Rio Grande River. By an interesting coincidence, staying at the park lodge at the same time was our friend from Austin, Stan Biderman, with his father and his son Zach who was a couple of years older than our David. Stan's father from Dallas was a Holocaust survivor of World War II concentration camps. We had dinner together at the local Starlight Theatre restaurant in Terlingua and had a lovely time. We had the opportunity to hear Stan's father's astonishing survival story of escaping from the Nazis, in the presence of Winnie Helen who probably had never in her life personally met a Holocaust survivor.

As it turned out, without planning ahead, the next day we ended up being on the same raft with the Bidermans, floating down the Rio Grande River going through the spectacular Santa Elena Canyon. While enjoying the scenic remote wilderness and stunning cliffs dominating the path of the river, I was chatting with our guide from Far Flung, the outfitter, while he paddled our raft. An idea crossed my mind that maybe it would be a great idea to get a few friends from Austin and plan our own group outing to float and camp for a few days on a river somewhere. That is how the idea of "Jews in

Canoes" started taking shape, and soon thereafter I began working on a list of friends who might share my love for outdoor adventure and join me on a rafting and camping expedition.

Soon thereafter, in the spring of 1993, I organized and put together a group of local Jewish friends for our first trip. We flew to Phoenix, Arizona, and were met at the airport by our outfitters from Far Flung Adventures. We drove a couple hours toward the headwaters of the Salt River. This first group of guys included me, Rob Warenoff, Irwin Schneider, David Wishnew, Stan Biderman, Ben Marz, Mark Simon, and Bruce Eisenman.

As we got on our way the next day, riding in our van to the put-in on the river, we had to pass through higher elevations and cross a mountain pass before getting to the river gorge. We soon realized a winter blizzard had moved in during the night, bringing with it some serious snowfall and freezing temperatures. Not exactly the late spring Arizona weather we had anticipated for our first float trip.

Our plan was to float the Salt River and its many rapids, rafting for four days and camping three nights. Once at the put-in and after consulting with our guide, it was decided that due to the sudden change of weather, the option of rafting had become a big risk with the possibility of hypothermia in the case of anyone falling into the frigid waters. After a short consultation and vote among ourselves, since we were all already in Arizona, Plan B was brought forward by our outfitters. Instead, we would go skiing at a nearby ski resort.

Half of us were somewhat experienced skiers and the other half were beginners. We had a great time on the slopes with a few intense moments trying to get the beginners among us to mind the more experienced ones. After a couple nights at the ski resort, we went back to float the river, spending one night on the water before getting back to Phoenix. Even though our first trip did not go as planned, everybody had a great time and the first funny stories, memories, and legends were being created and would be told for years to come.

The following year of 1994, we came back to do the Salt River as originally planned. This time the participants were me, Rob Warenoff, Irwin Schneider, Mark Simon, Johnny Warren, David Wishnew, Seth Brown, Mitch Brown, Randy Kunig, Yigal Saad, and Ben Marz. The experience of getting a small group of friends to venture into the outdoors on a rafting expedition once a year on average caught on and created some strong bonds among this small group of friends.

After my early years as a guide in the Sinai desert and with my strong attraction to the outdoors and remote wilderness, I was happy and thrilled to finally create in Austin my own little group and start this tradition that lasted for many years. The concept was to each time choose a different destination, preferably a remote, scenic river that we could float for four or five days and camp, escaping into nature away from civilization. I was in charge of putting together suggestions each time, and after a brief consultation with the "inner cabinet" of the group—composed of my two buddies, Rob and Irwin—I would proceed in making all arrangements for the eight of us.

After the first few trips involving inflatable rafts, we decided as a group that we were better suited for two-men canoes, usually four canoes for eight participants, and from then on we became known as the "Jews in Canoes" gang. The usual group of eight or nine guys was composed of Rob Warenoff, Irwin Schneider, Ben Marz, Tom Jensen, Seth Brown, Bruce Eisenman, Yigal Saad, Mark Simon, and me. The list of our destinations was quite diverse, including Costa Rica—our only international expedition—Colorado, Montana, Utah, Minnesota, Maine, Arkansas, and Texas. I was always looking for remote, scenic, wilderness rivers and a good outfitter to lead us there and make sure all the logistics were taken care of.

The yearly canoe expedition became a strong tradition involving not only the days floating and camping on the river, but also preparation meetings and a post-trip party once we returned home. I took particular pleasure in putting together a spectacular video or slideshow of our most recent adventure and made sure our wives were present to hear all about our outdoor survival skills. As the years went by, many fun memories of amazing experiences were created, and the bonds grew stronger among our little group of guys. We always looked forward to the next adventure.

Jews in canoes, Utah, 2007.
Front: Irwin, Robert, Seth, Yigal
Back: Rob, Tom, Bruce, Ben

Jews in canoes, Colorado, 2009
Front: Tom, Bruce, Rob, Robert, Irwin, Ben
Back: Yigal, Seth

Estepona

While David and Daniel were growing up, from the mid 1980s into the late 1990s, Deb and I took advantage of every opportunity to take with both of them long road trips, depending on their school schedule. Once our faithful, spacious Chevy Suburban was fully loaded and packed, we would drive off for weeks, on our way to explore the national parks and historical sites from the West Coast to the East Coast, often crossing into Canada as well. Our biggest, most memorable, and longest road trip was in the summer of 1996, when we decided to make it all the way to Alaska.

During the summer of 1996, a few months after we celebrated David's Bar Mitzvah, while Daniel was twelve and getting ready to have his the following year, we loaded up the family Suburban with our gear, including tents and camping gear, and started our long expedition to Alaska. Along the way we stopped at small-town hotels and motels. When around big national parks or national forests, we opted to break out the camping gear packed on the roof of the Suburban and set up camp to take in the magnificent vistas of the natural wilderness surrounding us.

Usually during the summer months we traveled to France to visit my family. As soon as school was out for the summer break, we were off on our way to Europe, landing first in Paris. There we would take possession of a leased car and spend the first week visiting my brothers and sisters there. We would then head to southern France to Aix-en-Provence where my brother Armand, and later my mother, were living. Most of our time spent in Europe was on the road, taking long trips to explore the main tourist sites of Europe, including in Italy, Spain, and Portugal.

My brother Sam and his wife, Aline, were living at the time in Madrid, Spain, having been transferred there for his job. One summer, Sam and Aline decided to invite my mother to join them to drive all the way from Madrid to Casablanca to spend a few weeks as guests of my mother's sister still living there. The plan was for them to spend a couple of weeks staying at a small beach bungalow that Aunt Perla and her Moroccan family made available to them. The bungalow, or *cabanon*, was located on a beach nearby, not far from Casablanca.

Upon arriving in Casablanca and checking out the bungalow, Sam and Aline were not too impressed with the lodging amenities for the four of them, including their toddler daughter, Audrey, and our mother. They decided to head back the way they came and go to southern Spain to look for other options for their summer vacation. After boarding a ferry to cross the narrow Strait of Gibraltar that separates Morocco from Spain, they landed in Spain in late afternoon and drove off north along the Spanish coast, better known as the Costa del Sol.

One of the small towns they came across was the coastal port of Estepona with a picturesque small marina in a beautiful setting. They decided to stop and inquire about lodging. They were able to rent a two-bedroom, furnished apartment overlooking the marina. During the following few days, Sam and Aline fell in love with the small town of Estepona. They decided to extend their stay and remain there for the rest of their summer break.

One day during their stay in the apartment complex overlooking the *puerto*, or port, my mother, while sitting around the pool, with her very limited Spanish struck up a conversation with another lady. Within a short time, my mother was able to understand that the lady was the owner of another small apartment in the complex with a nicer sea view, and she was actively looking to sell her unit. After visiting the apartment and being totally charmed by the location and view, Sam and Aline made an offer to purchase it. They became the proud owners of a two-bedroom, furnished apartment with two generous balconies overlooking the Mediterranean Sea and the lovely scenic boat marina.

A few months later, I received an invitation from my brother Sam to fly to Estepona and spend a few days with him and his family to discover for myself the beautiful little town. Sam made me appreciate everything that made him fall in love with this small corner of Andalucia. He took great pleasure in taking the time to show me every detail about his new daily routine there, from his morning visit to the beach below his apartment to the daily stroll at the end of the day.

The little pueblo of Estepona on the Costa del Sol has its own charm, with its palm-lined seaside promenade, the Paseo Maritimo, about a mile and a half long right along the sandy beach. Nearby are the restaurants and water sports facilities of the Puerto Deportivo. The port is the home of the fishing fleet of Estepona, with numerous small watercraft and fishing vessels that leave on a regular basis to harvest the rich bounties of the nearby Atlantic Ocean through the Strait of Gibraltar. The rest of the marina is filled with yachts, sailboats, and other recreational craft. Nearby is the sandy beach of the cove of Playa del Cristo. The whitewashed Old Town, with narrow streets full of flowers, has many picturesque small plazas. An old church that used to be a monastery is in the center of the Old Town section.

Around sunset, many of the town folks, will come out on the Paseo Maritimo in their best attire to stroll along the promenade, enjoying the caress of the refreshing evening breeze from the sea. As the sun set behind the Sierra Bermeja mountains just to the west of Estepona, shades of pastel colors from orange, yellow, red, and blue reflected on the surrounding hills and the open sea. We would take a leisurely walk toward the Old Town, from the puerto to the paseo, to join in the small gatherings of locals and summer visitors enjoying the traditional stroll as the sun slowly set behind the mountain. Old and young couples, families, groups of young people, children running in front of their parents, all enjoyed the promenade, occasionally stopping at the small kiosks for ice cream, candy, or small bags of sunflower seeds.

Sam made it almost a religious routine to culminate each day with the paseo walk to arrive at the Plaza de las Flores. This scenic little plaza located in the Old Town was filled with brightly colored flowering bougainvillea, rose bushes, and geraniums. Citrus trees surrounded the plaza, their flowers spreading a sweet, aromatic scent. Sam would find us a table in the center of the plaza and order refreshing cold beers or glasses of dry white sherry along with a few tapas, including the local *aceitunas*, the delicious Andalusian olives that religiously accompany any drink order.

We would sit with our drinks, enjoying the view of the tall, old church bell tower behind the plaza. Low flying swallows swooped above our heads in the last few minutes of daylight before they finally settled down to roost for the night in the canopies of two large avocado trees towering at the corners of the plaza.

Some evenings we would choose instead to find a table at one of the many *chiringuitos*, the little open-air snack bars, on the beach along the paseo. We drank cold refreshing "cervezas" with the traditional serving of Espeto de Sardinas—whole sardines on a cane skewer grilled over a bonfire—while enjoying the daily show of sunset vibrant colors; as the sky and the setting sun starts reflecting all the darkening shades of blue across the wide horizon.

The following summer while driving through Europe with Deb, David, and Daniel, after touring the main historical cities of Spain we drove all the way south almost to the tip of the Iberian Peninsula to Estepona. Sam, who was not in town yet, kindly offered to lend us his apartment. We stayed there for the length of our first visit as a family to the little town. After that summer, we started a tradition where each year, after arriving in Paris and spending a couple weeks driving around France, we would slowly make our way south to Spain to finish our summer vacation in a rented apartment overlooking the Mediterranean Sea and the little puerto of Estepona.

Word about Estepona spread among our family. Estepona became a focal point for family summer vacations, serving as a gathering place for a yearly family reunion for the Benayouns, Ben-Nuns, and Marcianos gathered from Paris, Montreal, Aix-en-Provence, and Austin. It was a wonderful opportunity for David and Daniel to spend time with the cousins that otherwise they had very little contact with the rest of the year. For me personally, having left my family in Casablanca as a young adolescent to immigrate to Israel and later move to Texas, I craved as well to reunite and spend time with my brothers and sisters, and especially to get to know the younger generation of nieces and nephews, all born and raised in France and Canada.

Estepona and the special setting of this little coastal town on the shores of the Mediterranean, right across from Morocco, was a good site for all the family, particularly for my brothers and sisters in Paris, to get away from their somewhat intense urban lifestyle. It encouraged all of us to spend quality family time together and become close as an extended family. All the Benayoun brothers and sisters got into the tradition of spending a few weeks each summer in Estepona.

In many ways the Spanish Andalusian lifestyle and the particular setting of the small coastal town of Estepona brought us back to early memories of our childhood in Casablanca during the late 1950s and '60s. The people, the Spanish food and dishes, the sound of flamenco music, and the Mediterranean Sea all combined to recreate for the Benayouns the traditional atmosphere and family-oriented ambiance that we experienced growing up in Casablanca. This was almost an experience of traveling back in time to reconnect with our distant childhood that took place in a particular Jewish-Moroccan bubble that no longer existed. That lifestyle we grew up with branded us, remained engraved in our common memory as we all left home and Casablanca to pursue different lifestyles, and start a new life, mainly in France but also in Israel, Canada, and Texas.

Deb, David, Robert in Estepona, 2013

Estepona

From left: Benjamin. Chloe, David Benayoun, David Assouline, with Sam in front. Estepona, 2008

*David, Robert, Deb, Daniel
Estepona, Plaza de las Flores, 2008*

From left: David, Daniel, Ben, Arik, David
Estepona, 2009

David, Daniel and Sarah with David, Benjamin, and Arik.
Estepona, 2005

During the early years of the 1990s, besides Sam and Aline who owned an apartment there, each couple or family usually made plans to rent a furnished apartment in Estepona during the summer in the area around the puerto, facing the sea and the marina. We made sure that our mother was included in joining us. In the late 1990s, two more of us decided to buy an apartment in Estepona.

One morning, Deb and I were taking our daily stroll to town. We approached the lighthouse that sits on a small rise above the marina. It is still-active and one of the few lighthouses along the Spanish Mediterranean coast. Nearby we noticed two small, portable buildings used as a sales office, and advertising future apartments in a new project to be built, appropriately named El Faro, which means the lighthouse. It didn't take us long to decide to commit to a two-bedroom, two-bath apartment on the fifth floor. The apartment was to be built within the next two years. As soon as my younger brother Michel arrived in town, having heard that we decided to buy an apartment in this new project, he decided as well to follow suit and committed to buying a one-bedroom, one-bath penthouse with a generous terrace. It was to be on the sixth floor, right above our unit.

When we finally took delivery of our unit a little over two years later, we were very pleased with the stunning vista from our balcony. It faced the marina, the coastline, and the mountains of southern Spain, all the way to the imposing Rock of Gibraltar, with a clear view on the horizon of the African continent and the Moroccan coastline. The El Faro apartment became our yearly ideal summer residence for many years and hopefully many more to come.

A few years later, our brother Simon decided as well to buy his own apartment. When Michel decided to move to a different apartment on the other side of the marina, Simon became the owner of the penthouse apartment on the sixth floor. We were now four brothers each with his own little apartment facing the puerto and the deep blue, shining Mediterranean Sea.

*Four brothers with nephews.
From left: Simon & David, Michel & David, Robert & Benjamin,
Armand & Arik Estepona, 1997*

As the years went by, the bond with the little pueblo of Estepona became stronger for the Benayoun siblings. Because of the family ambiance and joyful atmosphere of these annual summer gatherings, all our children also developed a strong, emotional connection to this special place and always looking forward to the next summer. David, Daniel, Nathan, Lionel, Michael, Davidoo, Chloe, Sarah, Arik, Audrey, Benjamin, David Benayoun, David Assouline, and Isabelle growing up accumulated their own fun memories of these family moments as the summers came and went. As the second Benayoun generation matured and turned into young men and women, Estepona became for them as well the place to invite a friend, girlfriend or boyfriend, or future spouse.

*From left: Audrey, Sarah, Benjamin, Arik, David
Estepona, 1999*

While in Estepona, I wanted to explore more of the area's countryside. I became familiar with the little inland mountain villages scattered in the region. On one occasion, by pure coincidence during one of my mountain hikes, I met a Spaniard from northern Spain, from the Pyrenees region. He had also been vacationing down here on a regular basis for many years. Manolo loved to hike and knew all the little country roads, hiking trails, and most importantly, where the natural springs, waterfalls, and swimming holes, or *charca*, could be found in the backcountry. Manolo kindly invited me to join him on hikes and outings and I took great pleasure discovering in his company so many beautiful, magical, hidden natural spots in the surrounding mountains. Soon it became another Estepona tradition to break up the summer routine, with me leading small groups of family members and visiting friends on special outings in the mountains. We would pack a picnic in a backpack and go on a mountain hike, many times finishing with a refreshing swim in one of the mountain streams.

*Refreshing swim at a water fall after a long hike
Estepona, 2012*

One summer, sometime around 2005, while enjoying our daily beach outing, we became acquainted with a nice, friendly couple. Abdel and Mounia were visiting from Morocco and were also regular summer visitors to Estepona for many years. They had, as well, recently purchased a new apartment in the puerto area. As we became close friends and got to spend much time with them each summer, we were introduced to their families.

Estepona

The Boukhriss clan included two brothers, Abdel and Omar, with their wives and children, some of their parents, and aunts and uncles and cousins like the Daoudis and Bendjelloul. Our summer family gatherings expanded to include now the two families, ours and the Boukhriss members coming from Casablanca and Virginia as well as their relatives visiting from Morocco. It became a tradition to get together almost every afternoon at the beach and later on in the early evening on the Paseo.

Sam, Robert, Simon, Michel, Nanou
Estepona, 2006

Deb and I also initiated a new tradition of organizing at least once in the summer season a happy hour gathering at night for a beach party. It soon developed into a full-blown banquet, with great food and dishes, tables, chairs, lanterns, dancing music, and a dress code of all whites. *Les Soirées Blanches*, the "white nights" on the beach became a big hit and a yearly event as everybody joined in the effort of putting it together.

The Benayoun and Boukhriss families on the beach. Estepona, 2012,

Jacqueline, my older sister living at the time in Paris, like most of us also developed a strong, emotional connection with southern Spain, having spent many summer visits there with her husband, Sylvain, and their two sons, Michael and Lionel. They decided to purchase a small apartment in the nearby bigger city of Marbella, where Jacqueline and Sylvain realized it would be a better fit for them as a possible year-round home once they moved away from Paris to enjoy their upcoming retirement.

Sadly, only a couple years after they started enjoying their frequent visits to the new apartment, Jacqueline was diagnosed with an acute blood condition. As one can only imagine, this was terrible news for our family. While Jacqueline was undergoing treatment in Paris to fight the disease, all she looked forward to was being able to spend as much time as possible in her little corner of the Costa del Sol. During her courageous fight to beat the disease, a fight that would last a little over a year, her Marbella apartment became the greatest source of comfort and joy for her, like a sheltering oasis.

Jacqueline couldn't wait to be in Marbella to just soak in the local atmosphere and Spanish ambiance. It was so fulfilling and soothing to her and helped her stand up to the tough fight for her life. As her condition unfortunately worsened and it became apparent that the cancer was gaining on her, one of her last requests was to spend her last few days there. I remember making a special trip from Estepona with my brother Armand to the Marbella hospital, to investigate if it was possible by any means to transfer her special weekly treatments and injections from the Paris hospital to the Marbella hospital. After a long, hard fight, Jacqueline passed away in Paris in November of 2010 at the age of sixty-two, may she rest in peace.

Robert, Simon, Jacqueline, Estepona, 2005

During the early summer of 2016, a very happy, special occasion took place in Estepona. Daniel decided to get married in Estepona. It was a joyful occasion to celebrate this big family event in this special Andalusian setting, our favorite little corner of the southern Mediterranean coastline of Spain. Daniel was married in June, with celebrations on the beach in Estepona and the big event taking place in Malaga in a castle on the mountain overlooking the city and port. They had a beautiful outdoor Jewish ceremony, with a view of the deep blue Mediterranean Sea as a magnificent sun was setting on the bay of Malaga.

I must add that as of lately, my two sisters, Evelyne and Nanou, both currently living in Montreal, Canada, are finally moving forward with acquiring a second home in Estepona. Both my sisters with their husband or partner and their children have been enjoying their summer times in Estepona, joining the annual Benayoun family gathering on the southern Spanish coast.

A few years ago, after returning to Texas from our yearly summer visit to Estepona, I was feeling a bit inspired and poetic and wrote a poem trying to put into words the special atmosphere that seemed to be present, motivating us to always look forward to the next visit. I wanted to capture the different images and feelings to try to immortalize the magic moments lived and shared over for the past thirty years. My brother Simon later improved on it by contributing a few words of his own. Originally composed in French, we have translated it to English.

It is titled "Senteurs et Saveurs d'Estepona," or "Scents and Flavors of Estepona."

Scents and Flavors of Estepona

The sky magnificent with shades of pink, orange, violet, and red at sunset reflecting on the Rock of Gibraltar and the mountains of Morocco on the horizon.

The sound of the purring rhythm of motors coming from fishing trawlers returning to port from the open sea, as small clouds of sea gulls trail above them.

The refreshing breeze at dusk, which caresses our faces as we walk on the paseo nibbling on pipas aguasal, admiring the twilight shades of blue sky fading over the Mediterranean Sea.

The familiar traits of the faces of the local townspeople strolling on the paseo. The young couples, the families whose children run in all directions, the older men and women—strangers, but whose faces resemble those of my own people.

The daily gathering of family on the beach. Siblings, nephews and nieces, young and old taking pleasure in rediscovering each other, each year starting over.

The traditional tuna sandwich wrapped in foil, with nineteen ingredients (some still secret), which we tackle with great appetite while sipping refreshing local beer, once after a quick swim in the sea.

The flavor of Cogoyo (minature heart of Spanish lettuce) sprinkled with lemon and herbes de Provence spices.

The nephews calling to aunts and uncles for double-chocolate ice cream bars from a nearby chiringuito, a sweet moment to savor after a day on the beach.

The particular aroma of the smoke drifting from a wood fire coming from the nearby Beach-bar grilling sardines and other sea food on a skewer.

The special taste of the first skewer of espeto grilled over a wood fire, accompanied by a small glass of manzanilla as we comfortably sit on the paseo watching the sea and admiring the full moon rising above the horizon.

The fragrant, sweet perfumes that drift in the evening from the flowers of la Dama de la Noche and from the orange trees that hang over the Plaza de las Flores.

The cries of the swallows circling above us at dusk while we sit and enjoy aceitunas and refreshing beer on the plaza.

The friendly atmosphere of La Escollera, a lively Greek-style tavern, and the taste of boquerones fritos, lenguados, and ensalada mixta with a tinto de verano (a memory from distant childhood), served at plastic tables covered in white paper tablecloths, our feet in the sand.

Sitting on the rock jetty at the harbor entrance, sipping a gin and tonic while nibbling on aceitunas, almonds, and peanuts, admiring the sunset colors on the Sierra Bermeja mountains, a stunning backdrop to the port.

The tranquility that empties our thoughts, reducing anxieties to zero . . . and to share this experience with family, this is pure bliss.

A relaxing stroll in the evening through the narrow streets of the nearby Casares village, with its rows of white houses appearing to be glued to the side of the mountain, and hiking up to the ruins of the old fortress, acknowledging along the way the old-timers sitting at the entrances of their homes and enjoying the evening breeze.

Strolling through the shaded pedestrian street in the heart of the city center to settle on the terrace of that small institution of Estepona—la churreria, the little café that serves hot churros which the children enjoy dipping in delicious, warm, dark chocolate.

We can't forget the other breakfast-on-the-go place farther up the street, on a terrace mostly frequented by the locals, serving a delicious pan con tomate y aceite y ajo.

What can we say about the annual summer event of making artisanal fig marmalade with love at Robert or Simon's place, made with fresh figs bought at the local open air Wednesday market.

La Charca, another magical place in the Andalusian hinterland where our family and friends often go on excursions. An enjoyable escapade of hiking in a small canyon or trekking in the nearby mountains and valleys, culminating usually in a refreshing dip under a waterfall, in a spring, or in a cold running stream.

Outings to the mountains always end in a happy picnic with fresh fruits and, of course, the famous tuna sandwich with its nineteen ingredients, prepared before departure.

Finally, the song of the Kiddush—the wine blessing—on Friday night for the Shabbat dinner on the terrace as all gather around a magnificent meal, with a view of sailboats and fishing trawlers gently rocking on the Mediterranean Sea, a dark blue sky strewn with bright stars. The Shabbat blessing with these lights and this backdrop takes us to a unique spiritual dimension.

In the sanctuary of Estepona, I have found a lifestyle which evokes similar feelings to what I remember of my childhood in the times of our Moroccan Jewish community of the 1950's and 60's which now no longer exists. So I have come full circle back to a semblance of my roots sharing close ties with my siblings accompanied by my beloved wife, children and grandchildren.

—Robert Benayoun Ben-Nun

Scents and Flavors of Estepona
Spanish word translations

pipas – sunflower seeds
coyogos – lettuce hearts
chiringuito – small open-air café on the beach
el sardinero – the sardine-catcher
espeto – skewer
manzanilla – a pale, dry Spanish sherry
Dama de la Noche – Lady of the Night, or Night-Blooming Jasmine
aceitunas – Spanish olives
boquerones fritos – fried anchovies
lenguados – flounder
ensalada mixta – mixed salad
tinto de verano – red wine with sparkling lemonade or Sprite
la churreria – a little café serving churros
pan con tomate y aceite y ajo – bread with tomato, olive oil, and garlic

www.ingramcontent.com/pod-product-compliance
Lightning Source LLC
Chambersburg PA
CBHW060041230426
43661CB00004B/616